Instructional Design for ELearning:

Essential guide to creating successful eLearning courses

Instructional Design for ELearning:

Essential guide to creating successful eLearning courses

Marina Arshavskiy

Second edition. Copyright © 2017.
Marina Arshavskiy
www.yourelearningworld.com
All graphics in this book © www.yourelearningworld.com

Trademarks

All brand names and product names used in this book are trademarks of their respective owners. The author is not associated with any product or vendor in this book.

Table of Contents

Introduction

When I first entered the field of instructional design, I reviewed a lot of literature and read many books on the subject. However, I did not find a single guide that offered a combination of theoretical and practical information. As a result, I had to supplement the theoretical knowledge I gained from these books and other resources with on-the-job experience. Instructional Design for ELearning: Essential guide to creating successful eLearning courses combines both theoretical aspects of instructional systems design and practical information from field experience to help instructional designers create the most compelling and effective courses. In this text, you will find the best knowledge, skills, and tools I could glean from the market. In addition to introducing theory and providing practical advice, this book aims to offer best practices drawn from many years of personal experience in the field of learning and development.

The Instructional Design for eLearning book can serve as a desk guide for instructional designers at any level and of any professional experience. Whether you are an aspiring instructional designer looking for a career change, a novice instructional designer trying to learn the basics of eLearning course development, a seasoned instructional designer needing a desk reference guide, or a human resources professional designing professional development training programs for employees, this book is your new go-to resource. Even though it concentrates primarily on designing eLearning courses for the workplace, curriculum developers and instructional designers who create face-to-face training programs can also benefit from it, as it covers all the important elements of course design regardless of the context.

The book is divided into four sections:

Part I – Basic Elements of Instructional Design
Part II – Designing Instructionally Sound ELearning Courses
Part III – Interactive Elements in ELearning Courses
Part IV – Advancing Your Skills

This text includes 27 exercises that will help you put your newly acquired knowledge into practice. Even though the activities will not be graded or reviewed, they are an excellent way to recap the information from each chapter and put it into perspective. Note that the first exercise sets the foundation for your project but does not provide all the content needed to create a project. Therefore, to complete the exercises, you will have to make certain assumptions about the topic and its content. Alternatively, you can use a project you are currently working on or simply invent one to complete these exercises.

In this edition, I have added and rewritten content to keep it current. I also added new chapters that reflect the changes in the field of eLearning and instructional design in general. Additionally, I added quizzes to help readers assess their understanding of the content. More templates and case studies found in this edition should also help eLearning professionals succeed in the field of instructional design.

Read each chapter, apply the knowledge you gain, and enjoy your learning quest!

Part I - Basic Elements of Instructional Design

"If you think training is expensive, try ignorance."
Peter Drucker

Chapter 1: Instructional Design for ELearning

This chapter will cover:

- Definitions of instructional systems design, eLearning, and blended learning
- Definitions of CBT and WBT
- Advantages and disadvantages of eLearning
- Situations when eLearning is an appropriate solution

Instructional Systems Design

Instructional Systems Design, also known as ISD, is a systematic approach to creating effective courses. ISD is both a science and an art—a science because it is based on learning theories, and an art because of the creativity involved in the design process. Furthermore, ISD is a tool that guides the structure of any course and promotes meaningful and active learning.

According to a renowned researcher and missionary, M. David Merrill, instructional design is the process of creating learning experiences that makes the acquisition of skill more appealing, effective, and efficient.

ISD follows standards similar to curriculum design; the chief difference being that ISD is mainly practiced in the workplace and concentrates on the how, while curriculum design applies to academic settings and concentrates on the why.

Even though there are many different approaches to designing courses, experienced instructional designers typically combine a variety of methods and incorporate technology and multimedia to enhance instruction.

Instructional designers are interested in knowing how people learn and retain information. According to Marc Rosenberg, a leader in the world of ISD training, performance is ultimately more important than training. There are many factors involved in creating eLearning materials that enable learners to retain information and, more importantly, transfer their newly acquired knowledge and skills to their jobs.

To people new to the field, ISD may appear easy. In reality, however, creating effective courses is rather complex. Skilled instructional designers focus on creating learning solutions that bring value to the organization by managing a project's time and cost. The success of their learning solution is measured by the performance improvement of their learners.

ELearning

ELearning is a form of learning conducted via internet, intranet, network, or CD-ROM. Successful eLearning courses are interactive, energetic, dynamic, and appealing to the learner's auditory, visual, and tactile senses.

ELearning can be synchronous or asynchronous. Synchronous eLearning is done in real-time with a live instructor. The synchronous eLearning experience is similar to that of a regular classroom, except learners can take courses anywhere in the world as long as they have a computer, internet connection, and access to audio or video conferencing. Some of the tools associated with synchronous eLearning are instant messaging, application sharing, and polling. While synchronous eLearning has the value of having a real instructor and ability to communicate with other participants in the course, it requires learners to virtually attend the course at a specific time.

Many instructional designers and distance learning educators find synchronous eLearning challenging to design. Since there is no face-to-face communication, online teaching requires a lot of effort not only from the instructor, but also from the learner. To ensure that each learner receives individual attention, instructors must recognize various types of learners in the class and adjust to their unique needs. For instance, there are learners who are clearly leaders; they always post comments and responses to other people's questions. There are also learners who always ask many questions, and expect to receive quick and thoughtful responses almost immediately. Furthermore, there are learners who take online learning very lightly, and do not participate in any discussions.

Through establishing high expectations from the beginning, and reinforcing deadlines and requirements for successful course completion, instructional designers will ensure that learners are on track and their goals and expectations are met. It is also a good idea to provide continuous feedback to each learner using the "pull up a chair" approach. In other words, you can send a quick email message once a week asking learners to reflect on their feelings about the course and offer thoughts and feedback about their overall progress. Additionally, it is critical that you check your emails regularly and respond promptly. Even if you are unable to provide a complete response right away, always acknowledge the receipt of the email and assure learners that you will get back to them with a complete answer to their question.

In order for a synchronous online course to be successful, it must be interesting and engaging to learners. It must also follow adult learning theories and principles. To increase learner success in a synchronous eLearning environment, consider addressing multiple learning styles and ensuring that all auditory, visual, and kinesthetic learners are able to fully participate in the learning experience. Since true learning occurs by encoding of new information in long-term memory, you should build in multiple opportunities to ensure retention. For example, you can offer games, interactivity, simulations, demonstrations, and provide constant feedback and reinforcement to all learners based on their individual needs.

Because adult learners are busy, many of them find synchronous eLearning impractical. To address this problem and to target a wider audience, instructional systems designers began recording synchronous eLearning courses and making them available to learners unable to attend live sessions. This is where asynchronous eLearning originates. Asynchronous eLearning is self-paced. It allows learners to go through courses as quickly or as slowly as they desire at their convenience.

Some of the most commonly used tools in asynchronous eLearning are forums, blogs, and webcasts.

Which ELearning Approach to Select – Synchronous or Asynchronous

Most clients who request eLearning courses are unaware of these two options. Furthermore, most of the time, they seem to think that asynchronous is the way to go. However, this is not always true. Before deciding on the delivery method, instructional designers should look at the advantages and disadvantages of both options.

When it comes to learners' preferences, the best delivery method often depends on their learning styles. Younger generations tend to enjoy asynchronous courses better because they are so used to all the "clicking" on computers and their mobile phones that learning on their computer at their own pace is like a second nature to them. Generations who grew up without computers, the internet, or smartphones, typically prefer synchronous eLearning experiences in which they are able to ask questions and participate in real time.

While audience analysis should be conducted prior to deciding on the delivery method, content and type of course also play a major role in the decision making process. If, for instance, the content is overly complicated and elicits many questions from learners, synchronous eLearning may be the way to go. Alternatively, if the purpose of the lesson is to provide a review or brief overview of a topic, then asynchronous eLearning may be your best bet.

Costs also play a major role. Because synchronous learning events require a real life instructor, they tend to be more expensive in comparison to asynchronous, on-demand experiences. So, when you need to make a decision about the delivery method for your course, you need to consider the learners, content, and purpose of your course as well as the available budget.

Marina Arshavskiy

Computer-Based Training vs. Web-Based Training

Computer-Based Training (CBT) and Web-Based Training (WBT) are among the most popular eLearning delivery methods. CBT is a form of education in which learners take training courses on the computer. CBT courses are typically packaged into a CD or DVD format, and are intended for asynchronous delivery. WBT courses, on the other hand, operate on the internet and are intended for both synchronous and asynchronous delivery.

WBT's best feature is also one of its disadvantages. Not all countries are gifted with high-speed internet. People from Third World countries may find CBT programs a more convenient option. Installing software through a CD-ROM will be faster than waiting for a WBT program or page to load.

On the other hand, people with jobs that require them to go to other places will find WBT more useful and more convenient as they won't need to bring their own PCs with them. WBT content can be accessed anywhere— even through personal portable devices, such as smartphones, laptops, and tablets.

WBT is also useful because learners from different locations can share their thoughts and knowledge about a topic being presented in the course. Some skills, such as learning a new language, will be more effective if the learner actually has the opportunity to interact with other learners via chats or discussion boards.

Blended Learning

Case Study

When Techne IT Company decided to create a training course to help employees learn the latest security standards, the choice of format seemed simple. An eLearning course that could be accessed whenever the employees needed it and completed at their own time would meet everyone's preferences.

"The course will include the basics, and we can also add a glossary and resource list for people who haven't been able to keep up," said the instructional designer. "That way the course will be adaptable depending on the learner's familiarity with the topic."

"We can also include simulations to guide them through all the best practices," said another member of the team.

But one of the ELearning developers had an issue. "What about updating the course?" he said. "Security standards change all the time. Soon enough, we'll need a new one."

This was a good point. As the team hashed out their options, it became increasingly clear that the best solution would be to have updated training every quarter— and that it was also way too much effort to finish four ELearning courses a year.

Finally, the developer had an idea.

"How about we make simulations every quarter, but leave the actual training to an instructor who can easily adapt the curriculum?" he said. "That's much more effective. The meeting time will stay minimal, but we won't have to constantly overhaul the content."

The team implemented blended learning in the form of a mixture of online resources and instructor workshops, and the training was successful.

Even though eLearning is a popular solution for many performance problems, it is mostly appropriate for increasing knowledge and developing cognitive skills. Even if the course follows the most solid instructional design principles, it cannot teach people how to drive a car, for example, because driving is a psychomotor skill, which requires real-life practice for best results.

Teaching interpersonal skills that change learners' attitudes and behaviors can be effective through eLearning if instructional designers add simulations, serious games, and role-plays. This is where the blended learning approach comes into play. The ultimate goal of this method is to combine several media in one course. In most cases, blended learning is a combination of face-to-face delivery with eLearning activities. For example, learners might have to complete the lecture part of a particular course via eLearning, followed by the instructor-led training for practice and hands-on activities. This blended instructional approach is becoming popular in higher education and can help instructional designers address different learning styles as it combines the needs of more traditional learners with the needs of the net generation.

So, to give you an example of a blended learning approach, let's assume an instructional designer needs to create a professional development course for physical therapists. For maximum effectiveness, the course will be divided into two parts. The first part will be delivered via eLearning, and consist of mostly theoretical content. It will include many real-life examples along with high-level games and simulations. The second part will be conducted in the classroom. Participants will complete applicable hands-on activities that will help them acquire psychomotor skills.

Advantages and Disadvantages of ELearning

When stakeholders identify the need for a training course, they often wonder whether they should choose eLearning over traditional learning. As an instructional designer, you should be aware of advantages and disadvantages that eLearning provides and share them with your clients.

Some of these advantages include being able to:

- Access courses at any time;
- Take courses anywhere;
- Learn at any pace;
- Go back and review course materials as needed.

Essentially, eLearning is a good option:

- If there is a need to disperse information to a diverse group of people who have trouble finding a common schedule to attend a session together
- If the learner has limited mobility, such as the elderly or someone with disabilities
- If the learner doesn't have a lot of time to devote to learning
- If the training is meant to develop one's cognitive skills
- If a traditional classroom setup is more expensive for the learner and the instructor than creating interactive, online content

Finally, if you are still unsure whether eLearning is an appropriate solution, consider these two questions:

- Will it be more cost-effective to take this route rather than a face-to-face setup or on-the-job learning?
- What skills are you trying to teach?

Although eLearning can be suitable for some courses, it is not always a substitute for traditional classroom training.

The disadvantages of eLearning include:

- Low retention levels by learners with limited motivation;
- Lack of immediate assistance when ambiguous information is presented; and
- low computer literacy may prevent learners from fully benefiting from the learning experience.

While the development of eLearning is much more expensive than the development of classroom training solutions, the implementation costs are significantly lower than those for the instructor-led training (ILT). For classroom training, some of the implementation costs are typically associated with paying the trainer, renting a training room, printing hard copies of all course materials, and many more. Alternatively, expenses associated with implementation of eLearning are typically limited to the costs of web servers and technical support.

When Will ELearning Work?

The questions below should help you determine whether eLearning is the appropriate solution for the content and requirements that stakeholders provide.

- What types of skills does the training address?
- What are the goals of the training?
- What is the motivation level of your target audience?
- What is the learners' level of computer literacy?
- Which generation do most learners come from?
- What is the geographic location of your learners?
- How many learners will the training course target?
- How much money is available for the training?

Test Your Knowledge

1. Instructional Systems Design (ISD) is a term describing a:
   A. Systematic approach to creating effective courses.
   B. Method for designing computer-based learning.
   C. Systematic approach to implementing a learning management system.
   D. Method for identifying new and innovative instructional design methodologies.

2. Skilled and experienced instructional designers (Choose all that apply):
   A. Are able to create a large number of courses in a very short amount of time.
   B. Typically rely on various technologies and multimedia to enhance their courses.
   C. Focus on providing value to the organization by managing a project's time and cost.
   D. Know that the success of their learners is measured by their performance improvement.

3. ELearning is a form of learning conducted via:
   A. Internet
   B. Text messaging
   C. Mobile device
   D. Webinars

4. Which of the following statements about eLearning are TRUE? (Choose all that apply)
   A. In order for eLearning courses to be successful, they must use standard templates that contain very little multimedia distraction.
   B. Successful eLearning courses are interactive, energetic and dynamic.
   C. ELearning courses must appeal to the learner's auditory, visual, and tactile senses to ensure effective knowledge transfer.
   D. ELearning can be either synchronous or asynchronous.

5. Why can synchronous eLearning be impractical, particularly among adult learners?
   A. It requires learners to attend at a specific time.
   B. It requires audio and video conferencing capabilities.
   C. It requires learners to attend at a time of their choosing.
   D. It takes place in real time, making it hard to re-visit the content.

6. Asynchronous eLearning allows learners to (Choose all that apply):
   A. Attend at any time.
   B. Ask live questions during the training.
   C. Pace themselves throughout the training.
   D. Use application sharing and video conferencing to communicate with the instructor.
   E. Learn via the use of forums, blogs and webcasts among other tools.

7. Which of the following statements about blended learning is FALSE?
   A. Blended Learning courses often utilize simulations, games and role plays as activities to help reinforce face-to-face classroom training.
   B. Blended Learning typically only caters to tactile learners and can be less effective for auditory and visual learners.
   C. Blended learning combines the needs of traditional learners with the needs of younger learners.
   D. Blended Learning helps cater to a variety of learning styles by offering different auditory, visual and tactile experiences.

8. What are the primary advantages of eLearning? (Choose all that apply)
   A. Access to an instructor in real time.
   B. Access courses at anytime, anywhere, at your own pace.
   C. ELearning allows you to access the material without an internet connection.
   D. ELearning allows you to go back and review course materials if you need to.

9. What are the primary disadvantages of eLearning? (Choose all that apply)
   A. Unmotivated learners may not retain information.
   B. Lack of immediate assistance when ambiguous information is presented may hinder learning.
   C. Low computer literacy may prevent learners from fully benefiting from the learning experience.
   D. Access courses at anytime, anywhere, at your own pace.

10. Which of the following statements about the costs of eLearning are TRUE? (Choose all that apply)
   A. The development of classroom training is much cheaper than eLearning, however the implementation of classroom training is much cheaper than that of eLearning.
   B. The development of eLearning is more expensive than classroom training, however the implementation of eLearning is much cheaper.
   C. Overall, eLearning is cheaper than ILT.
   D. Overall, ILT is cheaper than eLearning.

11. Why is it important to ask your stakeholders questions about their desired eLearning solution prior to starting? (Choose all that apply)
   A. You will uncover vital information about the audience, the budget and the goals of the training, which will inform what type of solution you build.
   B. By asking more questions, you will increase the number of hours you can bill your customer for because you have taken up extra time with this process.
   C. Understanding the skills, goals, geographic location and budget available for a training solution will allow you to advice on whether eLearning is the appropriate solution compared to traditional ILT.
   D. By understanding the learner's level of computer literacy and generation, you'll be able to tailor the solution toward the computing skills of the intended audience.

Exercise 1

Your company just signed a contract to develop an eLearning course for the department of finance in a large business firm. Your program manager assigned this project to you. The client wants to train employees on a new salary-calculating tool. The stakeholders believe that they know exactly what they need and do not want you to spend time, money, or resources on needs analysis. You have six months to complete the project.

Based on the information you have so far, which approach (synchronous, asynchronous, or blended) should you most likely use, and why?

Chapter 2: Instructional Design and ELearning – History of their Marriage

This chapter will cover:

- Evolution of instructional design
- Major contributors to the field of instructional design
- Innovations in the ISD field

The study of how people learn began with Ebbinghaus and Pavlov's studies on the effects of classical conditioning and how people forget. Then, B.F. Skinner, an American psychologist and behaviorist, built upon their studies and developed the behaviorist approach to learning. Well-known psychologists, including Piaget and Vygotsky, studied learners' development stages as well as the cognitive processes associated with learning. As a result of their studies, the cognitive theory of learning evolved. This theory included the role of metacognition and the importance of connecting learners' background knowledge with newly acquired knowledge.

Even though the aforementioned psychologists played a vital role in the development of ISD, actual instructional design is a fairly new field. It was founded during World War II when the U.S. military needed to mass train people to perform complex technical tasks as quickly as possible. Training programs created for these people were based on B.F. Skinner's theory on operant conditioning and observable behaviors. Specifically, large tasks were broken down into subtasks. Then, each subtask was treated as a separate learning objective. The training focused on rewarding correct performance and remediating incorrect performance. Many researchers, psychologists, and educators worked together to create an efficient and effective training program. Together, they discovered the importance of designing a form of instruction that met learners' needs. After the war, many of these researchers continued their work and developed a systematic approach to learning. This approach included the three major aspects of course design—analysis, design, and evaluation—which became the foundation for the popular ADDIE model.

Later, in the late 1950s and early 1960s, B.F. Skinner's studies on learning influenced instructional design. Short, to-the-point lessons with frequent question and instant feedback were introduced into the educational design. Because these lessons were measurable and could easily be revised based on the assessments, formative evaluation became part of the design process. This behavioristic approach to learning required clear, instructional objectives. Robert Mager taught educators how to write measurable and observable objectives. Later, Benjamin Bloom used Mager's guide to develop his taxonomies of learning. He created key verbs for instructors to use when writing objectives, known as Bloom's Taxonomy. The purpose of these verbs is to help learners move toward the highest possible learning domain.

Robert Gagné also played an important role in instructional design. His work described the five domains of learning outcomes, including verbal information, intellectual skills, attitudes, motor skills, and cognitive strategies. He then determined specific conditions for each of these domains.

Additionally, Gagné developed the Nine Events of Instructions, which became a major part of effective lesson design.

As time went on, other theories emerged. Educators and researchers created their own instructional theories for developing effective learning materials. Some of the popular models that emerged as a result of their efforts are the Dick and Carey Systems Approach to instructional design, and the Seels and Glasgow ISD model.

With the emergence of the computer age, instructional design experienced major changes that resulted in new theories, models, and learning modes. Many organizations decided that traditional learning was no longer the answer to their training needs. They wanted their learners to have access to training at any time and any place. Therefore, they began using eLearning and blended learning approaches.

In recent years, access to education has grown significantly. The advent of computers, internet, and mobile devices has played a major role in expanding the reach of education into far-flung places. This development enabled learners who normally would not be reached by traditional teachers to learn new things. More and more people use social networking tools such as Facebook, Twitter, and LinkedIn not only for socializing, but also for education purposes. It is becoming obvious that instructional design is an ever-changing field highly dependent upon technological innovations.

As with education's expansion to reach a wider market, instructional design has also kept pace in its evolution to ensure that teaching methods are in line. Defined as the process of taking in information and delivering it in a way that makes it easier for learners to understand, its evolution stayed in line with education's aim of equipping every learner with knowledge that is useful in their daily lives. It has grown exponentially from the aftermath of the WWII to the early 21st century, when several instructional models are available and ready for implementation in learning environments.

B. F. Skinner, Benjamin Bloom, and Robert F. Mager were among those who first introduced the marriage of instructional design and eLearning. In his article "The Science of Learning and the Art of Teaching," Skinner introduced the public to programmed instructional materials where he advocated the inclusion of smaller steps, frequent questioning, and immediate feedback for improved learning. Bloom, on the other hand, was an advocate of developing and identifying three principle domains of learning, which include cognitive, affective, and psychomotor.

The boom of online education was in the 2000s. A more powerful computer, a wider internet service reach, and instructional design elements that fit the needs of learners were some factors that drove eLearning into heights it never saw during this decade.

It was the decade when advancements in technology made instructional design more experimental while maintaining its effectiveness. With the advent of simulations, micro-learning, and mobile learning, access to information was not only easier for most learners, but also made it more convenient for them to learn whenever and wherever they were.

What started as a concept to help educators and designers develop a curriculum where learners can easily take in and process information, instructional design has been an integral part not only in online education, but also in traditional methods of teaching. It has been a significant tool in designing methods that would enable learners to better take in knowledge and process it.

The technological advancements that started in the '80s until the '90s contributed much to the fast-paced evolution of instructional design. They enabled designers to include new ways to deliver information using technologies like computer simulation, artificial reality, and the internet.

With better understanding of factors affecting learning combined with rapid technological advancements, instructional designers are now armed with more powerful tools that could take them into uncharted territory of eLearning.

Chapter 3: Instructional Design Models

This chapter will cover:

- ADDIE model
- Seels and Glasgow ISD model
- Dick and Carey Systems Approach model
- ASSURE model
- Rapid ISD model
- Four-Door (4D) ELearning model
- SAM model
- Merrill's Principles of Instruction
- Kemp's Instructional Design model
- Action Mapping

Case Study

The instructional designer in charge of the training department at the Techne IT Company was frustrated. For years, they'd faithfully followed the ADDIE model, but their current project seemed stuck in the Analysis phase. The problem was that the software the course covered hadn't been introduced to the team yet.

"We don't have any in-house SMEs, and we don't have enough information to tell how each of the departments are going to be using the software," the instructional designer explained to his manager when he asked about the delay.

"Well, maybe you need a new approach to things," said the manager. "Just do it without worrying about all of that."

Knowing how important learner analysis was to the success of a project, the instructional designer was, at first, resistant. However, thinking about the manager's idea of finding a different approach, he began to research instructional design models beyond ADDIE. Some, like Dick and Carey or the Kemp model, emphasized instructional goals. Others, like ASSURE, were similar to ADDIE, but with added or rearranged steps. Finally, he discovered Iterative Design.

Iterative Design allowed for a development process that involved rapid prototyping and implementation. Meaning, the instructional designer could implement a basic training for the software and solicit feedback. Then, refine the system based on feedback, and continue the process until the training finally worked. The instructional designer had found the right model for his project!

As you already know, instructional design is the process of analyzing learning needs and goals as well as the development of a delivery system to meet those needs. Instructional design involves the development of instructionally sound materials and activities, and evaluation of learners' knowledge. To create valuable courses, designers must understand why and how people learn. It is also important to analyze audiences and their needs to tailor the training to meet those unique needs. Instructional design models help to create a framework for developing effective and efficient training solution that helps learners achieve their individual goals. Additionally, instructional design incorporates the best ways to build the instruction and deliver learning. This is where instructional design models come into play. They help to outline the process that should be taken for training development, and guide course creators as they move through the design and development process. There are as many instructional design theories, techniques, and models as there are instructional designers. Therefore, it is nearly impossible to cover all of them in one chapter. This chapter describes the most popular ones.

As you read, please keep in mind that top instructional designers do not adhere to any one approach, but instead choose whatever technique best suits the specifics of a course's audience and content.

The ADDIE Model

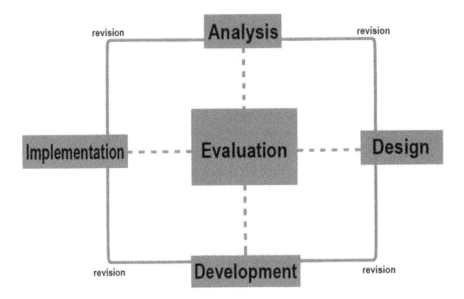

ADDIE is the classic model. All other instructional design models are rooted in the ADDIE model. It traces its roots to the 1950's Waterfall methodology of software design, where the development process gradually flows from one step to another, just like a waterfall.

ADDIE stands for

A – *Analysis*
D – *Design*
D – *Development*
I – *Implementation*
E – *Evaluation*

In the *Analysis* phase you clarify problems, define goals and objectives, and collect necessary data. You also define audience characteristics, the content to be included, the learning environment, and the technical requirements. It is important that your training program is aligned with your goals and objectives. This can be easily achieved through asking yourself, what should the learner know at the end of the training. In this phase, you should also look at your timelines, scope, budget, and delivery method. For example, you may find that training is not the best solution for the problems you have been asked to solve; or that computer-based training will be a better fit for your audience than web-based training. Your findings might not meet your stakeholders' expectations, so it is important to capture the details of your research and back up your training suggestions with solid data.

In the ***Design*** phase you write objectives, and craft the structure, duration, and sequencing of the course. During this phase, you will also create learning objectives for all modules and sections of your course. You will outline exercises, interactions, games, simulations, and assessments that will be included in the course. Additionally, depending on how your course will be delivered, you may also create storyboards, prototypes, and graphic design elements. You will also create a project management plan with deadlines, milestones, implementation details, and possibly budgeting. When you are done, you will have a blueprint for your course and its delivery methods.

In the ***Development*** phase, you bring your design to life by using text, storyboards, graphics, audio, and/or video, and by assembling all these elements into a compelling course. Not all instructional designers will fully participate in this phase. Oftentimes, you will have to work with programmers, videographers, audio talent, and editors in this stage of course creation. Any deliverables that you decide to include in the course, such as desk reference guides or assessment tools will also be developed during this phase.

In the ***Implementation*** phase, your course is delivered to its audience. Either you or your project manager is responsible for ensuring that all the resources needed for this training are readily available.

And, in the ***Evaluation*** phase, the effectiveness of your course is assessed by measuring the level of your audience's learning and retention, as well as how well your project's goals have been met. During this phase you are evaluating the goals and learning objectives you set prior to creating the course. Although this is the final stage of the ADDIE model, you should actually be performing evaluation throughout the design process.

Even though it may seem like each phase of the ADDIE model is independent, in reality the model is not always linear, and each stage may look different depending on your requirements, your project, and the way you manage it. You may even notice that you are skipping or combining some phases of the model to meet your client's needs.

Now, let's take a look at how ADDIE may work in real life. We will assume the team of instructional designers is tasked with training new IT specialists on new software installation for the Real Estate agency. They should begin by analyzing the problem, so that they can figure out what the problem is and why training is needed. There are many questions that instructional designers should seek answers to. For example, they need to gather information about the current knowledge of software installation, and what is expected of the learners as a result of taking this training. Instructional designers may also want to find out about barriers these IT specialists are running into as they try to install the software. There are many different ways to collect the required information and identify the gaps. Some examples include conducting interviews, sending out surveys, or observing several IT specialists on the job. By collecting information through needs analysis, instructional designers should be able to accurately identify problems, and determine the best possible training solution.

After conducting the analysis, ISD specialists are ready to start writing learning objectives, which should cover everything learners' need to know and be able to do as a result of completing the course. It is important to make objectives measurable and observable and align them with the company's business goals.

Now that all the objectives are in place, the next step is to look at a budget and a timeline. Unfortunately, most of the time, neither budget nor deadlines can be changed; therefore, instructional designers should use these as guidelines to decide on the delivery methods, break-down of activities, level of interactivity, and assessments.

The next step in the process would be to design the structure that works for the content and goals. When the structure is in place, ISD professionals are ready to move on to the most interesting part, which is storyboarding the course. In addition to storyboarding, the Design phase includes planning scenarios, interactivity, exercises, and assessments.

When all the planning work is completed, instructional designers can move on to the Development phase. Here, they will work with programmers and graphic artists to bring storyboards to life.

Finally, the training has been developed and it's time to implement it. As instructional designers create training, they must keep in mind that Evaluation plays a huge role in training success. Therefore, ensuring that all assessments align with objectives, and crafting relevant and appropriate evaluations are some of the most crucial aspects in obtaining great training outcomes. Instructional designers may also decide to evaluate training based on the pre and post-test results as well as on the feedback provided by the IT specialists who already completed the training. Not only that evaluations will help to measure learners' knowledge and understanding of the material, but they will also help instructional designers incorporate all the feedback into their future designs.

Even though ADDIE is the most widely used ISD model, it has some drawbacks. For example, some designers feel that ADDIE is too linear, time consuming, and expensive. This is why some instructional designers prefer newer, more Agile models such as Dick and Carey, Kemp, and SAM.

Seels and Glasgow ISD Model

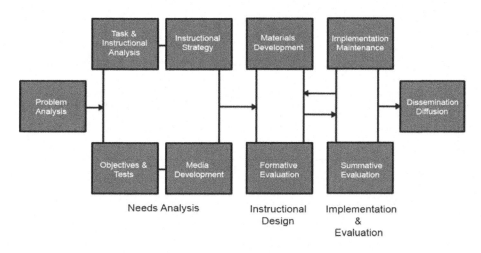

The *Seels and Glasgow* ISD model places design within the context of project management to ensure a course stays within time and budget constraints. Under this model, you conduct front-end analysis, develop the course, and perform evaluations.

The Seels and Glasgow ISD model consists of three phases:

- *Needs Analysis Management Phase* – Analyzing and documenting instructional requirements and goals.
- *Instructional Design Management Phase* – Formulating instructional strategies, breaking down development into tasks, selecting delivery systems, and performing formative evaluations.
- *Implementation and Evaluation Management Phase* – Developing and producing the course materials, delivering, and evaluating the results of the course.

Dick and Carey Systems Approach Model

The *Dick and Carey Systems Approach* model focuses on selecting and organizing the appropriate content for each module. This model incorporates the learner's needs, skills, and learning context into the course design. The Dick and Carey Systems Approach is based on theoretical principles of learning and Robert Gagné's conditions of learning. This model is widely implemented by curriculum developers in higher education.

The Dick and Carey Systems Approach is composed of ten steps, which include nine basic steps and an evaluation of the effectiveness of instruction.

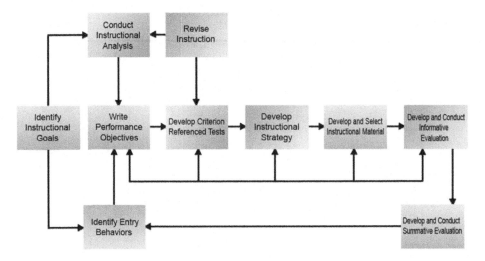

Step 1 – During the first step, you conduct needs assessment to identify instructional goals.

Step 2 – Instructional Analyses are conducted to determine the skills and knowledge required for the goal.

Step 3 – During the third step you analyze learners in terms of skills, attitudes, prior knowledge, and motivation.

Step 4 – After collecting and analyzing all the required information, you begin writing performance objectives specifying the skills, the conditions, and the criteria for learning.

Step 5 – The fifth step involves the development of assessment instruments.

Step 6 – The sixth step requires you to develop an instructional strategy for presenting the information, testing, and learning activities.

Step 7 – Now that there is strategy in place, you can develop and produce instruction.

Step 8 – The eighth step involves collecting data for conducting a formative evaluation.

Step 9 – The ninth step requires you to revise the lesson using the data collected from the formative evaluation, analysis, objectives, assessment instruments, and instructional strategies and content.

Step 10 – The final step involves conducting a summative evaluation to measure success of the instruction.

ASSURE Model

The *ASSURE* model, developed by Heinich, Molenda, Russell, and Smaldino, is based on Gagné's Nine Events of Instruction. The model assumes that the course design uses different types of media and is especially useful for designing eLearning courses. ASSURE stands for:

A – *Analyze Learners* – You research the general characteristics of learners, including their gender and age. Additionally, you learn more about participants' learning styles and preferences focusing on the motivational aspects of learning.

S – *State Objectives* – You develop specific and measurable objectives for the course.

S – *Select Media and Materials* – You select the materials and media for the course and develop and modify already existing materials.

U – *Utilize Media and Materials* – You implement the selected materials. However, prior to the implementation, you should pilot test them to ensure that the selections meet your objectives. In this phase, you also confirm that the course works the way it should and that the learners can easily access all materials.

R – *Require Learner Participation* – You elicit participation. You can do this through discussions, games, simulations, or assessments. You should ensure that all the activities allow learners to apply their knowledge and understanding of the content.

E – *Evaluate and Revise* – You evaluate whether or not the objectives were met. You can do this by revisiting presentation methods to see if the media and materials selected are appropriate for the lesson. After conducting a thorough evaluation, you should consider editing your materials and revising the course based on your findings during this process.

Rapid ISD Model

Today, instructional designers are searching for ways to create their courses quickly and effectively. At the same time, they want the learning to be engaging and interactive. The Accelerated Learning *Rapid Instructional Design* (RID) model, created by David Meier, is ideal for those who work with tight deadlines, a limited budget, and constantly changing content. This model is all about accelerated learning design strategies and shortcuts. Meier believes that traditional ISD models are too time-consuming and controlling. He also believes that these models are presentation-based rather than activity-based. According to RID, people learn more from application with feedback than from presentations. It replaces media-heavy courses with activity-based courses. Even though the RID model makes courses more interactive and engaging, it does not incorporate analysis and evaluation phases, which are crucial in the development of an eLearning course.

There are four phases in the RID model.

- *Preparation* – Arouse interest and motivate learners by stating goals and removing learners' barriers
- *Presentation* – Encounter new knowledge and skills by appealing to all learning styles and incorporating interactive presentations and discovery activities into the learning experience
- *Practice* – Integrate new knowledge and skills by incorporating games, hands-on activities, and skill-building practice exercises as well as providing substantial corrective feedback to the learner
- *Performance* – Allow time to apply the new knowledge and skills and reward the use of these skills.

The Four-Door (4D) ELearning Model

The *Four-Door (4D) ELearning* model was developed by Dr. Sivasailam "Thiagi" Thiagarajan. This is a simple model that allows professionals to develop eLearning courses cheaply and rapidly while addressing different types of learners. According to this model, learners have full control of course navigation.

The four doors in this model are the *Library, Café, Playground*, and *Evaluation Center*. However, you can change these names depending on the training needs. Learners can enter any of the doors they want based on their personal preference, background knowledge, and experience.

Library – In this area, learners will find all the information and resources they need to master objectives and to complete the assessment. Some of the materials that can be found here are presentations, slideshows, videos, and audio recordings.

Café – The social learning takes place here. Discussion boards, blogs, and wikis are types of tools found in the café. This area includes open-ended questions that help learners apply content presented in the library.

Playground – In this area, learners can play games to recall and apply the content they learned in the Library. The games can be played as many times as necessary until the content is mastered.

Evaluation Center – In this area, learners take assessments and performance tests. Most of the time, instead of giving regular assessments with multiple choice questions, learners have to complete real assignments related to the job.

Successive Approximation Model (SAM)

As a result of new developments in how eLearning is viewed by training professionals, and significant enhancements in supporting IT and multi-media technologies, Agile methodologies have now sprung up. Agile eLearning:

- *Promotes* a "parallel" way of developing courseware, as opposed to the serial **Waterfall** (ADDIE) approach
- *Endorses* the use of team-work as opposed to specialist roles (Designers, Developers etc.) that worked in insulation; and
- *Infuses* flexibility, speed and cooperation into the development process

The Agile approach, which is based on short, iterative, full-cycles that deliver usable components of the courseware, eliminates the biggest drawback to ADDIE, which is a time-consuming and often process-driven method of developing courseware. Agile methodologies, such as Rapid Content Development (RCD) and Successive Approximation Model (SAM) introduce goal-oriented, action-driven efforts that result in:

- More collaborative approach to eLearning content development
- A move to the "fail early, succeed earlier!" approach to content development—all issues are identified and fixed much earlier in the Agile approach than ADDIE
- The ability to reuse, recycle and reprocess previously developed content, saving lots of time and money for eLearning project sponsors

Agile not only speeds up courseware design and development, but also adds a dimension of better quality that is not possible with ADDIE. Moving away from the Waterfall and into Agile is definitely a windfall for eLearning projects.

The need for useful instructional design models has always been on the forefront of all types of educational experience. Throughout the years, various instructional design formats have been introduced to assist with the process of creating curricula and course planning options that would prove successful in helping people learn. Although some of these models, such as ADDIE, have proven the test of time, currently the use of the Successive Approximation Model has become quite popular for its unique, flexible approach to producing learning modules that have proven quite successful in application.

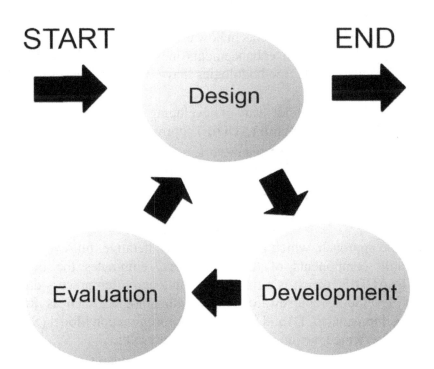

Successive Approximation Model (SAM) was created by Michael Allen, a recognized pioneer and leader in the design of interactive multimedia learning tools and applications. The model emphasizes collaboration, efficiency, and repetition. According to Allen, there is no perfect project; therefore, to create the best possible outcome, instructional designers should focus on producing usable products as quickly as possible. The model focuses on prototyping more heavily than other instructional design models do. With SAM, the goal is to take smaller, more flexible steps within a larger framework to achieve high quality in training and learning, as opposed to following the step-by-step process. SAM expects that mistakes will be made throughout the project. It also expects that stakeholders will change their minds or decide to make corrections along the way. Because of all these issues, SAM considers collaboration and early evaluation important to successful completion of any project. The model enables instructional designers to move quickly through the initial phases of course design to a rapid prototyping. There are essentially two SAM models.

SAM1 is for small simple projects that do not require extensive development or any specialized skills such as programming or graphic design. SAM 1 is composed of the following three steps:

- *Evaluation/Analysis*
- *Design*
- *Development*

The process cycles through three iterations, modifying and testing prototypes along the way. Because ideas are frequently evaluated, instructional designers can create usable courses relatively quickly and effectively while avoiding costly mistakes.

SAM 2 is for large projects that require advanced development skills. This model is divided into the following three phases:

Preparation Phase – Instructional designers gather background information and brainstorm ideas about the project together with stakeholders and their entire team.

Iterative Design Phase – Further broken into the following three steps:

Prototype Evaluate Design – During this phase, instructional designers and their teams rotate through design, prototype, and review, making decisions and refining their prototype prior to making critical mistakes.

Iterative Development Phase – Further broken into the following three steps:

- *Develop*
- *Implement*
- *Evaluate*

The *Iterative Development phase* begins with the design proof, and produces three deliverables known as alpha, beta, and gold releases.

Now that you are familiar with the SAM model, let's take a look at its advantages and disadvantages.

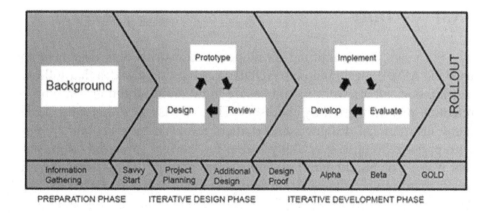

Advantages of the Successive Approximation Model

- It is less linear and more "true to life" when considering the building of a learning or training course
- It considers various points of views allowing for the

35

consideration of options that could improve the learning or training experience

- Uses iterations, small steps during the development process, which make room for evaluations and necessary changes as needed
- The goal is to find out where energy and resources should be placed immediately to create projects/material that can be used at once
- Very collaborative/teamwork based

Disadvantages of the Successive Approximation Model

Just as there are many reasons why people prefer SAM over other instructional design models, there are some disadvantages. They include:

- The idea that mistakes are "inevitable" may result in overlooking potential issues in a project
- Doesn't acknowledge and account for risk in relation to the effectiveness of a project in comparison to other instructional design models
- One must consider a variety of input which can lead to less cohesiveness if not monitored correctly
- There is a need for a considerable amount of collaboration to ensure the cohesiveness of the project

SAM vs. ADDIE

For years, many training developers and instructional designers have used the ADDIE design model. ADDIE was built on the idea that following a strict, linear framework would ensure high quality training, learning and retention of information by the users. The only issue is that with ADDIE many instructional designers and trainers felt as if they couldn't progress with projects because everything had to be "perfect" to avoid the mistakes that would potentially derail an entire project. With the understanding that this method can be somewhat limiting, many are leaving ADDIE for SAM. The flexibility of SAM allows for the development of learning and training materials that account for possible mistakes at each step that is often rectified with collaboration and team work.

Using SAM for learning and training purposes allows for the creation of materials that take into the consideration their real world application. Nothing is perfect, but flexibility creates results.

Merrill's Principles of Instruction

Merrill's Principles of Instruction model is also known as the First Principles of Instruction. It was developed by M. David Merrill, a researcher and professor at the Utah State University. It is an instructional theory derived from earlier learning theories and models, and is based on hands on experiences.

The model focuses on the premise that learners tend to understand content better when the instruction is centered on real-world problems and tasks.

If you are developing an eLearning course for employees of a call center, for example, you have to incorporate topics that help them deal with situations that they will most likely encounter as call center agents.

For example, when teaching the trainees the effective way of communicating with clients, you can make a list of scenarios that they might experience later on, and then illustrate how they should respond to each scenario. You can also integrate simulated calls into your eLearning course.

Kemp's Instructional Design Model

This instructional design model was created by Jerrold Kemp, along with other researchers, in the 1980s. The model is also sometimes called Morrison, Ross, and Kemp Instructional Design Model. It was considered as an innovative approach to education because of its circular and nonlinear structure. This means that this instructional design model is extremely flexible.

The model is based on the principle that the instructional designer should not only consider the learning objectives in creating a learning system, but also consider other factors, such as the personality and characteristics of the learner, the needs of the learner, the learner assessment, and instructional resources.

When using this instructional design model to create eLearning programs, you should follow these steps:
- Identify the problems in the existing instructional programs.
- Determine the characteristics and needs of your learners.
- Identify the learning goals for each learner.
- Identify the available resources. Can the learners learn at home using mobile devices? Do your learners have access to a desktop computer?
- Design an instructional system that addresses the needs of the learner and helps you achieve the learning goals.
- Develop an evaluation system to check the effectiveness of the

structional design to assess the aptitude of the learners.

Action Mapping

Action mapping is one of the newest instructional models. It was developed by Cathy Moore in 2008. It is a visual approach commonly used in corporate training. Its goal is to increase efficiency and performance. This instructional design model has a linear structure.

To use this model in your eLearning courses, you need to create an action map (or flow chart) to follow these steps:

1. Identify the problem or the business goal. What do you want to achieve? What problem do you want to address? This problem is the center of your map.
2. Identify the actions that employees must take or the job behavior that they must have to reach the business goal.
3. Identify the bottlenecks and problems that keep your employees from doing tasks that would help you achieve your business goals. Why aren't they doing it?
4. Determine what information your employees need to overcome these bottlenecks and challenges.

Let's say that you own a construction supply firm and you are losing your clients. This probably means that your goal is customer retention. To use the action mapping model to solve this problem, you need to identify what your employees need to do to increase customer retention. Recognize the challenges that keep them from doing what they need to do. Lastly, determine the information that your employees need to overcome these challenges. Your action map should look like this:

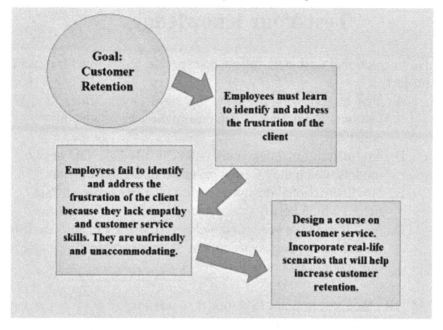

All of the models mentioned above have their pros and cons; however, you should always choose a model that aligns your company with the workflow of your team and your content. For example, if you are working with quick turnarounds and short deadlines, SAM may work best for you. On the other hand, if your team is flexible, Rapid Prototyping may be your best choice. By using a combination of instructional design models you should be able to achieve your learning goals and come up with a relevant, timely, and practical eLearning curriculum.

Test Your Knowledge

1. Do instructional designers follow one specific ISD model for every project?
    A. Yes, by following the same ISD model every time, instructional designers can ensure they are producing consistent work.
    B. No. Instructional designers will typically have one or two models which they follow based on how busy they are.
    C. No. Instructional designers will typically choose an ISD model which best fits the project they are working on.
    D. Yes. It can take years to develop proficiency in any one ISD model, so the best instructional designers typically choose one model to work with.

2. ADDIE, the most popular ISD model stands for:
    A. Analysis, Development, Design, Implementation, Evaluation
    B. Analysis, Design, Development, Iteration, Evaluation
    C. Analysis, Design, Development, Implementation, Evaluation
    D. Analysis, Development, Design, Iteration, Evaluation

3. The Design phase of ADDIE includes writing objectives and structuring the course based on your analysis. What other key activity is included in this phase?
    A. Creating a Go To Market strategy for launching and marketing your course.
    B. Creating a project management plan to track milestones, deadlines, implementation details and budgeting.
    C. Creating a style guide for this course including fonts, colors and image assets you intend to use for this course.
    D. Creating a template for the course, including the overall structure and objectives of the curriculum.

4. The Seels and Glasgow ISD model consists of three phases:
    A. Needs Analysis, Instructional Design, Delivery
    B. Needs Analysis, Planning, Instructional Design
    C. Needs Analysis, Instructional Design, Implementation & Evaluation
    D. Planning, Instructional Design, Implementation & Evaluation

5. Which of the following statements concerning the Dick and Carey Systems Approach Model is TRUE?
    A. This model is much simpler than the ADDIE model.
    B. This model is widely implemented by curriculum developers in higher education.
    C. This model is widely implemented by curriculum developers in the armed forces.
    D. This model is based on the principles of software development methodologies.

6. What does RID stand for?
    A. Rapid Interactive Development
    B. Rapid Intelligent Design
    C. Rapid Instructional Development
    D. Rapid Instructional Design

7. The RID model focuses on rapid development of interactive, activity-based learning content. What does this model NOT incorporate into its development process?
    A. ELearning
    B. Analysis and Evaluation
    C. Accelerated development timelines
    D. PowerPoint

8. What is the correct order for the four phases of the RID model?
    A. Preparation, Presentation, Practice, Performance
    B. Preparation, Practice, Presentation, Performance
    C. Presentation, Preparation, Practice, Performance
    D. Presentation, Practice, Performance, Preparation

9. SAM stands for:
    A. Success Approximation Mentorship
    B. Successive Approximation Mentorship
    C. Successive Approximation Model
    D. Successive Apprehension Model

10. The SAM model focuses on _____ and expects that _____ will be made throughout the process.
    A. prototyping / assumptions
    B. prototyping / mistakes
    C. proofreading / mistakes
    D. team building / assumptions

11. Which of the following statements below is TRUE with regards to SAM?
    A. SAM is an Agile instructional design model created by Michael Allen.
    B. SAM is a slow and meticulous instructional design model focused on perfection.
    C. SAM expects that stakeholders will not change their minds throughout the design process.
    D. SAM is an Agile instructional design model created by Bill Turnbull.

Exercise 2

Select an instructional design model for your new salary-calculating tool training course. Explain why you think the model you selected fits your project's needs.

Chapter 4: Learning Theories

This chapter will cover:

- The principles of behaviorism, cognitivism, and constructivism
- The concept of andragogy
- Malcolm Knowles's six principles of adult learning

Case Study

An instructional designer was tasked with teaching a team about cultural awareness. The team was comprised of communication experts who worked for a non-profit organization responsible for getting the latest medical research to disabled population. In an exciting new venture, they were going to partner with a French organization to help both nonprofits gain access to research outside of their native countries. This would involve a fair amount of travel to their offices overseas.

At first, the instructional designer, a trained behaviorist, focused on his usual techniques. He came up with checklists of faux pas and tips to distribute as job aids, described and modeled good cultural awareness practices, and had the team role play all possible scenarios.

When the team left for their first meeting, they felt confident in their abilities. When they returned from abroad, however, the feedback was less positive. "There were just so many little things about working with the team that we didn't cover," the project lead told the instructional designer. The team requested a new training.

Thinking about what kind of training would work to cover numerous situations, the instructional designer realized that what he needed was not so much to teach a behavior, but to help the team cultivate a mindset that could deal with cultural awareness issues as they arose. Researching alternative methods, he considered cognitivist and constructivist approaches.

Cognitivism did address the mindset of the learner, but the methods it used, lectures and memorization, did not seem appropriate for a team effort. Constructivism, though, emphasized mindset through group work, self-guided learning, and peer review—perfect for a team learning together. The instructional designer decided to rework his training with constructivist principles.

While Instructional Systems Design (ISD) models are essential tools that help instructional designers create effective courses, knowing how to apply learning theories to course design is equally important. There are three learning theories typically addressed within the scope of effective instructional design. These theories are *behaviorism*, *cognitivism*, and *constructivism*. Each learning theory has its strengths and weaknesses; therefore, to choose the theory that suits the needs of a specific course, you should take multiple aspects of learning into consideration, including your goals, learners, and situations.

Behaviorism

Behaviorism is based on observable and measurable changes in behavior. It assumes that the learner's behavior is shaped through positive or negative reinforcement. Both positive and negative reinforcement increase the probability that the behavior will reoccur. Punishment, on the other hand, decreases the likelihood that the behavior will happen again.

So, what role does behaviorism play in instructional design? The development of objectives is the main area where behaviorism affects instructional design. According to behaviorists, objectives indicate whether learners mastered the knowledge presented in the course. In other words, if the learner mastered the objectives, then their behavior changed, and learning took place.

Many people incorrectly assume that eLearning and behaviorism theory contradict each other. However, if done correctly, behaviorism can, in fact, improve learning outcomes.

Repetition plays a vital role in behaviorism. For example, we all know that many people learn best through observation, so video presentations are an efficient way to help learners understand the subject, organize their thoughts about the topic, and ultimately present their own analysis of it.

In behaviorism, only the response to the information received can be measured, so instructional designers should consider developing short drills, exercises, and quiz questions. Additionally, ISD professionals should consider presenting a series of steps that eventually lead to expected outcomes.

In this example, we will assume that you are developing a data management course. Your lessons would entail presentation of various data types as well as the commands for specific functions. You will also design step-by-step video tutorials, guiding learners through each step of the process and showing them what information to input to get the results they need. This is the theoretical part of the lesson. If you want to make this part of the course even more interesting, consider including drag and drop exercises, allowing learners to easily "move" the steps around as they try to figure out the sequence. Then, to completely master the process, you can ask learners to repeat the steps multiple times, using various instructional design methods and techniques. The principle of behaviorism dictates that learners should be able to make connections when they see a familiar process and need to draw certain conclusions. Feedback and reinforcement are the hallmarks of behaviorism. In addition to quizzes and exercises, certificates of achievement provide intrinsic reinforcement that further encourages learners to succeed.

Cognitivism

According to cognitivists, learning involves the reorganization of experiences. It is considered an active learning process. Cognitivism assumes that an existing knowledge structure is used to process new information. This theory believes that the information is received, stored, and retrieved. When cognitivists design their courses, they focus primarily on the learner. As opposed to behaviorists, who focus mainly on learning objectives, cognitivists concentrate on making learning meaningful through using learners' background knowledge. Cognitivists also believe that it is easier to remember items mentioned at the beginning or at the end rather than somewhere in the middle. Therefore, instructional designers who follow this theory focus on presenting the "must-know" content both at the beginning and at the end of the course.

Cognitivism Principles for More Effective ELearning

The wise application of cognitivism principles in the design of learning materials result in more effective learning for both children and adults. In any kind of learning environment, the needs of the learners need to be taken into consideration, so that ways can be devised to ensure optimal absorption and understanding of new information. In a nutshell, cognitivism principles have to do with optimizing the way adult learners are able to think about and understand new information so they can integrate that information into what they already know.

Adults learn more effectively when they know why they are learning in the first place. They must understand how the concepts and ideas that they are going to learn can be applied to their own lives. At the onset, the why is often more important than the how. Applying this cognitivism principle to eLearning modules, designers should ensure that their content and materials serve a clear and specific purpose in the life of the learners.

They should relate to the situations and challenges that the participants are facing. Theories presented should be followed by practical examples to show their relevance.

The cognitivism theory espouses that adults are primed for learning when they have established a learning goal or objective for themselves. Self-directed learning can be achieved by asking learners what they want to learn and what expectations they have for the course or module.

ELearning professionals should provide learners with the necessary tools to focus their efforts and facilitate learning. These should allow the learners to direct their learning based on their personal and unique needs and pace.

For instance, a general technical course on the use of MS Excel would have different uses for learners of different backgrounds. An accountant would require more information on functions related to bookkeeping, while a sales manager would need functions for trending, monitoring, and data analysis. The course should point these learners to where they can get the specialized information that they need.

According to Cognitivists, the design of the eLearning modules should promote the discovery of new information through inquiry. The right questions should be posed to stimulate critical thinking and drive the need to find new knowledge. Adults are usually more receptive toward problem-centered learning that gives them an idea of how to overcome challenges swiftly and effectively.

The modules should tap into the learners' cognitive information processing by more actively involving them in the discovery and analysis of new knowledge. Among the activities that apply this cognitivism principle to eLearning are role plays and case studies.

Adult learners should be given the chance to collaborate with each other and share insights as well as to bounce off their own ideas and opinion for didactic discussion.

Constructivism

Constructivists focus on how learners construct knowledge based on prior experience. They believe in experiential, self-directed learning. Therefore, instructional designers who follow this theory should understand what learners bring to the table in terms of prior knowledge and interests.

Here are some examples of how adults can learn through online education with a constructivist approach:

Interactivity provides a way to motivate and stimulate learners. In online learning, this can be done through video chat, voice calls, or in any other medium where the learners will not feel isolated. Constructivist thinking also suggests that learning is a social activity associated with the connection of an individual with other human beings. Using this principle, online instructional designers should conduct activities that will make a community of adult learners. Some examples of such communities are threads and group chats.

Motivating learners is also a huge factor that helps ensure transfer of learning. According to Gass & Seiter, there are eight types of motivational appeals that can push or pull an individual's performance. These eight types include: Fear, Humor, Warmth, Shame, Reward, Pride, Ingratiation, and

Guilt. So, how can instructional designers apply these appeals when designing eLearning? One way is for an instructor to remind learners about incentives that they could get if they successfully complete the training program. This is an example of Reward Appeal. Alternatively, an instructor may also remind learners about the consequences they would face if they will not complete the course successfully. This is an example of Fear Appeal. Another form of motivation, which frequently works better than most other forms, is reminding learners of why they are pursuing the course. Is it for money, for self-improvement? Or, for potential career opportunities?

Another principle states that all learning is contextual. A constructivist instructor must not impose to learners that there is only one correct perspective in the world. Instead, the instructor must give learners an opportunity to share their views.

Constructivists also believe that learning is non-instantaneous. Considering this, instructors should allot enough time for recap activities before continuing with the next lesson. It is also expected that eLearning courses should be designed using a subjective approach meaning that all learners and their abilities are different; thus, instructional designers must be considerate of designing courses for all levels.

Constructivist principles also suggest that a person needs some background knowledge to learn. Therefore, instructional designers should never assume anything and always give a brief background of any topic before digging deeper into it. Better yet, the instructor may give simple scenarios that prepare learners for absorbing new content.

Table 1 - Which Approach to Choose?

Approach	Suggested Use
Cognitivism	• Helps learners retain information • Helps learners familiarize themselves with policies and procedures
Behaviorism	• Teaches learners how to do something • Helps learners focus on specific skills
Constructivism	• Teaches learners how to develop interpersonal skills • Focuses on experiential activities

Adult Learning Theories

Case Study

Because he was an instructional designer, Frank thought that teaching his son's scout troop how to build a fire for their upcoming camping trip would be easy. He offered to lead a workshop on the topic and spent several evenings going over best practices, thinking about how to get the kids motivated and to give them opportunities to guide their own progress.

On the day of the workshop, the kids were restless, distracted by the park surroundings and the nearby playground. Undeterred, Frank began by describing all the reasons why the kids would want to learn how to build a fire. "You'll get to hang out around it all night long when we're on the trip," he said. "And then, when you go camping in the future with your families, you'll be able to build a fire for them."

He then explained the fire-building techniques to the kids. He separated them out into three groups, directed them to their fire pits, and gave them an instruction sheet.

The kids politely made a few attempts at making a fire, but quickly lost interest due to the lack of structure. They got so unruly that Frank eventually gave up and called the workshop off. Watching the kids run off toward the playground, he considered how much easier adults were: all you had to do was convince them the training was important, give them the tools and the information, draw on their lifetime of experience, and help them measure their progress. I'll stick with adults, he thought wryly.

To create truly beneficial training courses, you need to understand adult learning theories and methodologies. Andragogy, or adult learning, is an adult learning theory that describes assumptions about the learners. The concept of andragogy was pioneered by Malcolm Knowles, a theorist of adult education. He defined andragogy as "the art and science of helping adults learn." Knowles identified six principles of adult learning. According to him:

- *Adults are internally motivated.* Typical adult learners are satisfied with such extrinsic motivators as promotions and bonuses. However, satisfying intrinsic motivators such as self-esteem, power, and achievement is equally important. As an instructional designer, you should create learning activities that nourish those intrinsic motivators by demonstrating how the new knowledge and skills would be beneficial for the job.

- *Adults bring life experiences to new learning situations.* Adults have more experience than young learners do, and apply this background knowledge to the new learning that they acquire. Your training activities should reflect the actual work the learners perform and provide exercises that allow learners to apply their prior knowledge and experience to the theoretical aspects of the training.
- *Adults are goal-oriented.* Adults must have a need for learning. If an employee is expected to have certain skills or knowledge, the level of interest in training will be higher than if the same skill is not required for successful job performance. Providing just-in-time training is very important for the success of the course.
- *Adults are relevancy-oriented.* Adults must know the reason for learning. They want to know the benefits of acquiring, and the cost of not acquiring new knowledge. For this exact reason, you should base your courses on the intended audience and include all objectives and goal statements in the lesson plans and activities as well as on real work experiences.
- *Adults are practical.* Adults have a task-centered orientation to learning. Most school-age children have a subject-centered orientation to learning and focus on the content just to pass the test. Additionally, most children are not interested in retaining the information they learned in class. The ultimate goal for adult learners, however, is to retain as much information as possible from the training course; therefore, adults seek task-centered training experiences. If you satisfy this need and develop your courses around problem solving, then adult learners will most likely learn the content with the intention of actually applying it to the job. Your eLearning courses should allow learners to solve problems or perform tasks similar to those encountered on the job. This can be done through games, simulations, and various problem-solving activities. It is important to avoid information dumping and design activities that focus on practicing the information rather than simply memorizing it.
- *Adults like to be respected.* Adults like to be self-directing. In other words, they need other people, such as management, to see that they are capable of taking responsibility for themselves. Incorporating "search and discovery" elements in training courses can address this need.

Young learners may be open to receiving helpful guidance or critiques from their teachers, but adult learners tend to have a much different perception of their own abilities. (If you doubt this, think about the last time you received criticism or "guidance" from a manager or peer at work. How did you react?)

Therefore, when you see adult learners struggling to understand new concepts or failing to quickly grasp a new training topic, your intervention as an instructor should be implemented appropriately but tactfully.

Nuances to Remember when Assisting Adult Learners

Adults consider themselves to be responsible, so your intervention should not automatically treat them as though they are not.

Adults are more sensitive about being "called out" for their errors, so you should design your intervention to be perceived as facilitative as opposed to authoritative.

Adult learners often work best with specific targets or goals, so clear roadmaps of what each learner should expect during the course will be helpful as clear reference points during any intervention.

That said, any learner regardless of their age or skill level may still struggle with an online training for a wide variety of reasons. If you see that a learner is struggling, intervening sooner rather than later may be the key to getting that learner back on the right track for success.

Here are some best practices to consider when learners exhibit challenges during a course.

- **Know WHEN to Intervene** – If you intervene too late in a learner's struggles, you risk cementing their unwanted behaviors or substandard learning outcomes. However, premature corrective action could disillusion a learner if he or she feels they're being doubted or micromanaged. To help you take the pulse of each learner's progress, use early warning systems like pre-module assessments, mid-point evaluations, and other frequent appraisal techniques to assess when an intervention may be necessary. (When in doubt, acting sooner rather than later will help avert detrimental behaviors faster.)
- **Know WHAT KIND of Intervention Should Be Used** – Making evidence-based decisions is critical to any intervention's success. Use your "WHEN" (in point 1 above) to determine your WHAT. For instance, some learning challenges may require interventions in procedural aspects of learning like time management or a quick refresher on a prerequisite topic like how to use a particular piece of software for submitting assignments. Others might call for greater remedial intervention to address more systemic habits. Let your early assessments and tests guide your decision on what specific assistance you need to offer a learner.

- **Know HOW to Intervene** – In most cases, adult learners are adept at self-correction when they realize that they have a learning challenge. Here's how you can assist this process:
  - *Ensure you inform learners* about a "challenge" when you notice it. Do not be vague in your assessment, but point to specific areas that need focus instead.
  - *Be aware of any sensitivity* around exposing the need for intervention. In some instances, such exposure can have a detrimental impact on a learner's confidence.
  - *Be discrete.* This is where private communication may be most helpful, as opposed to attempting to correct someone's behavior in class.
  - *Offer universal help.* If personal discretion is not an option, you may prefer to make a universal offer to your entire class: "I'll be online after class for the next 2 hours. Any learners who want to discuss their grades or any of my feedback can contact me [through designated channels]."
  - *Be encouraging, not condescending.* When providing remedial instruction, it's important to make your learners feel as though it is okay for them to struggle with the concept/idea being discussed—"…Incidentally, you are not the only one who needs help with this topic… although you do already seem to understand a lot of it!"

The best way to manage your intervention is to first make sure your learners know right at the outset of a class what they must accomplish. Course outlines and expected learning outcomes help form each learner's expectations and set a guideline by which they know their own progress will be judged. Timely and appropriate intervention can then go a long way to making learners feel good about their ability to successfully complete your course, and your attention will feel more like welcome aid instead of an expression of doubt in their abilities.

Being a Tactful Helper at Work

Workplace learning opportunities are often perceived as privileges that are extended to only the deserving or "special" employees. As such, if learners falter or do poorly during a course or training, their confidence could be severely damaged once they return to the workplace and interact with other colleagues. This could not only be bad for their short-term productivity and morale, but also for their long-term prospects with your company.

By employing some of the intervention strategies discussed above, your instructors, teachers, and HR managers can gently, tactfully, and promptly step in and mediate or correct a potentially damaging situation. When implemented correctly, the challenged learner will not feel marginalized and the lesson's learning objectives will be successfully accomplished.

Test Your Knowledge

1. What are the three learning theories that are typically addressed during effective instructional design (Choose all that apply)?
   A. Behaviorism
   B. Abstractionism
   C. Cognitivism
   D. Constructivism

2. True or False: When designing curriculum for a course, you must only focus on one primary learning theory.
   A. True – Other learning styles will catch on eventually.
   B. False – You must design with all learning theories in mind.
   C. True – Most learners fall into the 'Behaviorism' category anyway.
   D. False – You actually shouldn't focus on any of them, as they are just theories.

3. Behaviorism is based on _____ and _____ changes in behavior.
   A. comprehensive / measurable
   B. observable / measurable
   C. observable / realistic
   D. comprehensive/ realistic

4. Cognitivism believes that information is:
   A. Relevant only when learned in the classroom.
   B. Received, retrieved and recited.
   C. Received, stored and retrieved.
   D. Received in small, bite-sized training modules.

5. Prior to designing content for Constructivists, instructional designers must first:
   A. Take deep breaths because this is the hardest audience to design effective training for.
   B. Have an understanding of what previous experience the learners are already bringing to the table.
   C. Strategize on how the same piece of content can be used in both the classroom and virtual setting without any edits.
   D. Have an expert level understanding of the topics to be covered in the training.

6. Which of the following statements is FALSE with regard to the learning theories you learned about in this lesson?
    A. Instructional designers should focus on leveraging a learner's background knowledge to make the learning meaningful.
    B. Instructional designers can engage Behaviorists by focusing on strong learning objectives.
    C. Instructional designers should leverage strong visual elements in their content in order to cater to Behaviorists.
    D. Instructional designers can tailor their content toward Constructivists by leveraging a learner's prior experience.

7. Andragogy, an adult learning theory that describes assumptions about learners, was referred to by its creator, Malcolm Knowles as:
    A. "The art and science of helping adults learn"
    B. "The science of learning and the art of behavior"
    C. "The art and science of human capital"
    D. "The natural desire for adults to learn"

8. All of the following are part of the Six Principles of Adult Learning as defined by Andragogy EXCEPT:
    A. Adults are internally motivated.
    B. Adults like to be respected.
    C. Adults bring life experiences to new learning situations.
    D. Adults like to be treated like children.

Exercise 3

Explain how you will adhere to the six principles of
adult learning in your new salary-calculating tool
course.

Chapter 5: Learning Styles

This chapter will cover:

- The VAK model
- David Kolb's Four Learning Styles
- Howard Gardner's Nine Multiple Intelligences
- Generational learning styles
- Presentation methods that address multiple learning styles

Targeting as many learning styles as possible is necessary for designing solid eLearning experiences. Even though all people have a preferred learning style, to maximize the efficiency and quality of learning, all learners must be exposed to all learning styles to one extent or another.

VAK Model

To better process new information or learn a new skill, one must hear it, see it, or try it. Most learners' preferences fall into one of the three categories. There are people who learn better through seeing; there are also people who prefer to learn by hearing; yet, there are other learners who must do hands-on activities to understand and retain new information. These three learning preferences are known as the visual, auditory, and kinesthetic learning styles and are part of the VAK model.

Visual Learning Style – These learners learn best by seeing. If you design courses that have no visual aids, they will be lost. In order to satisfy visual learners, you should include images, handouts, videos, slides, and demonstrations in your courses.

Auditory Learning Style – As opposed to visual learners, auditory learners understand and retain information by hearing it. To accommodate their needs, you should include lectures, discussion groups, and presentations as part of your course design.

Kinesthetic Learning Style – Kinesthetic learners learn best by doing. To accommodate these learners, you should consider adding hands-on activities to your courses. You may also incorporate board games, experiments, and role-plays in your training.

To ensure better retention among learners, you should accommodate all three learning styles by adding at least one activity that fits each style. Table 2 illustrates some of these activities.

Table 2 - Learning Styles

Learning Style	Tactics
Visual	• Pictures • Diagrams and charts • Written instructions • Videos • Demonstrations • Infographics • Downloadable handouts • Animated GIFs • Pictographs and Comics
Auditory	• Group discussions • Lectures • Podcasts • Audio instructions • Voice-over recording
Kinesthetic	• Games and simulations • Hands-on activities • Experiential learning activities • Role Plays

David Kolb's Four Learning Styles

David Kolb, an American educational theorist, developed the learning style inventory. His inventory is comprised of a four-stage cycle of learning and four learning styles. The stages of Kolb's learning cycle are as follows:

Concrete Experience – These learners are intuitive, they take an artistic approach to learning, are open-minded, and do not like structure. To accommodate these learners, training instructors or eLearning presenters should serve as motivators.

Reflective Observation – These learners are good at understanding different points of view, they understand the meaning of situations by observing and describing them. To accommodate these learners, training instructors or eLearning presenters should serve as experts.

Abstract Conceptualization – These learners analyze information to formulate theories and take a scientific, systematic approach. To accommodate these learners, training instructors or eLearning presenters should serve as coaches.

Active Experimentation – These learners like to learn actively. To accommodate these learners, training instructors or eLearning presenters should serve as facilitators and allow them to learn through experimentation and discovery.

Based on the four-stage cycle, Kolb developed the following learning styles:

- *Convergers* – Prefer to learn through games and simulations
- *Divergers* – Prefer to learn through hands-on exploration followed by constructive feedback
- *Assimilator*s – Prefer to learn through lectures, experiments, and conceptual models
- *Accommodators* – Prefer to learn through hands-on activities, presentations, role-plays, and debates

Howard Gardner's Nine Multiple Intelligences

The psychologist Dr. Howard Gardner pioneered the Multiple Intelligences theory. Based on his theory, people are born with certain aptitudes for learning new information and solving problems. According to Gardner, most people are only comfortable in three or four intelligences.

Table 3 lists and describes these intelligences and learners' preferences for each one of them.

While it is not always possible to address all of these intelligences in one lesson, you should aim toward including activities for as many intelligences as possible. For example, you can create both oral and written activities that require learners to "think outside the box" and analyze the information presented in the lesson. You can encourage collaboration through setting aside time for group work or participation in chats or forums. Presenting information visually through images, diagrams, skits, and videos can also help you address the needs of learners. At the end of each lesson, you should consider providing written summary of main points, keeping in mind that learners may interpret the same concept differently based on their background knowledge and skills. Providing clear objectives and evaluation methods at the beginning of the training can minimize misinterpretation of the intended message in the lesson. Whenever possible, consider giving your learners an option between writing, illustrating, or giving an oral report on the same topic.

Table 3 - Howard Gardner's Nine Multiple Intelligences

Intelligence	Description	Learners' Preferences
Linguistic Intelligence	Aptitude for writing and speaking	Learners prefer to learn through written and oral communication
Logical/Mathematical Intelligence	Aptitude for math and logic	Learners prefer to learn through logical analysis, strategizing, and creating a process.
Musical Rhythmic Intelligence	Aptitude for music and sounds	Learners prefer to learn through music and sounds.
Spatial/Visual Intelligence	Aptitude for visualizing things	Learners prefer to learn through imagines, shapes and visual designs
Bodily/Kinesthetic Intelligence	Aptitude for physical movement	Learners prefer to learn through movement, touch, and feel as well as through physical experience.
Naturalistic Intelligence	Aptitude for being with nature	Learners prefer to learn nature through working with things as well as with different features the natural world. This aptitude is especially valuable among biologists, botanists, and farmers.
Intrapersonal Intelligence	Aptitude for working alone	Learners with this aptitude learn best through self-discovery.
Interpersonal Intelligence	Aptitude for working with others	Learners prefer to learn with others through team work and communication.
Existential Intelligence	Aptitude for understanding one's purpose	Learners prefer to learn through posing and answering questions about existential realities such as life and death.

Do Learning Styles Really Exist?

Case Studies

Sarah was not used to a great deal of oversight in her job as an instructional designer. Her previous manager was very supportive of her ideas and methods if the training proved to be effective, but the manager had left the team to move across the state. Her replacement was very kind and enthusiastic, but Sarah quickly found that he had strong opinions. Specifically, he wanted her to implement *learning style theory* in her design.

"The graphic designers will probably think visually or kinesthetically, and everyone else is a grab bag," said the manager. "We should poll everyone and find out who has what learning style, so we can tailor the training and make it even more effective."

Sarah gently tried to tell the lead that learning styles were, in fact, a myth. Some evidence could be found to support it, she said, but most studies showed that all people learn in a variety of ways.

"I've heard of learning styles in conferences, from experts, and in everyday life," the manager insisted. "There might be some controversy, but no way it's completely wrong."

As Sarah began to design and develop new training, she thought about ways to both appeal to the manager and keep her training effective. After all, it was not like engaging the different ways of learning—visual, auditory, and kinesthetic —was a bad thing to do. Quite the contrary: the more ways of teaching a concept, the better the training. Regardless of whether learning styles were real, she could engage all the senses and produce great training.

The study of learning styles aims to understand the different ways that learners are able to take in and process new knowledge. It seeks to find the best practices to help a learner absorb, comprehend, and retain pieces of information. One big question in the world of learning styles, particularly among skeptics, is: Do learning styles exist?

The lack of reliable studies looking over the effectiveness of learning styles is one big issue that continues to plague it. While there are several researches on learning styles, they have "poor reliability, poor validity, and a negligible impact on teaching and learning." Additionally, abundance of learning style theories in the 21st century makes things even more complex, and many of these theories contradict each other.

The commercialization of learning styles is a new issue that haunts the concept. Dr. Steve Draper, a senior lecturer at the University of Glasgow's

Psychology School in the UK, said that commercialization poses a big threat in measuring the effectiveness of learning style theories. Another study backed this claim and found that while many of those bought a learning module based on their personal preference, the lesson never delivered the results expected from someone who fits the said learning style.

In their study, Coffield and his colleagues concluded that educators and designers should put more attention on learners' personalities as opposed to learning style theories. They suggested that there should be greater promotion on how people can enhance their learning, and supported the claim that self-development has great potential for a learner to acquire advantages and disadvantages of a specific learning style theory. However, sticking to a learning style might create some restrictions to changes in teaching.

The lack of reliable data is one cause that continues to fuel questions on the existence of learning styles. The "personalization" trend in the 21st century has even added another problem to this discipline, as it has made it more complex and much more difficult to assess.

Coffield and his team said it best: "In order for learning styles to bury concerns over its existence and effectiveness, instructional designers and scholars need to exert extra effort to discuss problems faced in learning styles research." This includes the need for deeper research on the psychological aspects of learning theories and creating unity among researchers over recommendations on teaching and learning styles.

Generational Learning Styles

Cultural changes influence people's tastes, preferences, and beliefs. As a result, a generational gap between older and younger generations occurs. Because of a rapidly changing culture and wide generational gap, instructional designers have realized the need for taking different generational learning styles into consideration. While all generations are able to learn through a variety of media, each generation has certain preferences. The four generational learning styles are:

- Traditionalists
- Baby Boomers
- Generations X
- Generations Y or Millennials

Table 4 illustrates the learning preferences of each generation.

Table 4 - Generational Learning Styles

Traditionalists	Baby Boomers	Generations X	Generations Y or Millennials
Ages 66 and over	Ages 47-65	Ages 29-46	Ages 18-28
Prefer learning through lectures	Like to learn through lectures and workshops	Prefer eLearning to traditional learning	Prefer eLearning to traditional learning
Dislike role-plays and games	Enjoy small group activities	Enjoy experiential learning activities	Prefer hands-on learning
		Prefer self-studying	Prefer learning through social networking tools such as wikis, blogs, podcasts and mobile applications

How to Satisfy Different Generations of Learners?

As an instructional designer, one of the main challenges that you will face is creating a successful learning experience geared toward all generations. While it is nearly impossible to create one perfect solution that would close the gap between generations, there are certainly ways to build courses that satisfy most learners' needs. Understanding the VAK model is one way to cover the needs of most generations. According to studies, traditionalists prefer an auditory approach to learning because most of them grew up listening to the radio. Baby Boomers, on the other hand, prefer visuals because they grew up watching TV. Most learners who fall under Generation X and Y are both kinesthetic and visual as they grew up playing video games, writing emails, and using different types of social media tools such as Facebook and Twitter. As you create your courses, you should consider incorporating a variety of activities that appeal to all learning styles. Additionally, you should focus on making your courses meaningful by choosing a blended approach to learning and mixing strategies to accommodate both younger and older generations.

When instructional designers create eLearning courses, they do their best to address all learning styles. However, what many course creators forget is that it is necessary to address learning styles across all generations. To do this, you should first conduct target audience analysis. If during the analysis phase, you discover that most of the learners are from Generation Y or Millennials, you should then gear your course toward these generations making their learning as interactive as possible. For example, you could encourage collaboration by incorporating a wiki or a Facebook page. Additionally, as you design your course for younger audience, keep in mind that both Millennials and Gen Y do not like to hear what they already know and they also do not like repetition. Young learners just want to know what they need to know now! When younger generation signs up for any training, the expectation is that the same course will be also available in the eLearning and Mobile Learning formats. So, to please a younger generation of learners, instructional designers should keep their lessons short and to the point. They should also try to gamify the training material as much as possible.

On the other hand, even if most learners represent younger audience, it is still important to keep the older generation in mind. If during the analysis phase you discover that older people will be taking your course, you should ensure that the eLearning piece you develop satisfies the needs of Baby Boomers and the X generation. It is no longer a secret that most older generations like learning through lectures and many of them think that gamification and interactivity are simply a waste of their time.

While it is nearly impossible to make everyone happy, it is always possible to find a compromise. For example, consider including a PDF file with most of the information found in your interactivities or add short lectures through video or audio narration. Another approach that some instructional designer may choose is to create two different versions of the course: one interactive and one passive. If you decide to go that route, you should understand that while flexibility will please learners, it may not be very practical from both budget and resources stand point. Therefore, as an instructional designer, you are responsible for finding a middle ground, so that all groups of learners can be satisfied.

Test Your Knowledge

1. Which of these statement about Learning Styles is FALSE?
    A. Learners typically fall into the following three learning style. categories: Auditory, Visual and Kinesthetic.
    B. The visual learning style denotes an individual who would rather see something to learn it, rather than purely listen to it.
    C. To accommodate the three learning styles, it is important to produce three different versions of the content you are creating.
    D. The kinesthetic learning style denotes an individual who needs to actually do or participate in what is being taught in order to retain the information.

2. David Kolb's Learning Style Inventory is comprised of the following four-stages of learning: (Choose all that apply)
    A. Concrete Experience
    B. Attentive Capitulation
    C. Reflective Observation
    D. Passive Internalization
    E. Abstract Conceptualization
    F. Active Experimentation

3. According to Kolb's learning styles, Divergers tend to learn through:
    A. Lectures, experiments and conceptual models.
    B. Games and simulations.
    C. Hands-on activities, presentations, role-plays and debates.
    D. Hands-on exploration followed by constructive feedback.

4. Generation X and Generation Y/Millennial learners:
    A. Prefer eLearning to traditional learning.
    B. Like to learn through lectures and workshops.
    C. Prefer learning through lectures.
    D. Enjoy small group activities.

5. Which of these generations prefer self-studying and enjoy experiential learning activities?
    A. Traditionalists
    B. Baby Boomers
    C. Generation X
    D. Generation Y/Millennials

6. Which of these generations prefer hands-on learning through social learning tools such as wikis, blogs, podcasts and mobile applications?
    A. Traditionalists
    B. Baby Boomers
    C. Generation X
    D. Generation Y/Millennials

7. Which of these generations prefer learning through lectures and dislike role-plays and games?
    A. Traditionalists
    B. Baby Boomers
    C. Generation X
    D. Generation Y/Millennials

8. Different generations tend to learn differently. Which model will ensure that you are catering to auditory, visual and kinesthetic learners in the same solution?
    A. ADDIE
    B. VAK
    C. Andragogy
    D. SAM

Exercise 4

What types of activities will you include in your eLearning course to ensure that you address the auditory, visual, kinesthetic, and generational learning styles?

Chapter 6: Motivation

This chapter will cover:

- Intrinsic and extrinsic motivation
- Abraham Maslow's Hierarchy of Needs and its influence on training courses
- The WIIFM principle
- John Keller's ARCS Model of Motivational Design and its application to course design

Case Study

When Paean Insurance Company had to revamp its call center processes only six months after the last overhaul, their instructional designer faced a team full of frustrated employees reluctant to engage in training. Though the revamp was necessary since important legislation had been passed that affected how they could talk to customers, the constant need for new training felt like a distraction from the job. Though no one said anything overtly, the instructional designer knew they were wondering why they couldn't just learn it on their own.

To deal with their frustration, the instructional designer went back to the basics of motivating adult learners.

First, when outlining the course, he included as much of the content as he could into a job aid. Call scripts, tips, hints and terminology explanations could all be made available separately to respect the learner's time and experience level.

Second, the instructional designer worked to keep the course content focused on real-world applications by creating case studies, games and role-playing exercises that reflected the way calls worked in real life.

Third, the instructional designer respected the learners' agency by allowing them to jump to any aspect of the process. Some learners may have done their own research on the changes, he reasoned, and shouldn't have to go through material they already knew.

Finally, the instructional designer took the time to explain why the course would be helpful to them by breaking down the new processes and providing resources. With these motivation strategies in place, the training was a success.

Designing highly motivational learning experiences is the challenge that most instructional designers face. After all, each learner has different goals, desires, and needs. Therefore, creating a course that motivates all learners is nearly impossible. However, certain aspects of motivation must be considered to ensure the effectiveness of course design. Motivation can be either *intrinsic* or *extrinsic*. Intrinsic motivation refers to internal drives. Specifically, learners take the course because they enjoy it or because they want to develop a particular skill. This is the type of motivation you should aim for when creating your courses. Extrinsic motivation, on the other hand, refers to performing activities to get something in exchange such as monetary rewards, certificates, or good grades.

More often than not, interestingly designed courses with lots of examples, interactions, and assessments will keep learners motivated. As an instructional designer, it is your job to create learning materials that are enticing to both the mind and the heart.

First and foremost, never underestimate the power of visuals. Visuals range from photos and infographics, to videos and simulations. Remember that blocks of text can be too overwhelming even for learners with long attention spans. A short but informative video in between texts, for example, may lighten the mood and enable learners to digest more facts and figures.

Keep in mind that multimedia is at the heart of eLearning. There's no room for monotony and repetition when concepts or topics are presented in varied forms.

Interactivity is also key when it comes to capturing the adult learners' discerning mind. Keep in mind that learning is not all about getting answers. It also involves acquiring questions to ponder. Adults do not expect to simply be spoon-fed. To make the most out of their learning experience, design a program that will spark meaningful questions in your learners' mind. These questions are usually related to their personal and professional life.

For instance, if the topic is modernization in Asia, make sure that the discussion flow elicits questions about how technology in one continent can be applied to another part of the world. In other words, tap the learner's curiosity by tying a subject matter with real-life applications.

Of course, proper education means having access to learning materials that are accurate and updated. Never sacrifice content for creativity. Find a way to balance the two. This will allow adult learners to enhance their critical thinking skills while satisfying their craving for amusement.

The more mature generation, compared to the younger one, generally has more experience in life. Therefore, they want and need to be challenged. Add value to their existing knowledge by adjusting lesson outlines according to their level. As an example, if the course is about agriculture, go beyond the basics of farming and include recent works on growing crops more effectively.

Overall, when motivational appeals are applied to eLearning, learners come out more intelligent and more confident in their field of expertise or interest. Additionally, when creating eLearning content always remember that imparting knowledge to learners involves getting them to act on their newfound facts and figures.

Abraham Maslow's Hierarchy of Needs

Abraham Maslow is known for developing a hierarchy of human needs. According to Maslow, five basic human needs must be satisfied in order for internal motivation to occur. *Physiological needs* are considered the lower level needs and must be met first. They include the need for food and sleep. *Safety needs* come into play when all the physiological needs are met. When both physiological and safety needs are satisfied, the *need to belong* becomes important. This involves the need for *family and friends* as well as the need to feel like one belongs somewhere. Typical eLearning courses satisfy the need to belong by offering a safe environment for answering questions, receiving feedback, and making decisions. Once the lower levels have been satisfied, the need for *esteem* surfaces. This involves the need to be highly regarded by others. Finally, when all four levels are completely satisfied, people begin looking for *self-actualization*, or the need to be "all that they can be." See the graphic below.

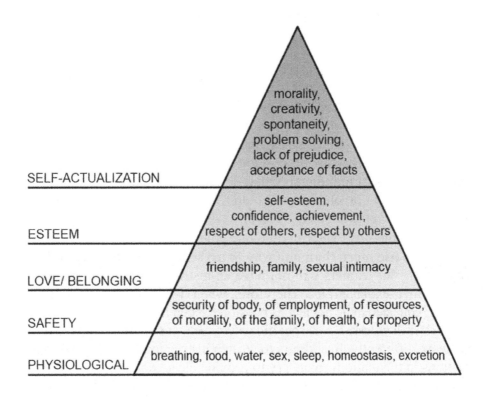

Even if you create the most fascinating course, if learners' physiological needs are not met, they will not gain much from it. This is why it is highly recommended that learners get enough sleep and eat a good breakfast prior to the training. Establishing a safe learning environment is an important factor in training success. Additionally, the learning environment should satisfy participants' needs to belong. Learners also expect to be respected by the trainer and other participants. Once the training is completed, learners expect to be able to utilize their newly acquired knowledge to grow on either a personal or professional level. In other words, the need for self-actualization typically takes place after completing the training course.

When designing, consider motivation, goals, experience, and culture of learners as these four elements play a crucial role in course development. Successful trainings are designed with the question *"What's in it for me?"* or *WIIFM*, in mind. You should aim to combine internal and external needs and motivators. Internal motivators arise from the sense of accomplishment people feel from learning something new. Alternatively, external motivators are associated with tangible outcomes such as money or awards. Creating training courses that satisfy both internal and external needs usually get the best results and receive good evaluations.

Most adults are eager to learn when they need to achieve a goal. Adult learners want to be able to immediately apply their new knowledge and skills to real-life situations.

As we have already discussed, adult learners bring a lot of experience and background knowledge and expect to apply them to the new material. Most adults are kinesthetic learners; therefore, whenever possible, you should incorporate hands-on activities into your lessons.

Even if you take WIIFM, goals, and experience into consideration, the course will not be successful unless cultural aspects are incorporated into the design. It is important to remember that designing training requires a lot of initial research as organizational culture varies from department to department, and even from team to team.

Here are some ways you can motivate your learners:

1. Always use more than one way to present instructions/directions – Remember, your learners will not have an instructor who will be able to provide further explanations. Therefore, when you want learners to do something, you need to be as clear as possible. When it comes to instructions, more is better than less. Be as specific as you can, and do not forget that all people learn differently. In addition to written instructions, consider offering instructions in the audio format. Try to provide clear examples of what you want your learners to do. Lastly, always use plain language when writing instructions. Your learners should not spend too much time thinking about the assignment. In fact, your instructions should be so simple that learners should immediately understand what they need to do without having to re-read the instructions multiple times.

2. Communicate your expectations and objectives – We all do better when we know what is expected of us. Expectations help us understand if we are performing better or worse than we should. Furthermore, clear objectives and expectations help us progress in the right direction. If adults are unsure why they are learning a particular skill, they will most likely give up, and think of training as a waste of their time. Course expectations do not necessarily have to be written as bullet points. Instructional designers may consider showing a motivational video, telling a story, or even displaying an image that emphasizes the real-world benefits. Throughout the course, try reminding your learners of goals and objectives. Remember, when we know the goal, or the reason we need to get to our goal, we will be more motivated to succeed.

3. Feedback, feedback, feedback – We all know that feedback is a crucial part of learning. Even kids in school know about their successes and failures through test scores and report cards. Obviously, adults do not need grades to feel motivated. What they need is constant clear and immediate feedback. While it's hard to provide truly valuable feedback in an eLearning format, there are some ways to do that. For example, instructional designers may create short quizzes or "test your knowledge" activities after each segment or objective. These knowledge checks may be in a form of a question, or designed as a game or simulation. You may even consider breaking your game into levels, and have learners participate in the level that is right for them.

4. Avoid cognitive overload – Break your course into as many chunks as you can. If you present a lot of information at once, your learners will be overloaded and their retention level will decrease. To increase retention, you should deliver your course in small segments. In eLearning courses, allow learners to go back, and review sections that they missed, or need more time to comprehend. Even if your course is short and to the point, never expect your learners to remember all the content. Whenever possible, provide a downloadable reference guide that contains all the must-know information from the lesson.

5. Personalize learning experiences – While eLearning is not easy to personalize, there are some ways to do so. For example, you can speak directly to your learner. This can be done by using the pronoun "you" throughout your presentation. Always put yourself in your learners' shoes. Use relevant real-life examples and stories in your course. Your goal is to make learners feel at home. You want them to be able to relate to the material you are presenting.

As you can see, motivation plays a prominent role in eLearning experiences. While it is not always easy to motivate adult learners, if you apply the strategies outlined above, the level of engagement and retention among your learners will increase.

ARCS Model

John Keller's ARCS Model of Motivational Design is a systematic approach to designing motivational learning. It consists of the following four steps for promoting motivation in the learning process:

Attention – Elicit learners' interest and curiosity
Relevance – Show the importance and usefulness of the content
Confidence – Include challenging but doable activities
Satisfaction – Make the overall experience positive and worthwhile

Table 5 illustrates how you can apply the steps from the ARCS model.

Table 5 - ARCS Model

Attention	Relevance	Confidence	Satisfaction
Include games and role-plays	Use examples that learners are familiar with	Provide performance requirements and evaluation	Reward learners
Use a variety of presentation methods	Provide reasons why content is relevant	Provide feedback	Provide opportunities to practice what has been learned
Use a small amount of humor	Explain learning goals	Allow learners to control their learning	Provide reinforcement
Add visuals	Ask about learners' goals		
Ask questions			
Have learners solve problems			

Personalization in ELearning

Personalization is another excellent way to motivate learners. The concept of "Personalization" can easily be understood from taking a closer look at some of the existing digital technologies that all of us use. For instance, from the browser that you use to roam the internet, to the email and messaging systems that you use to stay connected with friends and family, to the digital boxes you use to watch TV shows and movies online—they all offer personalization and customization options.

However, when it comes to eLearning systems, "personalization" takes on a whole new meaning. Personalized eLearning is the act of customizing:

- The learning environment (e.g. how the content appears to the learner—font sizes, colors, backgrounds, themes etc.)
- The learning content itself (e.g. audio, video, textual, graphical etc.)
- The interaction between facilitator, learner and the learning content (e.g. mouse, stylus, tap/swipe, keyboard; e.g. using "Gaming," Quizzes, Online discussions, Demonstrate-do-check-reinforce, Adaptive learning approaches, Tutorials)

So, what does Personalized eLearning mean? Well, as it relates to eLearning, personalization involves not only providing the ability to customize the learning environment, similar to the "preferences" and "settings" options that most digital tools offer today; but also personalizing many other aspects of the entire learning experience. Personalized eLearning, therefore, encompasses the ability to customize aspects such as:

- What content should be delivered as part of the learning experience.
- How the content should be delivered.
- The sequence of its delivery.
- How learners will be evaluated.
- What feedback mechanisms will be offered.
- ...and much more.

While traditional eLearning was an extension to symmetric learning approaches, personalized eLearning espouses a marked shift from "facilitator lead" teaching to "learner centric" learning. Where conventional eLearning tends to treat learners as a homogeneous entity, personalized eLearning digresses from that path by recognizing learners as heterogeneous mix of individuals.

According to a previous study, many eLearning environments are not organically supportive of lifelong learning or personalization. Therefore, instructional designers need to re-evaluate current eLearning courses to find ways to personalize them.

As you already know, there are multiple factors that impact learners' ability to learn, including age, demographics, cultural background, and the level of education, to name a few. All of these play an important role in determining how eLearning personalization should be approached. Some points that should be taken into consideration when deciding to personalize an eLearning experience include:

- **Personalizing the learner** – Make the course "personal" to the learner. Capture his/her name as part of the registration process, rather than using a generic "Learner A." Ask your learners to sign on with their name, and then use the name throughout the course (e.g. "Welcome, Adam! or "Well done, Jill...you've cleared Level II!")

- **Personalizing the environment** – Let learners determine what their online eLearning environments should look like. Let learners pick avatars to represent either themselves or their "facilitators." Where possible, let the learners pick voices (male/female) for audio content.

- **Personalizing the content** – Whenever possible, incorporate content from learners' personal environment and reflect learners' browsing habits and preferences—such as Blogs, Social Media sites or other relevant content sources.

- **Personalizing the roles with the use of photographs and pictures** – Throughout the lesson, use a photograph of the instructor or even ask your learners to add their own photo to make the content more "personal."

- **Personalizing learning objectives** – Enable learners to make the learning objectives relevant to why they are taking the course. For example, if the goal is to move from Supervisor to Manager, then learning objectives must reinforce that goal.

- **Personalizing learning sequences** – Learners should be able to chart their own learning path. Creating "nonlinear" content allows learners to pick and choose how they will learn.

- **Personalizing the "conversation"** – Whether it is voice/video, or just text, using phrases like "Now, let's click 'Done' to end this segment," instead of "Click done to end," will make the content more personalized. Furthermore, "Now, click 'Done' to end this segment, Jill," is even more personalized than the previous two examples.

- **Personalizing the navigation** – Foster "inquisitiveness" by allowing learners to explore various parts of the content, even if they are not currently or actively studying/learning it. This will allow eager learners to explore segments they find personally interesting, just like they would if they were reading a text book.

- **Recognizing individual competency** – Allow learners to skip certain segments of a course (perhaps by directly going to the "Test your knowledge" section) and start learning the areas they feel they need to learn—instead of forcing them to learn what they already know.

- **Personalizing the media** – Some learners learn quickly if they watch a short video, others need to read a printed PDF file rather than viewing the same document online. Giving choices such as "View," "Listen" or "Print" will tap into each learner's individual learning styles and preferences.

When harmonized together, all aspects mentioned above will create a truly Personal Learning Environment (PLE) that will empower learners to manage and control their own learning.

Personalized eLearning is essential because each person learns differently. As a result, in order to be effective, the personalization must take into account each individual's needs, requirements, learning objectives, skill level and learning abilities.

The personalization process should also use a progress monitoring mechanism to validate whether the personalization is delivering effective results. If not, appropriate revisions must be made to course delivery (e.g. change content from text-based to video/audio content, etc.) to achieve the desired learning outcomes.

Test Your Knowledge

1. Learners who take a course because they enjoy learning are said to have _____ motivation while learners who take a course to get something in return are said to have _____.
    A. intrinsic / extrinsic
    B. intrinsic / holistic
    C. extrinsic / intrinsic
    D. holistic / extrinsic

2. Abraham Maslow's Hierarchy of Human Needs consists of five basic human needs in the following order of importance:
    A. Physiological, Safety, Love/Belonging, Esteem, Self-Actualization
    B. Physiological, Safety, Love/Belonging, Self-Actualization, Esteem
    C. Physiological, Love/Belonging, Safety, Esteem, Self-Actualization
    D. Physiological, Love/Belonging, Safety, Self-Actualization, Esteem

3. Even if you create the most fascinating course, if a learner's _____ needs are not met, they will not learn from it.
    A. Esteem
    B. Self-actualization
    C. Safety
    D. Physiological

4. The need for self-actualization is typically fulfilled after a learner has finished a course and consists of:
    A. Learners being able to brag to their peers that they have completed the course.
    B. Learners expecting to be compensated for the course they have just completed.
    C. Learners expecting to be able to utilize their newly acquired knowledge to grow on a personal or professional level.
    D. Learners being able to hang a certificate of achievement in their office after completion of the course.

5. Which of the following statements about WIIFM is NOT true?

    A. WIIFM stands for 'What's In It For Me'.

    B. Designing a course with 'WIIFM' in mind ensures the learner will be motivated to finish the course.

    C. A good WIIFM utilizes both internal and external motivations and needs.

    D. A course designed with the 'WIIFM' in mind typically ensures high assessment scores.

6. John Keller's ARCS Model of Motivational Design stands for:

    A. Attrition, Relevance, Coincidence, Satisfaction

    B. Attention, Relevance, Confidence, Satisfaction

    C. Attention, Routine, Confidence, Situation

    D. Attrition, Routine, Coincidence, Situation

7. The Relevance step in John Keller's ARCS Model of Motivational Design:

    A. Ensures that learners get relevant feedback throughout the course.

    B. Demonstrates the importance and relevance of the content through familiar examples and learning goals.

    C. Rewards learners for providing relevant examples of their own during training.

    D. Includes relevant games, questions and problem solving challenges to learners within the course.

Exercise 5

Using the WIIFM principle as well as some other methods of motivational design, decide how you will address motivation in your eLearning course for the department of finance.

Part II - Designing Instructionally Sound ELearning Courses

"Change is the end result of all true learning."
Leo Buscaglia

Chapter 7: Needs Analysis and Data Collection Methods

This chapter will cover:

- The importance of analysis in instructional design
- Audience analysis, performance gap analysis, and task analysis
- Data collection methods and techniques
- Steps in conducting needs analysis

The analysis phase is an essential part of instructional design. After all, without conducting a needs analysis, you have no way of knowing the reason for creating the course. Needs analysis discovers the target audience for the course as well as the true purpose for creating it. Based on data collected during this phase, you will be able to determine the approach you need to take in designing the course. You will also be able to decide on media and delivery method based on the findings. Moreover, the analysis phase will help you figure out what content should be included in the lesson, whether the training is for beginners or more advanced learners, or whether it is just a refreshment or a job aid. In addition to answering all these questions, the analysis phase helps to find out if the training is really a viable solution.

Oftentimes, instructional designers conduct a thorough needs analysis just to realize that there is a performance issue, which cannot be solved by a training course. Alternatively, some instructional designers do not conduct needs analysis at all. This approach can be detrimental to designing an effective solution to a problem. In real life, clients underestimate the value of needs analysis; therefore, they do not dedicate the budget for this phase. If you face this situation, you can either try to convince your client of the importance of doing analysis by explaining the risks associated with avoiding it, or conduct minimal analysis to get the information needed to design the course. Oftentimes, stakeholders already have most of the required information; therefore, conducting extensive needs analysis becomes unnecessary.

There are three major types of analyses. They are:

- *audience analysis*
- *performance analysis*
- *task analysis*

Audience Analysis

Conducting audience analysis is a critical step because knowing your audience is necessary to effectively present training material. Audience analysis should include information on demographics as well as on learners' motivation and background knowledge. Below are some questions you should consider during the audience analysis.

- Who is the target audience for this course?
- What is the average age of learners?
- Are learners in your audience either mostly men or mostly women?
- What is their cultural background?
- What is their education level?
- What experience do learners have?

- What is their motivation level?
- Why do learners need this course?
- How much time can they devote to training?
- Do they have any specific needs?
- What is their learning preference?

Performance, Gap and Root Cause Analysis

The ultimate goal of an eLearning course is to close the gap between the current and the desired performance. To identify and close that gap, you need to conduct gap analysis. Before conducting gap analysis and identifying the real reason for training, assumptions about training needs and requirements should not be made. Only after carrying out gap analysis will instructional designers be able to draw conclusions and propose solutions. To conduct gap analysis, you should have your goals in place, as they indicate the desired state. Not only should you find a solution to close the existing gap, but you should also figure out the reason the gap exists. By conducting a root cause analysis, you should be able to address the actual root cause of the gap and therefore treat the real problem instead of its symptoms. One of the best ways to collect information about performance gap and root causes is by using the *Five Why Technique*. The essence of this technique is to repeatedly ask *Why* until you arrive at the root cause of the problem.

During the performance gap analysis, you may discover that people in the organization do not achieve the desired performance because they lack necessary knowledge or skills. However, you may also discover that poor performance is due to the lack of motivation, appropriate tools, resources, or organizational support in the company. If your analysis shows that the problem lies in knowledge and skills, then you can safely proceed with training. However, if the problem is with motivation, lack of tools, or organizational support, then it is a performance improvement issue, and training will not be helpful. Training does not solve all problems associated with inadequate information, lack of resources, poor process, or management issues. If, during performance analysis, you discover the problem is not related to knowledge or skills, you should advise the client that even the most innovative training course will not effectively address the need.

Task Analysis

Task analysis identifies knowledge and skills needed to accomplish instructional goals. It helps you describe the tasks and sub-tasks that learners will perform as well as prioritize the sequence of these tasks and create appropriate terminal and enabling objectives based on the results. Below is a list of questions that should be considered during the task analysis.

- What is the complexity of the task?
- How often is the task performed?
- Is the task critical to the performance of the job?
- Is this task performed separately or as part of other tasks?
- What is the relationship between all the tasks?
- What is the risk associated with not being able to perform the task?
- What background knowledge and skills are needed to perform the task?

In addition to performance, audience, and task analyses, there are other types of analyses including instructional, environment, and technical analyses.

The *instructional analysis* breaks down the tasks of each goal and helps designers eliminate extraneous information. To conduct an instructional analysis, ISD specialists should work together with the Subject Matter Expert (SME) designated for that course.

The *resource analysis* collects information on the learning context to ensure that the instructional designer does not go beyond the available resources dedicated to the project.

The *environment analysis* identifies the environment in which the learning should occur. It can range from watching an instructional video to listening to an educational podcast.

Technical analysis identifies technical specifications needed to develop and implement the course.

As you collect specific data about the type of eLearning course the client is looking for, you should consider asking the stakeholder the following questions:

- Is your content already available?
- Do you have any materials developed?
- How many SMEs will work on this project, and what is their availability?
- Do you have already existing visuals that you would like to include in the course?

- How long do you expect this course to be? Do you want to include assessments?
- Do you have a Learning Management System? If not, how do you expect the course to be launched? (We will cover Learning Management Systems in Chapter 14.)

Data Collection Methods

There are many information-gathering strategies you can use to conduct your analyses. These strategies range from review of relevant literature and direct observations to conducting interviews and focus groups. All strategies have advantages and disadvantages. The method that suits the specific needs analysis depends on many different factors, including the intensity of analysis and the amount of time dedicated to the analysis. Whenever possible choose several different methods to ensure accurate data collection.

Literature and Document Reviews

When there is no budget for needs analysis, you should at least review relevant documents. This approach is inexpensive compared to most other methods and provides the background information necessary for carrying out a project. However, before choosing this method, it is necessary to understand that the information found in documents can be outdated, inaccurate, incomplete and disorganized.

Observations

This is an excellent way to collect data when the training goal is to teach a new skill or change a behavior. You can simply sit and observe the performance of the best, average, and worst employees in the organization. Then, document your observations of both the current and desired performance. The observation method works well primarily because it allows instructional designers to see for themselves what people do and how they perform. However, there are also disadvantages to this method. One of them is that people typically perform better when they know they are being observed.

Interviews

Interviews work very well for gathering information about current business needs, performance, and audience analyses. They are also useful for gathering stories for learning scenarios and simulations. The interviewing method can help you clarify confusing information collected by either observations or literature reviews. Unlike observations, interviews can be done over the phone, which is very convenient for both you and your interviewee. The main problem with interviews, however, is that they can be biased as they rely on the reactions and opinions of respondents. Further drawbacks to interviews are that they can be costly and time consuming.

Focus Groups

Focus groups are a good way to collect information from many different people without meeting with each one of them individually. Using this data gathering method has many of the same advantages and disadvantages as interviews. In addition to being resource intensive, it takes a lot of time to analyze the information gathered from the entire group. Therefore, it is best to limit focus groups to ten participants. Moreover, there are typically participants who dominate the discussion, leaving the opinions of less outspoken group members unheard. The most important drawback to focus groups is the lack of anonymity, which can lead participants to not sharing their opinions.

Surveys

Surveys are the most commonly used tool for conducting needs analysis. Surveys vary greatly in the amount of time and money they require. While they can help instructional designers obtain both qualitative and quantitative data, there are still many problems associated with them. First, oftentimes people mark their answers without even reading the questions. As a result, data gathered from this source is not always precise. Surveys also require clear and accurate wording of each question. In interviews and focus groups, participants have an opportunity to clarify questions, and instructional designers can even provide examples that describe the meaning of each question. With surveys, participants do not have the luxury of asking questions or clarifying ambiguous statements. Therefore, if they do not interpret the question correctly, the results will be skewed. There are different types of questions and rating scales used in surveys. Some of the most popular ones are the following:

- Likert Scale
- Dichotomous questions
- Multiple choice questions
- Semantic differential
- Open-ended questions

Likert Scales

Likert Scales are linear rating scales. These scales are typically used to rate attitudes. You provide statements that you want participants to evaluate along with the definitions of the scale. In most cases, Likert Scale ranges from 1 to 10 with 1 being the worst and 10 being the best possible option.

Example of a Likert Scale:

1. I am satisfied with my job

strongly agree   agree   neutral   disagree   strongly disagree

Dichotomous Questions

Dichotomous questions are yes/no questions. While they do not provide enough information for analysis, they work well as screening tools to identify people eligible to participate in the survey.

Example of a dichotomous question: *Have you ever had on-the-job training before?*
> *Yes*
> *No*

Multiple Choice Questions

Multiple choice questions can ask for one or more answers. This question type can be used to analyze attitudes and behaviors, as well as personal preferences and styles. However, multiple choice items are difficult to construct, and oftentimes people circle the response without reading the question.

Example of a multiple-choice question: *What is your preferred learning style?*

  A. Visual

  B. Auditory

  C. Kinesthetic

Semantic Differential

This survey is used to measure the meaning of concepts, events, and objects based on peoples' perceptions and attitudes. The scale typically provides two or more contrasting ideas and asks people to rate them as important – not important, valuable – useless, interesting – boring, etc.

Example of semantic differential: *What do you think about this training course?*

  (5) Relevant to my job

  (4)

  (3)

  (2)

  (1) Completely irrelevant

Open-Ended Questions

Open-ended questions are very effective because participants have to think about their answers before responding. These questions can provide a lot of valuable, qualitative information for analysis. However, it can be very difficult to elicit only pertinent information and avoid useless irrelevant comments and responses. In addition, open-ended questions require a lot of time for participants to complete and for instructional designers to analyze.

Example of an open-ended question: *What type of training are you looking for to improve your overall performance?*

Steps for Conducting Needs Analysis

To conduct a thorough needs analysis for your course, you should do the following:

1. *Define objectives* – This step answers the following questions:
   - What is the purpose of the course?
   - What are the performance issues?
   - What are the root causes for performance issues?
   - Is training the solution to the problem

2. *Identify Data* – This step answers the following questions:
   - What is the training need?
   - Who needs this training?
   - What are some of the strategies for designing and delivering this training?

3. *Select Data-Collection Method* – This step answers the following question:
   - Which data collection approach will be used for needs analyses?

4. *Collect Data* – During this step, you gather the information using selected methods.

5. *Analyze Data* – In this step, you use the data you collected and compare, organize, and analyze it.

6. *Prepare Analysis Report* – During this step, you document both the data you collected and your analyses of that data in the analysis report. In addition, your report should include conclusions made as a result of data analysis. Typical analysis report includes the following sections:
   - Overview of the project
   - Performance analysis
   - Tools used to collect data
   - Training needs analysis
   - Conclusions or recommendations made based on the analysis

Is Conducting Needs Analysis Truly Necessary?

> **Case Study**
>
> Vulcan Oil Company had a problem: their safety training compliance program wasn't working. Even though the online course simply covered the basic compliance standards that were in place company-wide, there wasn't an increase in people passing the post-training test, and evaluations were very low across the board.
>
> When the head of compliance approached their instructional designer about it, the recommendation was to conduct thorough needs analysis.
>
> "You have a huge company, and every department is going to see safety differently," said the instructional designer. "The finance office is going to see things very differently from the people out in the field. This course is straight out of the manual. No wonder people don't see it as relevant."
>
> "This is just about the basic, company-wide standards," said the head of compliance, frowning. "I don't see the point in tailoring each training to the department."
>
> But reluctantly, the head of compliance agreed to let a needs assessment be conducted. As the instructional designer suspected, the training was too generalized for each department, and seen as divorced from their normal safety training.
>
> By surveying and interviewing both employees and safety trainers, the instructional designer could identify the reason why the gaps were occurring (the employees didn't see the connection to their safety training) as well as how to fix them (by connecting the information from both trainings). At the recommendation of the instructional designer, the training was reworked as a workshop held at the end of normal safety training, instead of an online course.

Most, if not all, instructional designers at some point have developed training that was not really needed. Unfortunately, it is not always easy to convince clients that what they have in mind may not be the best solution from the training perspective. However, good instructional designers must be able to recognize the ultimate reason for training and seamlessly help the clients select the most appropriate training modality.

To do that, it is crucial that instructional designers review the available information about the company and the current need. It may also be necessary to talk with some of the employees and managers to get their perspective about the situation in the organization. After conducting analysis, instructional designers should formulate a measurable business goal and create an action plan to reach that goal. During the initial research, instructional designers should determine why people are not doing what they should and whether the real problem has to do with work environment, motivation, or lack of knowledge and skills.

Once the root cause is determined and the business goal is formulated, you should determine whether training is the right solution to begin with. For instance, if you concluded that the root cause has to do with culture, as opposed to lack of knowledge and skills, you can confidently recommend a performance improvement intervention. However, if you are certain that the problem lies in lack of knowledge or limited skills to perform the needed tasks, you should then continue your analysis to decide which training solution is appropriate. As you continue with your analysis, you may conclude that most of the knowledge needed to solve the problem should be stored in memory. In that case, creating a job aid or a desk reference guide will suffice. Alternatively, depending on your client's budget, you may decide to design a formal training course first, and then, offer a job aid as a supplementary material.

If you decided that a formal training course is needed, you should then analyze the content, your client's budget, and of course, your target audience to recommend the most viable solution.

Remember, while getting your clients "buy in" may not be easy, if you back up your recommendation by showing the results of your analysis along with the conclusions made during the analysis phase, your client will be much more receptive to your suggestions.

Test Your Knowledge

1. All of the following are an outcome of the Needs Analysis phase EXCEPT:
    A. Needs analysis helps discover the target audience for the course.
    B. Needs analysis helps to uncover the true purpose of creating the course.
    C. Needs assessment helps to determine the length of the pre and post assessments for a course.
    D. Needs assessment helps to determine the approach for designing the course.

2. What are the three types of analysis?
    A. Risk Analysis, Audience Analysis, Performance Analysis
    B. Task Analysis, Audience Analysis, Performance Analysis
    C. Risk Analysis, Task Analysis, Performance Analysis
    D. Task Analysis, Audience Analysis, ROI Analysis

3. What are the risks of NOT conducting a through Audience Analysis?
    A. You may end up developing a totally useless course.
    B. You won't address the real training need.
    C. You'll waste a lot of money, time and resources.
    D. All of these answers are correct.

4. One of the best ways to collect information about performance gap and root causes is by using the _____ technique.
    A. Gap Code
    B. Gap Analysis
    C. Five Why
    D. Two Truths and a Lie

5. If a Performance Gap Analysis reveals the root issue to be a lack of motivation, organization support, poor process or poor management issue, then:
    A. Development should proceed as planned as these are all training related issues.
    B. Development should cease as these are performance improvement issues and should be handled another way.
    C. Development should proceed as planned as all of these issues can be solved by putting a training program in place.
    D. Development should cease as the lack of organizational support can be solved by putting a training program in place.

6. Which of the following is another type of analysis you need to consider when conducting Learning Needs Analysis?
    A. Instructional Analysis
    B. Authoritarian Analysis
    C. Learner Analysis
    D. Attrition Analysis

7. When conducting a Learning Needs Analysis, which of these elements is considered the most important form of research: Review Literature, Conduct Direct Observations, Conduct Interviews and Focus Groups?
    A. None of the methods required to conduct a thorough learning needs analysis are listed as choices to choose from.
    B. Focus groups and interviews tend to lead to the most detailed picture of the root problem being solved and eliminates the need to review any other documentation.
    C. All strategies have advantages and disadvantages. One must try to choose several different methods to ensure sufficient data collection.
    D. Reviewing literature will typically give you enough information to conduct a thorough learning needs analysis.

8. If budgetary limitations force you to only be able to review documentation for your Learning Needs Analysis, what should you be aware of prior to starting?
    A. Documents typically provide the most unbiased information available.
    B. Documents can be outdated, inaccurate, incomplete and disorganized.
    C. Documents typically provide you with the most up-to-date information available.
    D. Documents can be hard to share and, if printed, hard to carry around.

9. The primary disadvantage of Observation as part of learning needs analysis is:
   A. People typically perform better when they know they are being observed.
   B. Watching people work can be a fairly uncomfortable task for instructional designers.
   C. People tend to underperform when they know they are being observed.
   D. Observing someone do their job in person does not give an instructional designer insight into their typical challenges.

10. Interviews conducted as part of learning needs analysis can be _____ and _____.
    A. exhausting / time consuming
    B. expensive / inaccurate
    C. expensive / time consuming
    D. exhausting / biased

11. What is the most commonly used tool for conducting Learning Needs Analysis?
    A. Word of Mouth
    B. Focus Groups
    C. Suggestion Boxes
    D. Surveys

12. Which one of these statements is NOT a disadvantage of using Surveys as part of learning needs analysis?
    A. People may mark their answers without reading the questions.
    B. Surveys require clear and accurate wording of each question.
    C. Collecting information digitally can be dangerous without using encryption.
    D. Participants cannot ask questions to clarify unclear statements.

13. Dichotomous questions are _____ questions and can work well as screening tools.
    A. Yes/No
    B. Open-ended
    C. Closed-ended
    D. True/False

14. What is the question type used in the following example?
    "What are the problems you are trying to solve with this training solution?"
    A. Yes/No
    B. Open-ended
    C. Closed-ended
    D. True/False

15. Open-ended questions are very effective because:
    A. They limit the participants answer to a smaller set of possible options.
    B. Participants have to think about the answer before providing a response.
    C. Participants receive more guidance to answer the question correctly than with other question types.
    D. They almost always eliminate irrelevant comments and responses for you.

16. What is the correct order of steps you should follow when conducting learning needs analysis?
    A. Define Objectives / Select Data Collection Method / Collect Data / Review Data / Compare, Organize, and Analyze
    B. Define Objectives / Review Data / Compare, Organize, and Analyze / Select Data Collection Method / Collect Data
    C. Define Objectives / Collect Data / Select Data Collection Method/ Review Data / Compare, Organize, and Analyze
    D. Define Objectives / Review Data / Select Data Collection Method / Collect Data / Compare, Organize, and Analyze

Exercise 6

Keeping in mind that stakeholders do not have budgets allocated for needs analysis, think about the information you need to find out about the course to address the clients' needs. Are you going to convince them that needs analysis is an important part of course design? If so, how? What questions will you ask? Which data-gathering tools will you use in your needs analysis? Once you made your decisions, design an interview, survey, or focus group questionnaires.

Chapter 8: Learning Objectives

This chapter will cover:

- Role of learning objectives in course design
- The A-B-C-D format of learning objectives
- Terminal and enabling objectives
- SMART objectives
- Bloom's Taxonomy and three learning domains

Case Study

For ten years, Dr. Hansen had taught a nutrition course at his university. A highly popular course, he always received excellent marks in his evaluations. When the head of his department proposed creating an online version of the course, Dr. Hansen responded enthusiastically, working to translate many of the activities he used in his class to the online format.

When his technology assistant told him he needed to write course objectives, Dr. Hansen figured that he just needed to explain what material the course would cover. He wrote objectives like "Students will understand the three macronutrient groups."

The course ended and he received evaluations. Dr. Hansen was shocked to learn that not only did the students not perform well in his online course, but his evaluations, usually excellent, were not good at all. The course seems disorganized, the feedback said. After doing some research, Dr. Hansen decided to talk to an instructional designer about it.

"Your objectives need to be measurable and observable," said the instructional designer after reviewing his course materials. "You can't measure or observe understanding as well as you can measure or observe your student's behavior. What do you actually want them to be able to *do*?"

After some careful thought, Dr. Hansen worked to change his objectives. "Students will understand the three macronutrient groups" became "Students will identify macronutrient groups and describe their function." In the revised course, students understood the objectives, and were more satisfied with the instruction.

Learning objectives are an indispensable part of any course. They describe what the learners will be able to do upon completion of the course. Learning objectives are also sometimes called behavioral objectives, performance objectives, or course objectives. The main goal of objectives is to define the scope of the course and help learners focus on specific outcomes. Prior to writing objectives, you should determine the overall goal for the course. Objectives should always be written after conducting a thorough needs analysis. The main difference between goals and objectives is that goals provide information about the purpose of the course while objectives are measurable instructional outcomes of the course. Objectives describe the knowledge, skills, or attitudes learners should demonstrate after completing the training.

Robert Mager is a key contributor to the field of instructional design and to objectives in particular. He believed that all objectives should be measurable and observable, as those that cannot be measured and observed will have little chance for evaluation.

All objectives should include four components, known as the A-B-C-D format. These components are:

- *Audience*
- *Behavior*
- *Condition*
- *Degree*

Audience

When writing objectives, it is crucial to know the target audience. For instance, if you are creating a course on Teaching English as a Second Language (TESL), the *audience* component of the objective is the TESL learner.

Behavior

The *behavior* element of the objective should state what the learner will be doing using action verbs to describe the behavior. Most behavior statements are worded *should be able to*. However, many instructional designers prefer the *will be able to* statement. While both statements are correct, it is highly recommended you use *should be able to* in your objectives. The "will be able to" statement automatically makes a promise while the "should be able to" statement does not promise any definite results. Whether or not learners achieve the objectives depends on many different aspects not always under your control. For instance, your learners may be distracted while taking your course.

When writing behavioral statements in objectives, you should avoid using such verbs as *know* and *understand* as they are not measurable and observable. Instead, consider using *apply*, *identify*, and *explain*.

Condition

Objectives should include the *condition* under which the tasks are performed. Conditions should provide context that supports all other elements of the objective. For example:

- given a desk reference guide, or
- after completing a real-life simulation

Degree

The last element of effective objectives is *degree*. It is the level at which learners must perform the task. Some examples of degree statements are:

- without error
- successfully five times within one hour
- by giving fact on two different issues

All of these degree statements are measurable and observable. After seeing them, learners should be clear of what they need to do to meet the objectives.

Terminal and Enabling Objectives

Each course should include both terminal and enabling objectives.

Terminal objectives describe what the learners are expected to be able to do by the end of the course. They focus on the result, not the process.

Example of a terminal objective:

Given realistic scenarios depicting the most common writing problems of high school graduates, you should be able to write essays without errors.

Enabling objectives support terminal objectives. They define the skills, knowledge, or attitudes learners must obtain to successfully complete terminal objectives. Enabling objectives are more specific than terminal.

Example of an enabling objective:

Given handouts and videos related to essay writing, you should be able to complete essay-writing activities with 100% accuracy.

Developing SMART Objectives

To ensure that your objectives are well-written, you should use the SMART approach. SMART objectives focus on the result rather than the activities and allow learners to measure their own success. SMART stands for Specific, Measurable, Attainable, Relevant, and Timely.

Specific – Objectives should clearly state the knowledge or skill the learners need to demonstrate as a result of training. Specific objectives define what needs to be done by answering the What, Why, and How questions. Even individuals without any background knowledge about the topic should be able to read the objective and interpret it correctly.

Example – *Increase enrollment of ISD learners in X University through participation in the local job fair*

Measurable – Focuses on the evaluation standards and includes some type of quantifiable measurement such as standards or parameters. Instructional designers should be able to evaluate this element through assessment.

Example – by 15%

Attainable – Even though your objective can be both specific and measurable, it may not be feasible during the proposed period or with the limited resources available. The attainable part of your objective is responsible for the capability of satisfying the expectation. Action verbs such as observe, identify, participate, demonstrate, and communicate can help represent the behavior the objective is trying to measure.

Example – Participate in the local job fair

Relevant – Emphasizes the practicality of the objective and clarifies why something should be done.

Example – Increase enrollment of ISD learners in X University over the next three months through participation in the local job fair

Time-bound – Identifies the time when something will be done.

Example – Over the next three months

To ensure that your courses meet the desired instructional objectives, start mapping various elements of the course (Modules, Chapters, Lessons, Activities, Assessments) to specific learning objectives. Be very careful not to confuse Training Objectives (which may be much broader in scope, like "obtaining a driver's license") with individual Learning Objectives for that course (like "understanding the rules of safe vehicle operation").

For each of the learning units that learners will be exposed to, your mapping will offer an overview of the competencies required, the topics to be discussed, and the activities to be performed.

Since learning outcomes must be successfully demonstrated by the learner, you must establish unambiguous pass/fail criteria for quizzes, tests, assignments and other individual or group activities.

By mapping each course unit to clearly-defined specific learning objectives, and then providing your learners with clear guidelines about what constitutes "success" in your course, you will give your learners everything they need to know in order to successfully meet those standards and ensure that your design successfully delivers the information that meets the required learning objectives.

Bloom's Taxonomy

In 1956, educational psychologist Benjamin Bloom identified three learning domains. These domains are:

- Cognitive (knowledge)
- Affective (attitude)
- Psychomotor (skills)

When you write your objectives for any of the three domains, you should always aim toward the most complex behavior.

Cognitive Domain

The cognitive domain includes content knowledge, which involves the ability to recall specific facts that help learners develop new skills and abilities. There are six levels in this domain. The lowest level is knowledge, and the highest level is evaluation. Table 6 describes each of these levels and provides action verbs associated with each learning outcome.

Table 6 - Bloom's Taxonomy – Cognitive Domain

Level	Description	Verbs
Knowledge	Being able to recall applicable knowledge from the memory	• Define • Describe • Identify • Label • List • Name • Recall • Recite • State
Comprehension	Being able to construct meaning from written, oral, and graphic messages	• Convert • Distinguish • Estimate • Explain • Predict • Summarize
Application	Being able to apply previous knowledge to carry out a procedure	• Compute • Demonstrate • Develop • Organize • Solve • Use
Analysis	Being able to identify the relationships among content elements	• Diagram • Differentiate • Illustrate • Infer • Outline • Relate
Synthesis	Being able to combine the elements learned in a lesson to produce something completely new	• Categorize • Compose • Create • Formulate • Predict • Produce
Evaluation	Being able to make judgements or suggestions based on specific criteria	• Compare • Contrast • Criticize • Justify • Support

Affective Domain

The affective domain includes feelings, emotions, motivations, and attitudes. The table below illustrates the five categories in this domain and the action verbs that describe learning outcomes. The receiving level is the simplest behavior; the internalizing level the most complex. The table below describes each of these levels and provides action verbs associated with each learning outcome.

Table 7 - Bloom's Taxonomy – Affective Domain

Level	Description	Verbs
Receiving	Being aware of something in the environment	• Attend • Control • Listen • Notice • Share
Responding	Showing a new behavior as a result of experience	• Comply • Follow • Obey • Participate • Practice
Valuing	Showing commitment	• Act • Argue • Debate • Express • Organize
Organization	Integrating a new value into an already existing set of values	• Abstract • Balance • Define • Systematize • Theorize
Characterization by Value	Acting regularly with the new value	• Avoid • Exhibit • Manage • Resolve • Revise

Psychomotor Domain

The psychomotor domain includes movements, coordination, and motor skills. Developing skills in this domain requires practice. The psychomotor domain consists of seven categories. Perception, the simplest behavior; and origination, the most complex. The table below describes each of these levels and provides action verbs associated with each learning outcome.

Table 8 - Bloom's Taxonomy – Psychomotor Domain

Level	Description	Verbs
Perception	Being able to use sensory cues to guide motor activity	• Choose • Detect • Isolate • Relate • Select
Set	Mental, physical, and emotional readiness to act	• Display • Explain • Move • React • State
Guided Response	Attempting the physical skill	• Copy • Follow • React • Reproduce
Mechanism	Learned responses of a physical skill become habitual	• Assemble • Construct • Fix • Measure • Sketch
Complex Overt Response	Skilled performance of physical activities	• Build • Display • Grind • Manipulate
Adaption	Modifying movements for special situations	• Adapt • Alter • Change • Rearrange • Revise
Origination	Creating new movement patterns to fit specific situations	• Arrange • Combine • Compose • Initiate

Revised Bloom's Taxonomy

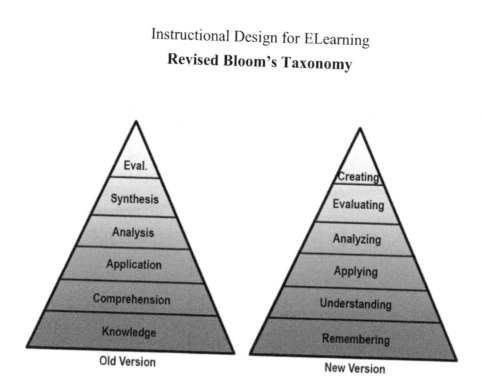

Since Bloom's Taxonomy was created for traditional classroom training, there was a need to reconstruct it to fit modernized approaches to training. Therefore, in the mid-90s, Lorin Anderson, Bloom's former student, revised the learning domain to reflect a more active form of thinking and make it more relevant to modern needs. The two major modifications are:

- change of names from noun to verb
- forms, and rearrangement of the levels

Table 9 illustrates the updated version of Bloom's Taxonomy.

Table 9 - Revised Bloom's Taxonomy

Level	Description	Verbs
Remembering	Being able to recall, recognize or retrieve information such as definitions, facts, or lists	• Acquire • Define • Duplicate • Label • List • Memorize • Recall • Recognize • Repeat • Reproduce • Retrieve
Understanding	Being able to construct meaning by correctly interpreting, classifying, summarizing, explaining or comparing information	• Classify • Describe • Give examples • Interpret • Locate • Paraphrase • Predict • Select • Summarize • Translate
Analyzing	Being able to break materials or concepts into parts	• Break down • Contrast • Compare • Deconstruct • Differentiate • Examine • Find • Illustrate • Outline • Separate
Evaluating	Being able to make judgements about materials, concepts, or ideas	• Appraise • Argue • Categorize • Critique

		• Compare • Conclude • Experiment • Hypothesize • Justify • Judge • Summarize • Support
Creating	Being able to combine elements to form a new meaning	• Assemble • Categorize • Combine • Compile • Formulate • Generate • Invent • Plan • Produce • Rearrange • Reconstruct • Write

Oftentimes, when instructional designers are tasked with designing a course, one of the challenges that they face has to do with the design approach they take. While experienced instructional designers seem to have a better grasp of this, novices often struggle with selecting the right activities and exercises that truly reinforce learning.

The best way to use Bloom's Taxonomy is to use the content of the course to develop measurable learning objectives. Then, categorize these objectives based on the levels of learning and include appropriate activities in each category.

Here is how you can apply revised Bloom's Taxonomy to creating effective eLearning materials.

Remembering is the first level of learning. It simply refers to being able to remember concepts to become familiar with them. Some of the activities that instructional designers can use at that level include PDF attachments, step-by-step lists, and webinars.

The next level of learning is known as **Understanding.** This level can be tricky, mostly because we all know that understanding cannot be measured and, therefore, we should avoid using that "term" in learning objectives. However, similar to *Remembering, Understanding* is one of the foundational levels of learning and can be taught through lectures, step-by-step user guides, PDF files, and by incorporating the "Click and drag" activities using rapid eLearning tools such as Articulate and Captivate.

Applying is the next level of learning. This is where learners take the concepts from the first two foundational levels and start doing something. While this level of learning works best in a classroom setting, where people can form small groups and carry out conversations, it is possible to do it through virtual classrooms, discussion boards, or by offering learners to complete a simulation.

The next level of learning is known as *Analyzing*. While activities for *Applying* can be easily developed and evaluated, Analyzing requires a lot of work. These activities are very time and resource consuming and, in most cases, cannot be evaluated in a virtual environment. Therefore, if you want your learners to be able to analyze something, you may want to consider a blended learning approach with, at least, a discussion board available to them.

The *Evaluation* level of learning also works best in a blended environment; however, can be achieved through asynchronous eLearning, too. At that level, you want learners to be able to make decisions about things through researching and evaluating their options. This can be done through such activities as scavenger hunts and web searches.

Create is the last level of learning. This is where learners physically do or create something they have learned in class using all the resources available to them. Clearly, *Creating* works best in a classroom setting, but, if you must do your training in the eLearning format, consider a blended learning approach with a discussion board, a forum, or even access to a conference line. You can also use a webcam or ask learners to record a short video with their smartphones showing the steps they take to complete the required task.

Note, that not all courses will require you to have objectives for all levels of learning. However, if you are new to instructional design, Bloom's Taxonomy should help you figure out the best presentation methods of the material.

Learning Objectives Makeover

There is no doubt that learning objectives play a very important role in course design. Typically, instructional designers use a classical approach to writing their objectives. As a result, the first element learners see when they start a course is the objectives. Even though the purpose of objectives is to help learners focus on their learning experience, most learners do not like to read the objective list and skip it whenever possible. Because of this, the value of objectives is diminished. However, if learners do not know the objectives, they cannot truly benefit from the course. The dilemma that instructional designers face lies in approaching learning objectives in the most interactive way possible while avoiding long and boring bulleted lists. So, what can you do to turn objectives into motivators?

First, before writing objectives, you need to identify a business goal for the course. Then, think about the actions necessary to reach that goal. Once a list of actions is compiled, the objective makeover can begin. Not only should objectives be measurable and observable, but they should also be motivational and relevant. Remember, you design courses for adults, and most adults are busy people. Therefore, you need to ensure that objectives meet your learners' needs. For example, even though the objective with an action verb *define* is measurable, it is most likely useless as in most cases people do not need to be able to define something to solve a problem or master a skill. While it is still a good idea to include definitions in training courses, turning them into objectives may be impractical for adult learners.

Incorporating scenarios will add meaning to your learning objectives. The goal of the objectives is to help learners understand the benefits of learning the content in the course as well as the risks associated with not learning it. Objectives that use the pronoun *you* instead of the word *learner* are more personal as they speak directly to the learner. For example, saying *"By the end of the module, you should be able to..."* is more personal than saying *"By the end of the module, the learner should be able to..."* Also, turning abstract concepts into real situations that learners will experience on the job adds meaning to objectives. For example, instead of *"After completing this module, you should be able to describe the four stages of the ARCS model of Motivational Design,"* consider, *"After completing this module, you should be able to design motivational courses for your learners."*

Test Your Knowledge

1. All of these are terms used for learning objectives EXCEPT:
   A. Behavioral objectives
   B. Outcome objectives
   C. Course objectives
   D. Performance objectives

2. Learning objectives should always be written _____ conducting needs analysis.
   A. before
   B. congruently to
   C. after
   D. along with

3. All objectives should be measurable and observable by incorporating the four components of the A-B-C-D format:
   A. Audience, Behavior, Condition, Degree
   B. Audience, Beliefs, Correction, Design
   C. Assessment, Behavior, Correction, Degree
   D. Assessment, Beliefs, Condition, Design

4. Which of the following words would satisfy the "Behavior" element of writing learning objectives?
   A. Understand
   B. Apply
   C. Will be able to
   D. Know

5. Which of the following statements does NOT satisfy the "Degree" element of writing learning objectives?
   A. Without error
   B. At some point
   C. Within the hour
   D. On two different issues

6. Which of the following learning objectives best satisfies the Measurable portion of the SMART objective writing model?
    A. Moderately increase participation of learners in health screenings.
    B. Increase participation of learners in health screenings through participation in local outreach programs by 15%.
    C. Increase participation of learners in health screenings through participation in local outreach programs by August 2017.
    D. Increase participation of learners in health screenings through participation in local outreach programs.

7. Which of the following objectives best satisfies all elements of SMART?
    A. Decrease the number of traffic accidents by 10% through implementation of community education initiatives in Q2 of 2017.
    B. Decrease the number of traffic accidents by 10% through implementation of community education initiatives in the future.
    C. Decrease the number of traffic accidents incrementally through implementation of community education initiatives.
    D. Decrease the number of traffic accidents by 10% in Q2 of 2017.

8. What are the three learning domains identified by educational psychologist Benjamin Bloom (Bloom's Taxonomy)?
    A. Cognitive Domain, Affirmative Domain, Psychological Domain
    B. Cognitive Domain, Affective Domain, Psychomotor Domain
    C. Constative Domain, Affective Domain, Psychological Domain
    D. Constative Domain, Affirmative Domain, Psychomotor Domain

9. Which of the following statements about developing learning objectives is FALSE?
    A. Learners tend to not want to read a list of learning objectives and skip over them.
    B. In order for a learner to get the most out of the course, they must understand the objectives.
    C. The problem instructional designers face is incorporating learning objectives in the most interactive way possible.
    D. Most learners prefer a bulleted list of learning objectives at the beginning of the course.

10. Which of these learning objectives is the most personable?

    A. After completing this module, you should be able to repair a bicycle.

    B. After completing this module, the learner should be able to understand the mechanical procedures involved in bicycle repair.

    C. After completing this module, the learner should be able to repair a bicycle.

    D. After completing this module, you should be able to describe the mechanical procedures involved in bicycle repair.

Exercise 7

Write terminal and enabling objectives for your course. Ensure that your objectives are SMART and include the A-B-C-D components.

Chapter 9: Designing the Learning Experience: Gagné's Nine Events of Instruction

This chapter will cover:

- Robert Gagné and his levels of learning
- Nine Events of Instruction
- Presentation methods that adhere to the Nine Events of Instruction

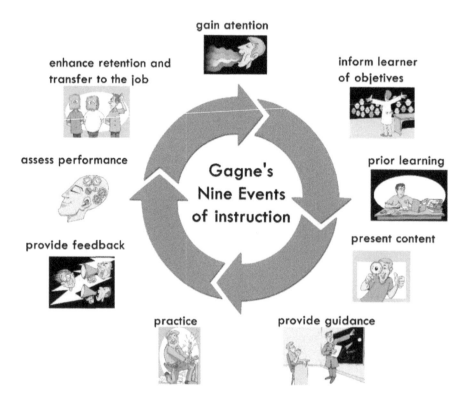

Case Study

An instructional designer was assigned an advanced course on chemical safety hazards. Thinking about the approach he would take, he knew that this course would have to satisfy a few requirements: to help the learners build on safety hazard knowledge they already had, to maintain the learner's motivation and interest to acquire new knowledge, to drill the information carefully, and to change their behavior around potential hazards. After some thought, he decided to use Gagne's Nine Events of Instruction as a template for course design.

First, he got the learners' attention with a scenario illustrating how careful the learners needed to be about safety hazards. This technique also demonstrated the topic's relevance.

He communicated the course objectives to the learners in a way that summarized, defined, and explained evaluation methods.

Then, in the first part of the course, the instructional designer related the new information to past knowledge. Since the course content built upon previous chemical hazard training, instructional designer spent some time on this.

The designer also worked to make the content orderly and goal-oriented, with measurable and observable objectives in each section.

The course offered ample guidance to learners with scaffolding, learning aids, peer discussion and case studies. The course provided plenty of reinforcement of the knowledge through reviews and feedback, as well as frequent assessments.

Finally, the course emphasized real-world applications, using real scenarios with realistic settings to prompt the learners to identify safety hazards and respond to them. The result was a dynamic, engaging course that prepared the learners for their jobs.

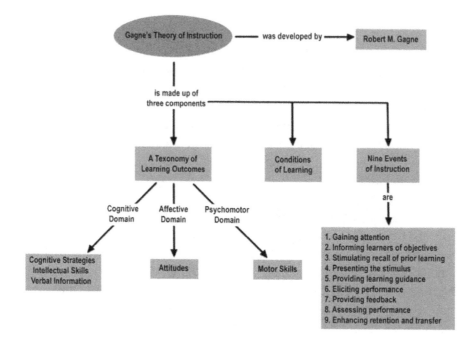

Robert Gagné is an American educational psychologist best known for his "conditions of learning for training applications." In 1965, Gagné published the book titled *The Conditions of Learning*. In this book, he explained the relationship between learning objectives and instructional design principles. According to Gagné's theory, there are five major levels of learning, including verbal information, intellectual skills, cognitive strategies, motor skills, and attitudes. Each of these levels requires a different type of instruction.

Table 10 - Gagné's Five Levels of Learning

Learning Outcome	Example
Verbal Information	Retrieve stored information such as poem recitation
Intellectual Skills	Perform mental operations such as problem-solving and rule-using
Cognitive Strategies	Develop new solutions to problems
Motor Skills	Perform a sequence of physical movements such as correct reproduction of musical pieces
Attitude	Hear persuasive arguments about a certain topic

Even though Gagné's levels of instruction cover all aspects of learning, his theory mostly focuses on intellectual skills. Based on this theoretical framework, Gagné developed a nine-step process known as the **Events of Instruction**. Together with the five levels of learning and learning outcomes, these events provide the necessary conditions of learning and play an important role in the development of instruction.

At their very basic, Gagné's Nine Events of Instruction can help eLearning professionals achieve the following goals:

- Help your audience relate to the content you are delivering by associating it with prior knowledge or experiences.
- Offer supporting online content (prompts, hints, flash cards, cues) in the form of building blocks for the new information you are delivering.
- Pose probing questions which make reference to content that has already been learned by the learner.
- Support learners in relating the new content to situations and examples from the real world.
- Make elaborate use of interactive quizzes, assessments, questions, and online drills at every stage of the course—before (Pretest), during (Touch-points) and after (End assessments).
- Help learners internalize the new concepts and knowledge, so they gain expertise of the content.

Gagné formalized the above thoughts into a set of nine instructional principles or events, which revolve around internal and external cognitive dynamics that directly or indirectly impact a learner's ability to learn and retain new information. Let's explore those **Nine Events of Instruction** in further detail, and talk about how eLearning content creators can leverage them to their advantage.

1. **Gain attention** – Start by gaining your learners' attention. This gives learners a framework into which they can organize the content that will be presented in the lesson. This instructional event is also used to motivate learners.

    Distance learners have more opportunities to get easily distracted—more so than classroom learners. It is, therefore, important to make sure that the learner is all "fired up" to start learning the new activity. To do this, you must stimulate their attention with compelling led-in introductions. For example, you can:

    - Use trending catch-words or attention-grabbing bylines.
    - Create a compelling story to introduce your topic.
    - Use thought-provoking phrases or sentences to force learners pay attention.
    - Get learners to pose and answer questions about the new content.

2. **Inform learners of objectives** – During this phase, designers should describe what learners should be able to do at the end of the course and what tools they may be using to achieve learning objectives. Objectives should create expectancy and describe the structure of the lecture. Some ways to notify learners about the expected outcomes and objectives of the course prior to course commencement include:
    - Summarizing course goal and content
    - Defining minimum standards (grades, marks, timelines)
    - Specifying evaluation methodology and criteria.

3. **Stimulate recall of prior learning** – Here, the instructional designer should relate the new lesson to situations that the learners are familiar with. For example, the previous lesson.

    You can relate new information to past knowledge or experiences by:
    - Linking content that will be explored in your course to previously learned or experienced knowledge/situations;
    - Eliciting samples of related content learners may already have learned; and
    - Helping learners relate those topics to what is to come in your (new) course.

4. **Present the content** – In this stage, the instructional designer should describe the key points of the lesson using a variety of techniques. Designers should try to vary the format to keep the learners' attention and increase comprehension of the material.

    Make sure the content is meaningfully segmented, with measurable/demonstrable goals following each section of your course:
    - Explore lexicon, vocabulary, and abbreviations before each segment.
    - Provide a summary of each segment.
    - Follow demonstrations/simulations with explanations.
    - Mix/match multiple online content (videos, slides, podcasts) for each topic.

5. **Provide guidance** – At this point, the instructional designer should present the lesson in small steps leading from simple to complex. It is important to begin the lesson with easy to understand information and add more difficult information as the lesson progresses. This gives learners an opportunity to build on their existing knowledge. As a result, they will understand the material better and retain more content.

    Support learners with online learning aids to help them understand, reinforce, and master the content presented in the course:

    - Develop online repositories of case studies.
    - Provide learning aids such as cheat sheets, flash cards, check-lists, mnemonics; and
    - Integrate online collaboration aids, such as chat groups, gaming platforms, and role-playing sessions into the course.

6. **Elicit performance** – Here, the instructional designer should involve learners in discussion and questioning to confirm that they have learned the material. Learners' active participation should increase understanding and retention of the material.

    The following strategies should help learners recall, remember, and reinforce what they have already learned:

    - Create pop-up boxes could help learners retain past knowledge.
    - Provide "Quick Review" tabs or access to online repositories can help with recap and recall.
    - Offer conveniently located options for lessons to be repeated/reviewed.
    - Develop Flash quizzes could force learners to recall prior knowledge.
    - Integrate real-world examples as part of the content.

7. **Provide feedback** – As learners respond to questions, instructional designers should provide them with reinforcement and remediation.

    As you plan your courses, you can plan to include automated means for learners to assess where they stand by providing:

    - Confirmative feedback: Acknowledging that the learner has completed required tasks (quizzes, assessments, assignments).
    - Corrective feedback: Notifying learners where they went wrong, and why.
    - Remedial feedback: Offering advice/encouragement on how to remediate deficiencies.
    - Informative feedback: Sharing useful information about performance improvement.
    - Analytical feedback: Delivering rule-based/fact-figures based feedback on individual performance.

8. **Assess performance** – To confirm mastery of the objectives, instructional designers should include quizzes or other assignments in their lessons.

Add milestone tests and assessments at every level:

- Pretesting could help learners find out how much they already know and whether or not they can/should skip certain sections of the course or focus on specific topics.
- Post-testing should confirm whether learners have mastered a specific content set.
- Use online quizzes, word games, and multiple-choice questions as well as text-based answers to assess learner understanding of topics versus predetermined criterion (criterion-referenced performance).
- Use normative-referenced performance to evaluate how learners perform.

9. **Enhance retention and learning transfer** – At this point, instructional designers should provide the opportunity for learners to apply the outcome of their training to a real-world situation. For instance, they might give learners some type of realistic assignment or provide a desk guide that learners can refer to at any time when they perform the tasks presented in the lesson.

Instructionally sound courses should help learners translate the knowledge provided by the course into real-world situations. Some of the ways to accomplish that include:

- Getting learners to map content learned to their everyday life activities;
- Making learners think of specific work-related situations where the new knowledge can be applied; and
- Providing simulated examples, "what-if scenarios" and "gaming situations" that require learners to respond with new skills/knowledge learned in the course.

The Nine Events of Instruction is an excellent framework for any lesson. However, although these events have been presented as a sequential list, in reality, the events will likely overlap, or even inter-mingle. Rather than trying to implement each event independently, in linear form, online content creators should look at weaving various events throughout the course—more in iterative or circular fashion.

For instance, depending on how your course is structured, you may want to invoke the principles behind Event 1: Gain Learners' Attention, at several points throughout the course rather than just at the beginning of the course.

Table 11 illustrates how you can use the Events of Instruction in your eLearning materials.

Table 11 - Gagné's Nine Events of Instruction

Instructional Event	Application Method
Gain Attention	icebreakers, slideshows, case studies, YouTube videos, podcasts, demonstrations, Flash presentations, storytelling, polls, images, analogy, paradox, anecdote, articles, charts, and diagrams
Inform learners of objectives	slides, instructions, discussion boards
Simulate recall of prior learning	review previous lectures integrate previous information into activities using slides, use discussion boards, YouTube videos, audio recordings, graphics
Present the content	lectures, articles, activities, discussion boards, wikis, blogs, podcasts, YouTube videos, storytelling
Provide learning guidance	activities that include rubrics and state clear expectations, demonstration of principles in action, discussion of common errors, case studies, analogies
Elicit performance	discussions, written assignments, case studies, simulations, drills, role plays, interactive questions
Provide feedback	immediate and detailed corrective feedback
Assess performance	assessments, written projects, games
Enhance retention and transfer to the job	additional practice activities, exercises, job aids, manuals, desk guides, forums

Your primary objective, as eLearning content designers and developers, is to produce courses that online learners can relate to, and which they will be able to engage with. Gagné's Nine Events of Instruction will help you craft carefully designed online content and truly motivate your audience.

By using the strategies mentioned in this chapter, you will ensure that your learners not only understand what you are teaching them, but that they actually take that knowledge back into their real world and apply the new concepts to achieve organizational goals and objectives.

Scenario

Mrs. Rosario is a Human Resource Specialist at the X Corporation. Upper management made a decision to purchase the SnagIt screen-capturing tool, and Mrs. Rosario is now responsible for ensuring that all technical writers know how to use it. Mrs. Rosario has many other responsibilities; therefore, she decided to make this training available in the asynchronous eLearning format. She followed the Nine Events of Instruction to create her course.

Gain attention – When learners access the lesson, the senior technical writer appears on the screen and introduces the course. She discusses the importance of staying on the cutting edge of technology and explains how the SnagIt tool will be beneficial for technical writers.

Inform learners of objectives – After the introduction, the objective slide with the voiceover appears. One of the objectives on that slide is "Upon completing this training, you should be able to use all features of the SnagIt tool without further assistance."

Stimulate recall of prior knowledge – At this point, learners are called upon to use their prior knowledge of other similar tools to understand the basic functionality of SnagIt.

Present the content – Next, using screen images, Camtasia demonstration, and audio narration, the training program describes the basic features of SnagIt.

Guide learning – With each new feature, learners are shown a variety of ways to use them. Complex sequences are chunked into short, step-by-step lists for easier storage in long-term memory.

Elicit performance – After each function is demonstrated, learners are asked to practice with realistic simulations.

Provide feedback – During the simulation, learners are given guidance and feedback as needed.

Assess performance – After all lessons are completed, learners are required to take a post-test. The assessment questions are tied directly to the learning objectives displayed in the lessons.

Enhance retention and learning transfer – Upon completion of the course, learners are presented with a downloadable desk guide, which includes step-by-step instructions on how to use the SnagIt tool.

Test Your Knowledge

1. Which of the following statements about Robert Gagne is FALSE?
    A. He is an American educational psychologist.
    B. He published a book called The Nine Events of Instruction.
    C. He published a book called The Conditions of Learning.
    D. He identified five major levels of learning: verbal information, intellectual skills, cognitive strategies, motor skills and attitudes.

2. The first of Gagne's Nine Events of Instruction is:
    A. Informing learners of objectives
    B. Presenting the stimulus
    C. Gaining attention
    D. Stimulating recall of prior learning

3. Enhancing retention and transfer, the last step in Gagne's Nine Events of Instruction typically includes giving learners realistic assignments, additional practice activities and:
    A. A job aid/desk guide
    B. An assessment
    C. An invitation to a future course
    D. All of these options are correct

4. True/False: An instructional designer should always include all Nine Events of Instruction into their courses.
    A. True – All nine events must be present in a course to ensure its efficacy.
    B. False – At least three should be present in a course to ensure its efficacy.
    C. True – All nine events must be present to make sure learners retain as much information as possible.
    D. False – It is not necessary to include all nine events; however, an instructional designer should consider each event as part of the design process.

Exercise 8

Follow the Nine Events of Instruction to create a lesson plan for your eLearning course. Remember to include motivational examples and activities.

Chapter 10: Creating a Design Document

This chapter will cover:

- The role of the design document
- Sections of the design document
- Information included in each section of the design document

Case Study

The training team at Techne IT Company used Iterative Design. Because so many of their courses were rapidly prototyped, released, and then revised, the team began to question the need for a design document. There are so many changes in the process—content, delivery, sometimes even authoring tools. Why waste so much time?

Their next project, an onboarding course, seemed relatively straightforward, so they decided to go without the design document and dive right into prototyping.

The problems began a month down the line. It was clear during group meetings that the instructional designers were doing well with content creation. However, their interactive exercises and quizzes were going to be incompatible with each other because they hadn't yet decided on a tool. They quickly identified this problem, but the ensuing discussions lasted some weeks because each member of the team was invested in the ideas they'd already created.

Later on, when the prototypes began to be developed, the feedback said that although the content did work, the look of the course just wasn't consistent. The team hadn't agreed on style or graphic standards, so this took more time to hash out and fix.

Finally, the delivery became problematic. The tool was chosen, but the delivery platform was not. Some members of the team wanted the course to be in the LMS for data tracking, but this would require reworking sections of the course that were designed for the web.

If the team had made and recorded these crucial decisions with a design document, these obstacles wouldn't have appeared. It would have taken more time at the outset, but the payoff would have been greater clarity for the project.

As the name implies, the Design Document is created during the design phase of the instructional design process. Its purpose is to document the entire design process for a specific project. The document provides all the necessary information about the course to instructional designers, graphic artists, multimedia specialists, programmers, project managers, and all other team members. Just like all other documents created for the eLearning project, the sections included in your design document will differ depending on course requirements. For example, if you are creating a linear course using the rapid instructional systems design model, the design document will not have as many sections compared to a full-fledged eLearning course filled with interactions, simulations, and games.

Generally, all design documents are based on the thorough needs analysis and include all the objectives and assessment items for the course.

In addition, these documents provide information about media and supplemental materials that will be included in the training as well as the screenshots of the layout of the course. The table below illustrates some major sections that a typical design document should include.

Table 12 - Sections of a Design Document

Section	Information
Background Information	• Course overview • Major topics • Overall goals
Scope	Short statement about the scope of the course
Target Audience	Who is the course designed for?
Prerequisites	• What should the learners know before taking the course? • Which course should the learners take prior to this course?
Interface of the Course	• Navigation • "Look and feel"
Compliance Considerations	• SCORM • Section 508
Project Management	• Development timeline maintenance requirements for this course • Project sign-off names and contact information
Objectives	• Terminal objectives • Enabling objectives
Evaluation Strategy	• Assessments • Kirkpatrick's Levels of Evaluation • ROI
Development Tools	Tools used to create this course
Interactions	Detailed descriptions of interactions
Testing and Assessment	• Questions • Answers • Detailed feedback
Technical Requirements	• Plug-ins/players

	• Memory • Operating system
Media Elements	• Graphics • Animation • Video • Audio
Course Outline	• Outline of course structure • Screenshots • Content

Test Your Knowledge

1. The goal of the design document is to capture the entire design process for a specific project and is typically based on:
    - A. The stakeholder's requirements.
    - B. The needs analysis.
    - C. The size of the instructional design team.
    - D. The intended training audience.

Exercise 9

Draft a design document for your course. Remember to include detailed descriptions and examples.

Chapter 11: Storyboarding and Rapid Prototyping

This chapter will cover:

- Origin of storyboarding and storyboarding components
- Ways to storyboard and prototype
- Benefits of storyboarding and prototyping
- Rapid prototyping
- Difference between storyboarding and prototyping

Case Study

When Swiftfoot Software Developers began the process of translating their instructor-led workshops to self-paced eLearning, they decided to carefully follow standard development procedures. They conducted a needs assessment, created a design document and began to storyboard the course. The instructional designer and developer painstakingly added graphics, development notes, and text to a PowerPoint storyboarding template.

The assumption had been that the course would have a fairly short turnaround since the content was set in stone. If anything, they thought, content could be simplified, since there was no need for tools like group exercises, and self-paced eLearning made it easy to reference external resources. When a month passed and the team was still in the storyboarding mode, the project lead approached them with a thought.

"Why are you two storyboarding at all?" he asked.

The designer was a bit surprised at the question. "So it's easy to review the material before we get into the weeds, and so we're on the same page when it comes to how the course is going to look," she said.

"But it's just the two of you, and your content doesn't need a big review. Why not just come up with a simple version of the course and add to it as you go?"

The instructional designer and developer were reluctant to let go of their work so far, but at the lead's insistence, they decided to test it out for a week. They quickly found that without storyboarding it was difficult to create the same "look and feel" of the course, decide on appropriate media, identify errors at an early stage, and most importantly, there was nothing to obtain client's sign off on.

The Development Phase of an eLearning course involves many complex steps and activities to guarantee a quality product. To ensure the outcome of all efforts meets the highest standards, ISD professionals use *storyboards* and *prototypes* to illustrate and communicate their ideas to team members and stakeholders.

Storyboarding

Storyboards are visual organizers that illustrate and communicate ideas to other professionals on the team such as graphic artists, multimedia specialists, and programmers. Typical storyboards include text, visual, and audio elements for every screen of an eLearning course. Instructional designers incorporate interactions, assessments, demonstrations, simulations, and games in their storyboards.

Historically, in the early 1930s, Walt Disney Studios started using storyboards to draw the scenes for their cartoons. By the late 1930s, all major studios had adopted the concept. Gone with the Wind was the first live-action film that was completely storyboarded. Nowadays, eLearning professionals use storyboarding as an aid to develop instructionally sound courses and learning materials. Many instructional designers provide storyboarding templates to Subject Matter Experts (SMEs), who use them to populate the content. It is then much easier for instructional designers to use the pre-populated template to rearrange the content and add interactivities and assessments.

There is no single way to storyboard. In fact, every organization uses its own template based on its unique needs. Even though many tools can be used to create storyboards, most templates are built in either PowerPoint or Word. Some instructional designers like to use multiple storyboards and choose the appropriate one based on their content. For instance, the template used to design a game or simulation would be different from a template for video development. Nevertheless, there are certain elements common to most storyboards. These elements include the following:

Content – This is the information that will appear on the screen. In addition to the on-screen text, this section contains instructions for learners such as *Click Next for more information.*

Audio – This is the narrator's script for each screen. In this section, the instructional designer writes out the pronunciation of terms and acronyms that might be unfamiliar to the narrator.

Graphics – This is where instructional designers either place images that they want to appear on each screen or, if they cannot find the image they are looking for, or need the graphic artist to create an original one, simply explain what they want. Alternatively, they can find a visual that conveys the message but is not exactly what is needed. This sample visual will guide graphic artists as they develop graphics or search for appropriate images.

Programming Instructions or *Developer's Notes* – This is the most complex element of a storyboard, primarily because it incorporates many sub-elements. In this area, instructional designers need to provide clear instructions about navigation. For instance, they should explain to the programmer where each screen should take learners and provide names for each button that appears on the screen. Additionally, in the *programming instructions area*, ISD specialists should provide detailed explanations of interactions, assessments, and feedback. It is important to keep in mind, however, that developers will be creating all the interactions, test questions, and remediation screens based on these descriptions; therefore, being very accurate and including as many details as possible is key. If the developer is responsible for creating assessment items, storyboards should include the question type and the question itself along with all answer choices.

Instructions and corrective feedback that would appear on the screen must also be included in the storyboard.

In addition to the above elements, storyboards often include:

- the name of the module
- page numbers
- screen references

These elements help instructional designers and developers communicate more efficiently when discussing specific screens. Most of the elements mentioned above are common to storyboards; however, because there is no single way to storyboard your eLearning courses, you should choose the elements that suit your specific needs.

Following are two examples of eLearning storyboards—one is text-based and one is visual.

Text-based Storyboard

Project Name: Audio:	Screen name: On-screen text:	On-screen graphics:

Visual Storyboard

Course Name:	Screen Number:		Module Name:
On-Screen Text			Graphics
Audio Narration			Programming Notes

Even though storyboarding is very time consuming, it is a major time saver at the end. Storyboarding makes it easy for the SME to review projects, and allows instructional designers to avoid rework.

Prototyping

While storyboards are very useful for visualizing a course, they only work well for linear courses. Because many eLearning lessons are non-linear, storyboards can be rather confusing to both SMEs and programmers. Sometimes it is excessively difficult or even impossible to describe all the interactions, non-linear navigations, scenarios, simulations, and other media-rich content in words. Storyboards do not always allow to fully capture all the nuances of the design, especially when it comes to games and interactions. Therefore, many instructional designers turn to *rapid prototyping* to develop an interactive model of their eLearning course. In addition to all the information found in storyboards, prototypes contain the overall course layout including buttons and navigation. When you have many projects on your plate and a very short timeframe to complete them, rapid prototyping can save a lot of time as some of the elements created previously for other projects can be reused.

There are three prototyping styles:

Nonfunctional prototypes – Do not have any functional elements but still have the look and feel that effectively communicates functionality of the future course.

Semi-functional prototypes – Contain interactions and can be used as screenshots in storyboards.

Fully functional prototypes – Include most of the content, interactions, and assessments and clearly demonstrate the functionality of the entire course.

Just like with storyboarding, there is no single way to prototype. Therefore, you should choose the prototyping approach that works best for your specific needs. There are many different tools that can be used to build prototypes; Articulate 360 and Adobe Captivate are just some examples. If, however, rapid eLearning tools are not available, you can use PowerPoint to build your prototypes. ISD specialists who are technologically savvy and want to create a fully functional prototype with advanced interactions can turn to Adobe Flash to lay out their lesson. Prototypes are not meant to be complete.

Furthermore, having the exact content is not required for building prototypes. Their sole purpose is to visualize the functionality and usability of the course.

When instructional designers submit their prototypes to stakeholders, they typically review them for the following:

Functionality and Navigation
- Do all elements of the course including videos and interactions play well at their workstation?
- Is the load time of all content and interactions acceptable?
- Do all buttons take the user to the correct place in the course?

Look and Feel of the Course
- Does the layout work for the purpose of this training course?
- Is the color scheme of the course appropriate?
- Are the fonts easy to read?

Interactions and Audio
- Are the videos and interactions appropriate?
- Do all interactions and videos play correctly?
- Do they meet instructional goals of the course?
- Are the voiceovers professional and audible?
- Is the tone of voice appropriate?
- Is the dialect easy to understand?

Nowadays, many instructional designers choose to use the rapid prototyping method in place of the ADDIE model. Rapid prototyping goes hand in hand with the rapid ISD model and allows you to create learning solutions quickly and effectively. This model focuses on developing a training solution rather than simply preparing for its development. In this model, you can immediately jump into prototyping and gather necessary information about learners' needs as you build your course and interact with SMEs.

Test Your Knowledge

1. Storyboarding and prototyping is used by instructional designers to:
    A. Take up additional project hours.
    B. Determine the need for additional instructional design staff for any given project.
    C. Illustrate and communicate their ideas to team members and stakeholders.
    D. Provide themselves with a personal boost and to prove that they can handle complex projects

2. Storyboards typically include:
    A. All visual elements necessary to convey the intention of each slide.
    B. All audio, visual and text elements to convey the intention of each slide.
    C. All audio elements necessary to convey the intention of each slide.
    D. All visual and text elements to convey the intention of each slide.

3. When working with Subject Matter Experts (SME), it is typically best practice to:
    A. Provide them with a storyboard template to populate the basic content, which the instructional designer can then arrange and add interactivity to.
    B. Provide them with a fully populated storyboard based on instructional designer's knowledge of the topic, so that they can make corrections to it.
    C. Work collaboratively with them in a one-on-one setting to populate a highly polished storyboard.
    D. Ask them to come up with a storyboard without much guidance from the instructional designer, which will help to preserve the original intention of the training.

4. Which of the following elements is NOT typically part of a storyboard template?
    A. On-Screen Text and Graphics
    B. Audio/Video Timecode
    C. Programming/Development Notes
    D. Audio Narration

5. Which one of the following is a disadvantage of storyboarding?
    A. It wastes a lot of time.
    B. It makes it harder for SMEs to review projects.
    C. Storyboards only work for linear courses.
    D. Storyboards necessitate a lot of re-work.

6. Rapid prototypes are _____ models of eLearning courses which contain the overall _____ including navigation.
    A. interactive / course layout
    B. detailed / course layout
    C. interactive / course instructions
    D. detailed / course instructions

7. Semi-functional prototypes:
    A. Do not have any functional elements but still have the look and feel of the actual course.
    B. Contain interactions and can be used as screenshots in storyboards.
    C. Include most of the content, interactions, and assessments and clearly demonstrate the functionality of the course.
    D. Include all of the content, interactions and assessments and if approved, will only need another 10% of development work to be completed.

8. If rapid eLearning tools are not available, you can use _____ to build prototypes.
    A. Microsoft Word
    B. Microsoft PowerPoint
    C. Microsoft Excel
    D. OneNote

Exercise 10

Using the example provided in this chapter, create your own storyboarding template, and populate it with appropriate content.

Chapter 12: Scripting Your ELearning Course

This chapter will cover:

- Basics of scriptwriting
- Plain language principles
- Style guides

Case Study

The project lead for Paean Insurance Company's training department was at the end of her rope. Her team had been tasked with creating easily digestible training that would be relatable to the learner, and they had been excited to try out something new for their team: videos. She and her team had worked hard to create skits that explained complicated healthcare processes in an interesting way, but the feedback from customers was that the training seemed unrealistic and irrelevant. Thinking through her options, she took one of the feedback comments to heart: "If the dialogue were more natural, it would be easier to take the course seriously." She decided to hire a scriptwriter to rework the scripts.

The scriptwriter she found had instructional design experience, and after reviewing the scripts; he told her that the problem wasn't the content but the story and dialogue. "I think they're just having problems taking the scenarios seriously. They're not realistic, they last too long, and the dialogue sounds wooden," he said.

"Well, do your best," the lead said. "If we need to shoot these videos again, we will."

The scriptwriter and the project lead sat down with the team to brainstorm new scenarios, focusing on ordinary situations where the customers would need to know about the claims process. As they came up with their ideas, the scriptwriter would often tell the group to keep the stories simple, short, and impactful. Then, he asked the team to read their own scripts aloud, pointing out the moments where the conversation didn't flow well. With a casual, conversational tone and stronger, simpler storylines, the training improved.

By now, you have analyzed learners, developed learning objectives, selected appropriate media, created a design document, and even built a prototype. Now, it's time to write a voiceover script. Even for experienced writers, voiceover scripting can be difficult as writing for audio differs from other types of writing and requires a unique set of skills.

To write a script that will bring all the points across and engage learners with the material, you must understand the content. Logical organization is the key to effective scriptwriting. To turn the content into the chronological, well-written script, it is essential to be able to follow the material. Most instructional designers work on projects they know very little about. Conducting additional research and communicating with Subject Matter Experts (SMEs) is the essential first step in making sense out of the information that will be included in the lesson.

Even though clients often believe one has to be an expert in the subject area to write a good script, this is not true. In fact, not being an SME can be advantageous primarily because most SMEs know so much about the topic that they often leave the important information out, forget to mention crucial steps in the process, or provide unnecessary content that confuses learners.

Instructional designers unfamiliar with the material will ask questions and clarify statements to get all the information needed for creating a clear and effective script. Alternatively, if instructional designers appear to be experts in the topic, finding a non-expert to review the script and provide feedback is recommended. Remember, as you seek clarification and answers to questions, you prevent learners from having the same questions and concerns about the content.

One of the most important rules in script writing is informality. Scripts are written to be heard, not read. Therefore, the writing style should be conversational. To add a conversational tone to the script, consider using contractions (e.g., *isn't* instead of *is not*) and pronouns to make the eLearning content more personal (e.g., *you* instead of *learner*). You should also consider the plain language principles as you write your scripts. Some of these principles include:

- Using active voice over passive voice
  Example:
  Active voice: *Amy wrote the letter to her boss.*
  Passive voice: *The letter to the boss was written by Amy.*
- Avoiding run-on sentences
  Example:
  Run-on sentence: *Amy is a great writer she writes well.*
  Corrected sentence: *Amy is a great writer. She writes well.*
- Avoiding sentences that express more than one idea
  Example:
  Sentence with more than one idea: *Amy likes writing letters and editing audio narration.*
  Corrected sentence: *Amy loves writing letters. She also enjoys editing audio narration.*
- Avoiding misplaced modifiers
  Example:
  Sentence with misplaced modifier: *If you only have time to write one letter, do it professionally.*
  Corrected sentence: *If you have time to write only one letter, do it professionally.*

- Avoiding double negatives
  Example:
  Sentence with double negative: *If Amy does not write a letter, she cannot send it to her boss.*
  Corrected sentence*: Amy can send a letter to her boss if she writes it.*
- Keeping subject and objects close to the verb
  Example:
  Sentence with subject and object far from the verb: *Amy, anticipating salary increase, wrote a letter to her boss.*
  Corrected sentence*: Anticipating salary increase, Amy wrote a letter to her boss.*

If, in the script, you use word combinations that are difficult to pronounce together, the talent may have a hard time reading them, and learners may have problems understanding what they hear. One way to avoid tongue twisters is to reread the script multiple times and make relevant changes to wording and grammar.

Remember, eLearning courses should address multiple learning styles and meet accessibility requirements (We will cover accessibility in Chapter 14). When your learners hear the audio recording, they should be able to tell when the topic is changing. To achieve this goal, instructional designers should check their script for appropriate transitions.

Another good practice for scriptwriting dictates that pauses should be incorporated into the script to indicate where the talent should stop and to give learners a chance to absorb the information. Additionally, using 12-point font and double-spacing the script will help the talent go through it more easily. Double-spaced scripts provide enough room for narrator to make notes when necessary. If the talent will be reading from a hard copy, it is best to use a serif font such as Times New Roman. Alternatively, using a sans-serif font such as Arial is preferred when reading from a computer screen. Another way to help the talent is to spell out all URLs as well as terms or acronyms that are difficult to pronounce. The same principle applies to dollar amounts and dates. By following these simple rules, you will save a lot of time for both your talent and yourself as the audio recording session will not be interrupted for questions and clarifications.

Refer to the following website for additional information about scriptwriting: http://www.screenwriting.info/

Lastly, proofread, proofread, and proofread. There is nothing worse than noticing errors in the script after recording it.

Style Guide

When you work with other professionals such as editors, graphic artists, and programmers, maintaining a consistent style can be problematic. Therefore, it is important to create a standardized guide for each project that all team members will use.

ELearning content needs to follow standards just like classroom manuals and material. When content is standardized, it makes it easier for the learner to understand and quickly process the information. They stop noticing inconsistencies and focus on what you would really like them to—the meat! You could also implement a final Q/A checklist to ensure they followed each standard.

Here is a list of "standardized items" you should include:

1. **Bolding**: Decide how to use bolding. Do you want to use it for emphasis? As a heading, for sections, to indicate actions?

2. **Italics:** Are hyperlinks italicized? What about names of documents, screens, and systems?

3. **Fonts:** Choose two to three fonts and decide which one is for headings, body text, and possibly image design.

4. **Colors:** Find colors that contrast well. There are many different websites that help create color schemes and check contrast.

5. **Layout**: Design five to ten different layouts and let the team use them. This saves time because each page does not have to be custom designed each time. It also trains to understand your pages.

6. **Grammar and tense:** Are you talking directly to the learner? Should you use past, present, or future tense? Should you be formal or informal?

7. **Images:** Will your images have shadows, rounded corners, feathering, borders, or reflections?

8. **Buttons**: What buttons will you always use? You might need buttons for next, back, job aids, exit, simulation, more info, tips, play, course, evaluation, get help, FAQs, feedback, and replay.

9. **Logos**: What logos will you have displayed? Company, department, none?

10. **Text size:** What size are the headings? How about the body text?

In addition, it might be helpful to include the following:

1. **Types of files allowed in the course:** .mov, .swf, .avi, .png, .wmv, etc.

2. **Icons:** Create a library of standard icons such as: caution, checkmarks, notes, numbers, arrows, etc.

3. **Interactivity:** How well do you tell the user to do something? Click the XXXX button or Click XXXX? Do you bold what action the user should take?

4. **Bullets:** What bullet shape will you use?

5. **Course player/GUI:** Create a standard interface for all courses. This allows the user to get used to the navigation within your course.

Test Your Knowledge

1. Not having expertise in the subject matter of the course you are developing can be helpful when writing scripts because:
   A. You will develop in a way that will make the learner thirsty for more information after they are done with the course.
   B. The questions you ask in clarification as you develop are likely to be the same questions a learner might have about the topic.
   C. The opinions of the SMEs you incorporate into the content will be taken even more seriously.
   D. Your content will have a fresh approach to the subject being taught, thereby helping to innovate in that particular field.

2. Scripts are written to be _____ and should be _____.
   A. seen, not heard / controversial
   B. read, not seen / conversational
   C. heard, not read / conversational
   D. read, not heard / controversial

3. To make the script sound more personable, consider using:
   A. Contractions like "isn't" instead of "is not"
   B. Contradictions in opinions
   C. Conversations between two people
   D. Commas to separate phrases for the narrator

4. All of the following are examples of the plain language principles EXCEPT:
   A. Using active voice over passive voice.
   B. Avoiding adjectives.
   C. Avoiding sentences that express more than one idea.
   D. Avoiding misplaced modifiers.

5. You will help your voice-over talent tremendously by:
   A. Incorporating several local vernaculars into the script.
   B. Involving a third party producer into the audio recording process.
   C. Incorporating many changes during the audio recording process.
   D. Incorporating pauses into your scripts and using 12-point, double-spaced fonts.

6. To ensure the narration is perfect after it comes back from the voice-over talent, make sure that you:
   A. Pay them in advance.
   B. Send them to a seminar on the topic so they can comfortably talk about it.
   C. Proofread the script multiple times.
   D. Break each line onto a separate piece of printed paper for easy reading.

7. A document which helps align all team members on things such as design, voice and image rules is called a:
   A. Storyboard
   B. Style guide
   C. Prototype
   D. Design guide

Exercise 11

Based on what you know about the topic for your
eLearning course (new salary calculating tool for the
department of finance), brainstorm the elements that
will be included in the style guide.

Chapter 13: Quality Assurance

This chapter will cover:

- Alpha, beta, and pilot testing
- Error log
- Checklists for identifying errors

Case Study

The Advanced Media, Inc. team was struggling with the end of a major project: a huge simulation designed to train officers in the military. Though they had a standard QA process, they were quickly finding that the usual process was inadequate. Their military clients were incredibly detail oriented and needed every aspect of the training to be perfectly accurate, clear to a wide variety of learners, and it should conform to protocol. The need for more and more reviews and revisions was creating tension with their clients and losing them money.

The team knew they should have clarified the process before the project had begun, but it was too late now—they were bogged down with work. Finally, the instructional design lead decided they needed a pair of fresh eyes. She brought in a QA Analyst from another project who was known for his ability to streamline and simplify the QA process.

First, the QA Analyst decided to have a meeting with the clients. He generated a checklist of items that they were concerned about and had the clients assign them a priority. With the project lead's help, he and the clients clarified what could be changed at this stage. He added to, and revised, the style guide to be a more intuitive and comprehensive resource for the team.

Next, the QA Analyst created checklists and review forms tailored to the project to facilitate good communication with the instructional designers and developers.

Finally, he had everyone thoroughly document the QA process to continue to improve it. He knew there was always room for improvement, especially with such a tricky project. With the QA Analyst's help, the project slowly picked up speed.

Once you have developed your course, you should **alpha and beta test** it before submitting it to the client. **Alpha testing** involves interface testing to confirm that the course functions the way it should. Very often, alpha testing reveals misspelled words, ambiguous directions, broken links, poorly developed interactions, and unsynchronized audio and video.

The second phase of testing is known as **Pilot** or **Beta testing**. During this time, the course is released to the small group of target audience, most likely Subject Matter Experts (SMEs), to ensure its quality and functionality. It is important to have the pilot testing participants avoid making on-the-spot changes to the problems they encounter. Instead, ask them to focus on the course itself and keep an error log of all the issues they want to address. Once the pilot testing is complete, instructional designers and testing participants can meet to discuss desired changes.

Below is a sample error log template that you can use for piloting courses.

Reviewer's Name	Module #	Screen Title	Issue Type (e.g., text font, graphic, navigation	Explanation	Assigned to	Date completed

Table 13 should help you identify errors as you test your courses. This quality assurance checklist can also be given to the SMEs to guide them through the problems they should keep an eye on as they conduct course review.

Table 13 - Quality Assurance Checklist

Question	Yes	No	N/A
Do all buttons work correctly and take learners where they should?			
Are all feedback statements programmed correctly?			
What happens if the learner answers correctly/incorrectly?			
Do all games and simulations work correctly?			
Are the directions clear?			
Do all videos play correctly?			
Are all videos placed correctly in the course?			
Is the audio level similar across the entire course?			
Are visuals relevant to the topic of the course?			
Is there a good balance of text, images, and multimedia?			
Is navigation simple and intuitive?			
Is design clean and there is a lot of white space on the screen?			
Is the content relevant to learners' needs?			
Is the content presented in an interactive way?			
Do interactions, games, and simulations support learning objectives?			
Are interactions, games, and simulations practical and realistic?			
Are the titles of all lessons clear and accurate?			
Does the course launch properly?			
Are all screens present?			
Are examples clear and easy to understand?			
Does each screen contain enough information?			

Test Your Knowledge

1. Before submitting your course to the client, you should _____ test it.
    A. alpha
    B. beta
    C. interface
    D. conversion

2. Often called Pilot testing, this testing phase releases the course to a small group of individuals to ensure its quality and functionality.
    A. Alpha and Beta Testing
    B. Alpha Testing
    C. Beta Testing
    D. Conversion Testing

3. The _____ will help you and your SMEs to identify errors as you test your courses.
    A. storyboard
    B. style guide
    C. Learning Needs Analysis
    D. Quality Assurance Checklist

Exercise 12

Brainstorm ideas for alpha and beta testing your course. Then, using the example in this chapter, create your own error log template.

Chapter 14: Implementation

This chapter will cover:

- Implementation of eLearning courses
- Learning Management System (LMS) and Content Management System (CMS)
- SCORM and guidelines for creating SCORM-compliant content
- Reusable Learning Objects (RLOs)
- Section 508

So, the course has been designed and developed, and it is now time to think about *implementing* it. During implementation, you upload all the content into the Learning Management System (LMS), Content Management System (CMS), or use another appropriate distribution method. Implementation also involves uploading the SCORM package and ensuring that it is tracking properly. Once you launch the course, you should test it to make sure it is fully functional.

During the eLearning implementation phase, you need to ensure that all the tools and equipment are readily available and work properly, and the learning application is fully operational.

This means all slides, interactions, games, assessments, and external links provided in the course should be tested. Some instructional designers upload their course and fail to review it again. Many of them are either too busy or do not consider this an important step primarily because they have already reviewed the course many times before uploading it to the learning platform. The importance of testing the eLearning course after uploading cannot be stressed enough. Once the course is launched, the operating system, web browser, and even the display settings on the computer may change the appearance and functionality of the course. Furthermore, there are can be many other technical reasons why the lesson may appear different after it is uploaded to the learning platform. Some of these reasons may go beyond the capability of an ISD specialist. However, it is still your responsibility to review the course for any possible errors, and have someone with the right skill set fix the issues.

Once an eLearning course is implemented, it will require continuous maintenance to ensure it functions effectively on the regular basis. In most cases, however, once you develop the course and confirm that it functions properly, you are no longer responsible for it unless the client comes back and asks for additional changes or upgrades.

The log should be kept throughout the implementation phase to record and fix errors. Table 14 is a checklist that will guide you through major functionality questions that should be addressed during that time. While it is not exhaustive, it covers most major elements that you should look for when implementing your projects.

Table 14 – Implementation Phase Checklist

Question	Yes / No / Not Applicable
Does the course launch properly?	
Are the learning results updated upon completion of the course?	
Does the menu play properly?	
Do all external links work properly?	
Do all attachments open?	
Does the scroll bar work correctly?	
Do all interactions in the course play correctly?	
Do all buttons take learners where they are supposed to take them?	
Is the load time of all screens including interactions and quizzes relatively quick?	
Are all buttons, links and objects displayed correctly on the screen?	
Do all videos play smoothly?	
Is the video quality acceptable?	
Is the audio audible?	
Do all audio pieces sound the same?	
Are all on screen elements such as text and graphics aligned correctly?	
Do all animations play smoothly and appear in the appropriate time and place?	
Is the color scheme consistent?	
Are the fonts easy to read?	
Is the spacing of paragraphs consistent?	

Learning Management System (LMS) and Content Management System (CMS)

Case Study

When his clients told him that he should "pick the LMS that costs the least," the freelance instructional designer working on the project knew he had to communicate the importance of LMS selection. The clients, an environmental non-profit named Ecoquest, were new to eLearning, and didn't realize how much an LMS could affect the success of the delivery of the project. That's why they were trying to rush delivery along as quickly and cost-effectively as possible.

The instructional designer planned a meeting that would go over the major aspects of LMS selection and guide them toward a decision. First, he looked through the needs analysis and found relevant observations about the learners and learning goals. The course was designed to train employees as wilderness guides for groups of elementary school students, and there were a lot of important details to memorize for the certification. The course as designed had many assessments, so the instructional designer knew he'd need good data tracking abilities.

Next, the instructional designer considered key features needed. Mobile delivery was best, he thought, since many of the employees were often out of the office and all of them had access to smartphones through the organization.

Finally, he knew he needed an established LMS with a strong customer support network since Ecoquest didn't have a training team in-house.

The instructional designer presented these considerations to the client and made his suggestions. Realizing that LMS selection was more important than they'd assumed, the client decided to take some time and find the best LMS for their needs.

A *Learning Management System* (LMS) is a software application used to plan, implement, and assess the learning process. LMS allows instructors and administrators to create and deliver content to the maximum number of people, monitor participation, and assess performance. Among some of the most popular LMSs are:

- Moodle
- Edmodo
- SumTotal Systems

Content Management System (CMS) is often the main function of a Learning Management System (LMS). Most LMSs encompass a CMS. As opposed to LMSs, CMSs do not have to be SCORM-compliant and act more like databases. Among some of the most popular CMSs are:

- WordPress
- Joomla
- Drupal

There are countless LMSs and CMSs on the market. To choose the option that best suits the needs of a specific organization, you should consider your target audience, budget, and requirements. The following questions should guide you through the process of selecting the LMS and CMS for your needs.

- What are the organizational goals?
- What are the organizational business needs?
- How many learners will have access to the LMS?
- Is content relatively stable?
- Is the LMS SCORM-compliant?
- How would the LMS fit in the overall structure of the organization?
- What tracking features do you need?
- How much money can the organization spend on LMS?
- What kind of technical support is available?

SCORM

SCORM stands for *Shareable Content Object Reference Model*. SCORM is a set of technical standards that ensure the course works well with other eLearning software. SCORM also ensures that the learning content and the Learning Management System (LMS) communicate with each other. Even though SCORM does not speak directly to instructional designers, as it only relates to technical standards, you should be familiar with it.

SCORM governs how content communicates with an LMS and how the user is allowed to navigate between parts of the content. SCORM speaks only to the interface between content and LMS. ELearning content that is SCORM-compliant should be:

- *Accessible* – The content should be easy to find and access from one location and deliver to another location.

- *Adaptable* – The content should be adapted to organizational needs and new content should be able to be added easily and cost effectively.
- *Affordable* – The time and costs involved in training delivery should be minimized while production should be maximized.
- *Durable* – New content should be added without having to redesign or recode the course.
- *Interoperable* – ELearning courses should easily run in any location and on any CMS regardless of the location and set of tools used to develop the training.
- *Reusable* – Instructional designers should be able to reuse any part of the course to create other courses or to present contents as standalone modules.

The best way to ensure SCORM compliance is to use a SCORM-compliant authoring tool. Among these tools are Adobe Captivate, Adobe Presenter, Camtasia, and Articulate 360.

Even the best eLearning modules will not be maximized if learners cannot access them. The same is also true if their features do not run on the devices that learners can use. This is why SCORM compliance is of utmost importance in designing eLearning materials.

Fortunately for eLearning designers, there are several reliable software programs that can be used to ensure that their outputs are SCORM compliant. This means that these materials can be made available to a wider audience and their features can be fully utilized regardless of the device they are being accessed from.

In finding the right SCORM compliant eLearning solution, you have to go through the following steps:

1. Know your audience – One of the best things about SCORM compliant eLearning is that it is more flexible when it comes to design customization. This does not only pertain to the aesthetics of your modules, but also to their flow and scope.

If you are designing a nursing course, for instance, your modules would require SCORM compliant eLearning solutions that allow you to upload video files of training demonstrations and simulations of patient care procedures.

Taking it further, you might have a chapter or a section of your module that you want your learners to read and understand before they view your video content. You can design your module in such a way that the learners cannot access these media until after they have completed a specific chapter or section.

2. Determine your own performance monitoring and assessment needs – Parameters can be set in the SCORM package and root manifest to include diagnostic pit stops. You can also set your own criteria and values for your grading scale. This allows you to measure your learners' performance, so that remedial measures can be undertaken as necessary. This also makes it possible for you to review and incorporate improvements in your online training strategy.

Among the diagnostic tools that you can include in your SCORM compliant modules are multiple choice test questions after each lesson or chapter, and simulation tests for skills assessment.

3. Find the right authoring tool – The conventional way of creating eLearning modules is using presentation programs that are readily available. It is possible to create your materials using Microsoft PowerPoint, and then later convert them into SCORM compliant modules. However, there are limitations to tools and functionalities that you can include in your modules. Plus, some design and programming components might not convert properly and cause problems later on.

A key component of making your eLearning materials SCORM compliant is the SCORM manifest. It basically contains an overview of the training content including all the resources, overall format, and design elements. This can be handled by a SCORM-friendly software suite. When all these are in place, it will be a cinch to import, upload, and migrate data to any LMS.

SCORM compliance makes it possible for you to distribute your eLearning resources in a more efficient manner. At the same time, it allows for closer monitoring of learner performance and more reliable tracking of the effectiveness of the resources.

Case Study

After the new fiscal year began, Petrol Oil Company embarked on the huge task of reworking its entire training library to reflect new standards and processes. Because it was a huge company with many departments, they immediately faced the issue of having to create generic training or tailor their training to each specific standard. The difficulty was that certain topics, like drugs and alcohol training or safety training or courses on branding standards, were required across the company, but generic training tended to lead to suboptimal evaluations. After all, each department dealt differently with issues like safety or branding.

After some discussion on how to rework the courses without costing the company a fortune, one of the instructional designers had an idea. "Why don't we focus on making Reusable Learning Objects?" she said. "They're customizable, so they can be used in a variety of different settings. They'd save us time and money."

The instructional designer explained her vision: to create standard RLOs for, say, drug and alcohol policy, and to also create some tailored content, like scenarios or assessments. That would combine the best of both worlds.

The team decided to try it. They identified key topics, which could be used across many or even all departments—for instance, the company color scheme, which had to be used in any department that dealt with communications. They focused on creating condensed, self-contained modules with their own clear learning standards that could easily be followed up with content specifically targeted to each relevant department.

Reusable Learning Objects

Instructional designers always look for techniques to develop their courses quickly and inexpensively. One of the best ways to save time and money is by reusing course components.

A *Reusable Learning Object* (RLO) is an instructional design element that can be used for multiple purposes. They are usually small components that are developed for a specific use in one course, but can be conveniently reused in multiple future projects, often with a few simple custom edits.

For example, a video that's produced for a particular eLearning course (e.g., a financial literacy course) could also be repurposed to serve an instructor-led classroom course, or reused in other self-paced courses that are related to a similar concept or topic (like Budgeting, Tax Preparation, etc.). Also, graphics and other visuals can be easily saved and reused when developing other courses. For course pieces to be reusable, they must be designed as standalone objects. For example, reusable objects should not have transitions, summaries, or information presented in another part of the course. Additionally, truly reusable objects should all be created using the same style.

So, where should the reusable content be stored? You can create folders that everyone on the team or in the organization would have access to and save your reusable objects there. Alternatively, RLOs can be stored in a Content Management System (CMS).

Thanks to many rapid eLearning tools available on the market, instructional designers are able to save time and resources by reusing learning objects such as eLearning modules, videos, and documents. However, the main problem with Reusable Learning Objects (RLOs) is that many training products are customized to address a very specific need, and become outdated relatively quickly.

Developing a library of RLOs means designing content with sustainability in mind. Another term used for this type of content is "evergreen," meaning that in a month, six months, or even a year, the content will still be relevant and applicable to learners. Evergreen content can eventually save a lot of time by not requiring extensive edits and updates.

Consider the content you may use for training products currently on your shelf—what pieces of information are easy to recycle and require very little maintenance? Here are some examples:

- Stable: compliance laws, harassment awareness training, and broad introductions to teams and organization culture will likely not change and require the least updates from the content perspective.
- Soft-skills training: because the approach to soft skills is not as fluid as technical systems training (which becomes outdated as soon as a new version is published), you may reuse this content for a long period of time.

Also, consider information that is not sustainable, and does not lend itself well to reuse. For example,

- Employee names and images: sharing the images of a team risks the need to revise the training quickly, if there is a change in title or structure.
- Descriptions of a technical or specific process: few processes within an organization stay the same for years; new systems, resources, and efficiencies are likely to occur many times in the course of a year, making any training products outdated and confusing.
- Walks through a business system: training and development

products for information systems are extremely useful resources, but the relevance of the training should be reviewed regularly to ensure it is up to date with all releases and changes.

Using an arsenal of authoring tools to build sustainable learning objects will save time in the overall development and launch of training products. Being mindful of the content put into each type of training product also makes the ability to reuse objects much simpler.

Not every course you make needs to be designed from scratch. In fact, if each one is, you may end up with some very confused learners who expect to encounter the same user experience (UX), same information delivery, and same visual design aspects each time they take one of your courses.

By comparison, imagine the dread you would feel if every car you drove had a different user interface. That might put you off driving for good. Instead, every car uses a variation of a core design template, so drivers of multiple vehicles will not have to waste precious time figuring out how each car works.

Good organization and time management are critical to producing efficient online training, meeting your deadlines, and staying sane. By looking at the bigger picture during your course design and development phases, you will start to see opportunities to build RLOs that can be creatively re-used for multiple applications. The time you invest now in creating those RLOs will pay dividends later, because each time you reuse an element you are saving future development time—and over the course of multiple lessons all those saved design hours really add up.

So, what can become an RLO? While not all training materials work well as RLOs, the following elements can often be repurposed:

- Quiz and test formats
- Visual layouts
- Icons and reference images
- Problem-oriented learning
- Exploratory learning modules
- Performance support courses
- Blended learning environments
- Job support tools, and
- Help systems

Here are a few tips instructional designers can apply when designing and applying RLOs.

1. Modularize your content – Just like modular furniture that is built using standardized components (nuts, bolts, screws, etc.), plan your eLearning courses in a modular fashion so they will rely on the same components (videos, graphics, assessments and quizzes) to come together.

2. Size appropriately – If RLOs are built correctly, they can fit neatly within almost any related curriculum. Therefore, when building reusable content, make sure your components are not too large. For example, do not create one single 60-minute video; create 10 six-minute segments instead. That way, each video can be conveniently plugged in wherever appropriate within the overall course design, rather than reusing a longer video that is only partially applicable to a related topic.

3. Be neutral – Wherever possible, create objects that are neutral without any specific cultural references. For instance, if your slides for a course about "Safety Procedures Around Fire Hazards" are gender neutral or industry independent, ISD professionals will be able to plug-and-play those RLOs for future courses designed for any audience or any industry.

4. Get help – A large collection of RLOs can quickly become unmanageable and overwhelming. Therefore, eLearning professionals should work with Content Management Systems (CMSs) that can help create, organize and track their component inventory. That way you will not have to go on the eternal "object hunt" each time there is an opportunity to reuse one of your previously developed components.

5. Leverage agnostic development tools – To benefit the most from your investment in RLOs, choose tools that are accessible, customizable, and responsive. Designing for the most commonly-used operating systems and browsers will also result in greater flexibility in course deployment while maximizing your return on investment (ROI).

Case Study

During the talks to develop a huge video simulation for military officers, the Advanced Media Company was stunned to learn how involved 508 Compliance seemed to be. Though they were excited to work on a project with such an ambitious scale and emphasis on innovation, it quickly became clear that Section 508 was going to throw a wrench into many of their plans.

Any background image, any video, was going to need to be accompanied by text or captions, for one, and other factors, like the requirement that no color coding should be used, affected some of the company's tried and true methods for conveying information. The team was overwhelmed by all the information.

But one developer wasn't deterred. "We'll just create really good processes to incorporate all the 508 requirements," he said. "Everyone can have a checklist on their desk, we'll review the checklist any time we want to make a design change."

"But what if something falls through the cracks?" one of the instructional designer asked.

"We'll make looking over the checklist a part of the QA process. In fact, we could even ask a QA Analyst to specialize in 508 compliance for this project."

Though the team was intimidated, the developer's confidence won them over, and they set to work. As he suggested, each member of the team took the time to get familiar with 508 standards. With time, the standards became second nature and didn't bog down the development process at all.

Section 508

Section 508 is part of the Rehabilitation Act of 1973 amended in 1998. According to Section 508, all electronic and information technology must be accessible by people with disabilities. In other words, all eLearning courses must meet the needs of people with visual, auditory, and motor disabilities. The output of most eLearning courses, even those created with rapid tools, is Flash, which is not Section 508-compliant. Therefore, to meet the accessibility standards, ISD professionals should consider other ways to comply with the law. Some of these ways include the following:

- Providing a text equivalent for every non-text element
- Offering synchronized captions for all audio and video files
- Ensuring that all the information presented with color is also available without color

171

- Avoiding elements that flash, whether text, graphics, or objects; Identifying row and column headers for all tables
- Providing a text-only page with information equivalent to that on the non-text version
- Adding alternative text for all images
- Designing accessible and consistent navigation
- Making a Camtasia movie of all interactive slides and elements

There are many assistive technologies available to accommodate people with disabilities and give them an opportunity to benefit from eLearning courses. For example, JAWS (**J**ob **A**ccess **W**ith Speech) is a screen reader that allows visually impaired users to read the screen with a text-to-speech output or on a refreshable Braille display. Braille displays, screen magnification devices, and speech recognition software such as Dragon Naturally Speaking, all help people with visual or movement disabilities receive a similar experience to that of learners who take the interactive version of the course.

Obviously, assistive technology can merely replicate the content from the course, not its interactive elements. However, when developing eLearning, instructional designers should strive to increase the accessibility of their courses by using the above-mentioned strategies.

Because most training courses are developed in Flash or using rapid eLearning software, the output is not 508-compliant. Even though most rapid eLearning tools claim to be 508 compliant, can learners with disabilities truly complete courses developed with this software?

Just like with everything else in eLearning, the answer is: it depends. If your course does not have any animations or other elements of interactivity, then it is probably okay. However, most eLearning courses come with quizzes, games, simulations, or other interactive components. If instructional designers take out interactivity from the learning experience, they receive complaints that their training is boring. If, on the other hand, they leave the interactivity in the course, they receive complaints that the courses do not meet the lawful requirements.

So, what are the alternatives? In addition to adding Alt text to all images and providing a transcript of everything being said, there are some other solutions that instructional designers may find helpful. First, as an alternative, consider publishing your courses in Word. In addition to the transcript, this option allows learners to see the screenshots; therefore, those who have hearing impairment can still benefit from your course.

Another solution is to record a Camtasia movie of the published presentation and read all the quiz questions, answer choices, and feedback aloud. This option works well when there is a lot of interactivity in the course. Learners with visual disabilities are able to have all the interactions and quizzes read to them. While this solution addresses the needs of most learners, it requires additional time and resources dedicated to the development of a 508-compliant version of the eLearning course. However, before creating a Camtasia movie of your published Flash presentation, you must understand that you are essentially creating a new version of the course, which will require additional time and resources. If you decided that Camtasia is the way to go, here are the steps:

Step 1 – Record the clicking.

Obviously, visually impaired individuals will not be able to do drag-and-drop or matching exercises. Therefore, you will be recording all the clicking yourself, so that people on the other end will be able to just sit and watch the presentation.

Step 2 – Read all the text on the screen.

When you arrive at quiz questions, you will have to read the directions slowly, then the question, and finally all the options associated with it.

Step 3 – Give learners time to form their response.

Once you finish reading the options, pause and wait about a minute or so to allow learners to think about the answer. Then, read the correct response.

Step 4 – Provide appropriate feedback.

Remember, because these learners selected their response mentally, you don't really know what their selection was. Therefore, your feedback should not say "good job" or "sorry, that's not the correct response." Instead, you should simply state what the correct answer is and explain why this answer is correct.

Because the corrective feedback for your audience with disabilities will be different, you may have to write a separate script and record additional voiceovers to accommodate the needs of these learners. If you do not want to overcomplicate things for yourself, the alternative would be to design one standard feedback for both groups of learners, eliminating the praise.

If you know that your course will require a 508-compliant version, before you start creating your content, review the following areas of your design:

- For learners with certain disabilities, keyboards are their only means of navigating through the course. While the "Tab" key is often used as the primary navigation command, you should also explore the use of alternate shortcut keys such as "Space bar."
- Some course designers may shy away from using videos because of the 508 compliance issues. Consider adding text prompts, descriptions, sub text, and closed captioning, to make video clips and animated content accessible to learners with disabilities.

- Content designed for people with visual impairments should provide voice over features that clearly read out and describe the information displayed on the screen. For best results, ensure that the learner is able to control the speed of the narration.

- For images and graphics in your course, make sure that detailed narrations are provided for each image displayed. For instance, a visually impaired learner might not respond well to instructions such as "…as shown on Figure 1." For the content to be 508 compliant, whatever appears on "Figure 1" needs to be described underneath the graphic in greater detail. This technique is also known as adding the Alt text to images.

- Instead of assuming that people with visual impairments will easily use browser settings or operating system commands to resize their content, consider providing text resizing configuration options within the course itself.

- While easing the sizing of text may be a step toward 508 compliance, designing textual content for learners with specific disabilities may need to go one step further. For instance, using sans serif fonts for those with dyslexia is recommended.

- Choose your colors carefully. While most color blind learners can see clearly, they find it challenging to discern text and images that feature red, green, or blue. Keep that in mind when you design your content and avoid these colors whenever possible.

- Use alternate approaches when producing materials that reside in linked and sub-linked sections of the course. For instance, a person with visual impairments will not benefit from instructions such as "Click here to learn more..." because they simply wouldn't know where to click. Use the word Select instead of Click, and describe the link. For example, "Select the History link to learn more about various historical sites in the park."

- Another object that is taken for granted by most course designers is drop-down boxes. Even though these widgets can enhance the overall design of the course, they are not Section 508-compliant and need to be avoided at all costs.

- Learners with cognitive disorders, such as Attention Deficit Hyperactivity Disorder (ADHD), may not respond well to purely single-modal lessons (e.g. video only). For best results, consider mixing video, audio, graphics, animated, and textual content.

- Learners dealing with Auditory Perceptual Deficit tend to have challenges with distinguishing similar-sounding tones, or may not be able to accurately hear sound over other background tones or noises. So, whenever possible, try to avoid using sound arbitrarily in the course.

- Interactivity, especially simulations, quizzes, and tests, can be challenging when designing 508-compliant eLearning courses. While we all know that linear courses that lack interactivity are boring, if 508 compliance is the most critical priority for your client, be sure to make your eLearning solution as simple as possible.

- Large segments of data, presented in tabular form, can be challenging for learners with certain types of disabilities. Therefore, whenever possible, restrict the use of tables; and if you really need to use them, break them up into smaller segments.

- Where heavily illustrated or complex graphic and video-based content cannot be 508-compliant, provide content in text-equivalent form. Users should then be given the option to either use the standard page or choose text-only presentations.

- Lastly, rigorously test for 508 compliance. Turn on all of your computer's accessibility features, and run your course from the beginning to the end.

Test Your Knowledge

1. LMS stands for:
   A. Learning Management System
   B. Learning Monitoring System
   C. Learner Mission Statement
   D. Learner Management Statement

2. What does the C in CMS stand for?
   A. Comment
   B. Course
   C. Content
   D. Certificate

3 After uploading a new eLearning course into an LMS or CMS:
   A. Only the first few slides should be checked.
   B. All slides and interactions should be checked.
   C. The course only needs to be launched to verify that it is there.
   D. The only check that needs to occur is that the course is present in the course catalog.

4. SCORM (Shareable Content Object Reverence Model) is:
   A. A set of rules dictating how non-linear eLearning courses communicate with an LMS.
   B. A set of technical standards for how an LMS should display completion status.
   C. A set of rules dictating how eLearning content can trigger additional courses to be assigned in an LMS.
   D. A set of technical standards for how learning content can communicate with an LMS.

5. Reusable Learning Objects (RLOs) are:
   A. Course pieces that can be used again in a different context.
   B. A way for a course to communicate repeat completion of a course to an LMS.
   C. Course pieces that must be used again before learning results can be seen.
   D. A way for an assessment question to be reused in a different LMS.

6. According to Section 508:
   A. All eLearning courses must be accessible to those who are visually impaired.
   B. All electronic and information technology must be accessible by people with disabilities.
   C. Learners with disabilities must be presented with options to take a version of the course suited to their needs.
   D. All electronic and information technology must be re-developed to comply with SCORM standards.

7. All of the following are methods for ensuring content is Section 508-compliant EXCEPT:
   A. Providing a text equivalent for every non-text element.
   B. Offering synchronized captions for all audio and video files.
   C. Offering captions in video sign language.
   D. Avoiding elements that flash, whether text, graphics or objects.

8. JAWS is a:
   A. Screen reader that provides visually impaired users text-to-speech or Braille outputs of the text on the screen.
   B. System which translates braille into audio files.
   C. Screen reader that allows visually impaired users to hear what is written on the screen.
   D. System which translates other languages into English.

Exercise 13

Think about the implementation of your course. Which questions are you going to ask your stakeholder? How are you going to ensure your course is SCORM and Section 508-compliant? Are you going to have any reusable learning objects? How are you going to create them?

Chapter 15: Evaluation

This chapter will cover:

- Formative and summative evaluation
- Kirkpatrick's Four Levels of Evaluation
- Application of Kirkpatrick's model to eLearning courses
- Relationship between Needs Analysis and Kirkpatrick's Four Levels of Evaluation
- Level 5 evaluation: ROI model
- Data Analysis in eLearning

Evaluation plays a vital role in training. It ensures that courses stay on track while they are being developed. It also ensures that training meets standards and expectations and helps instructional designers identify the strengths and weaknesses of their materials. Furthermore, evaluation ensures that all learning objectives have been met and the business goal has been achieved. A good system of evaluating training provides valuable information for the learner, management, and, ultimately, the instructional designer. Most training decisions such as those on additions, deletions, or modifications to the training programs are based on the information collected during the evaluation phase. Evaluations also help prioritize training needs at the organizational level. As a result of evaluation, resources can be shifted from training that has less impact on business goals to training that has a more promising cost-benefit ratio. In other words, evaluation ensures that training programs improve performance, which is the ultimate goal of all courses.

Formative and Summative Evaluation

The evaluation phase consists of two parts: formative and summative. Formative evaluation occurs in all phases of the design process and ensures that the training course stays on track while it is being developed. Some of the questions that instructional designers should ask as they evaluate each phase of the ADDIE model are:

Analysis – Is this a training problem? What must learners be able to do to ensure the desired change in performance?

Design – What must participants learn that will enable them to fulfill the goal? Are all objectives measurable and observable?

Development – What activities and interactions will result in the required performance?

Implementation – Have learners become performers?

During **formative evaluation**, instructional designers should conduct delivery method, content, and usability reviews.

Summative evaluation, on the other hand, is the process of reviewing a course after implementation. It measures training outcomes in terms of learners' opinions about the course, assessment results, job performance, and return of investment (ROI) to the organization.

Donald Kirkpatrick's Four Levels of Evaluation

Case Study

The new call center training for Paean Insurance Company was proving ineffective. Though the training was comprehensive, customer survey reports revealed complaints that the employees didn't know how to answer questions well once they were asked about a topic that wasn't in their script.

The instructional designer reworked the training, adding content, activities, and assessments that better covered the topics that could come up with spontaneous questions. To ensure that the employees learned this new aspect of the training, he resolved to measure the effectiveness of the course.

As the training rolled out, the instructional designer tracked the effectiveness of the assessments. Some of them were too easy or too hard, he noted. He also paid close attention to the results of the survey at the end of the course, which asked the learners to evaluate the training they had received.

In six months, when the employees were fully integrated into the training, the instructional designer started tracking behavior. By using manager's observations, personal observations, and peer reviews, he saw that the ways the new training was successful and the ways it could be improved.

Customer survey data and other business metrics provided the final look at the revised course effectiveness. Surveys showed a definite upward trend in customer satisfaction, though the surveys did also reveal a few other areas where employee awareness could be improved. With this knowledge in hand, the instructional designer could improve the course even more.

In the 1950s, Donald Kirkpatrick established the Four Levels of Evaluation model:

Level 1: Reaction
Level 2: Learning
Level 3: Behavior
Level 4: Results

Level 1: Reaction

Reaction is the first level of evaluation. It is the easiest way to evaluate any training program. At this level, you find out what learners think about the training. Reaction is typically measured through surveys, questionnaires, and verbal feedback. It is a fairly inexpensive way to gather information about the quality of the course. This level of evaluation is conducted immediately after the training event. Donald Kirkpatrick suggests asking for learners' feelings on all aspects of the course, including content and presentation methods. He also recommends making the reaction form anonymous to encourage honest feedback. When creating evaluation questions, consider including open-ended questions that allow learners to put their feelings and attitudes toward the course in writing.

Level 2: Learning

Learning is the second level of evaluation. It assesses the extent to which learners gained knowledge and skills and whether they learned what was expected of them. Pretests and post-tests are typical tools used to evaluate learning. If, however, the course is intended for beginners, there is no need for a pretest. Instead, you should assess learners in different ways throughout the entire course. For instance, you can create a game or simulation that would allow learners to evaluate their knowledge, skills, and attitudes in an interactive way.

Level 3: Behavior

The third level of evaluation measures the extent to which change in *behavior* actually occurred. It measures whether or not learners apply the knowledge and skills they gained at the training to their job. Whenever possible, measure the before-and-after behavior to determine whether the change took place. To ensure more accurate results, Kirkpatrick suggests allowing sufficient time for a change to occur. Then, conduct surveys or interviews with learners, their management, and with the other people who constantly observe the learners' on-the-job performance. Before drawing the conclusion that the desired change has not occurred, and therefore no learning has taken place, keep in mind that several factors can contribute to learners' behavior. For instance, even though learners may have learned a lot from the course, their supervisor may not have given them an opportunity to apply their new knowledge and skills. In addition, because of the lack of on-the-job rewards, learners may simply be unmotivated to use what they learned in the training session. Even though interviews and focus groups can provide a lot of valuable data, the recommended practice is to conduct surveys to measure the real change in behavior. Being able to provide anonymous responses is key to honest feedback, especially when it comes to a change in behavior. Surveys will allow you to get the feedback you need without intimidating training participants.

Level 4: Results

Results are the fourth level of evaluation. This final level is the main reason for taking the training course and is considered the most important of all levels. It measures whether the employee's performance improved as a result of completing the training, and whether the organization benefited from it. Like the third level, the forth level of evaluation should be measured both before and after the session. It is also advisable to measure results several times after the training has taken place. Before measuring the results, however, you need to measure the third level and determine whether the desired change in behavior has occurred. If the change in behavior has not occurred and training participants have not been applying new knowledge and skills to the job, then conducting the fourth level of evaluation is unnecessary. Some ways to collect information for the results level of evaluation include conducting follow-up needs assessments, interviewing managers, leading focus groups, and sending out surveys.

When conducting the Four Levels of Evaluation, aligning each level with a needs analysis is important. Table 15 illustrates the relationship between the needs analysis and Kirkpatrick's Four Levels of Evaluation.

Table 15 - Relationship between Needs Analysis and Kirkpatrick's Four Levels of Evaluation

Levels of Evaluation	Needs Analysis
Level 1- Reaction	Learners' Needs
Level 2 - Learning	Learners' Needs
Level 3 - Behavior	Performance Needs
Level 4 - Results	Business Needs

Prudence dictates that investment decisions for any new project, whether it is commercial or non-profit in nature, must be predicated upon a solid business case of value delivery. While some social programs might be justified even though there might not be a monetary value to them, most initiatives in the business world are tied to demonstrable value, either in productivity or monetary terms. Corporate training initiatives fall within that category.

Because of its perceived difficulty, many initiatives do not strive to complete a Level 4 evaluation. In reality, however, doing a Level 4 evaluation is not that difficult, especially given that the impact of the training initiative will have been deconstructed significantly as the team progresses through the previous 3 levels. Level 4 evaluations will have significant number data points to work with as a result. The best way to achieve success is to envision what success looks like. When a company's trainers start at Level 4, which initially defines what training results should look like once the program has been delivered, closing the loop (once training has been delivered) on the review process with Level 4 evaluation becomes much easier. For instance, some Level 4 results that a company may look forward to achieving might be:

- 60% reduction in customer order cancellation in the next two quarters
- Cutting staff absenteeism by half each year
- Decreasing scrap/wastage quantity by 2000 lbs each month
- Slashing high-school dropout rates by 25% annually

Having such Level 4 outcomes defined in advance gives training evaluators a solid basis for working backward to quantify what Level 3 metrics are required to be achieved to hit the Level 4 evaluation criteria. This process continues through Levels 1 and 2. In every case, however, it is imperative to ensure that the proposed metrics are observable and measurable. For instance, a "poor" set of Level 4 evaluation metric might be:

- Reducing customer order cancellation significantly, or
- Considerable decline in staff absenteeism

By starting at the end, and defining clear and measurable Level 4 evaluation criteria, instructional designers can clearly demonstrate to company management and training sponsors the precise value that a training program can bring to the organization. It is that kind of precision that senior management like to see before approving a program.

It is important to understand that a Level 4 evaluation of training results requires a certain framework to be credible to company management. Merely publishing test scores of the trainees will not cut it. Management needs to see demonstrable change before they acknowledge that a training exercise was a success. Here are some broad guidelines to consider when setting up a Level 4 evaluation:

- ***Points of Reference*** – Make sure to have before training and after training measurements of the evaluation metrics

- *Time frame* – Change takes time, so allow an acceptable time period for training to prove its worth
- *Validation* – A single evaluation might not be sufficient. Repeat the measurements at appropriate times to validate that results have actually taken root
- *Controlling the Evaluation* – Where practical, the use of control groups produce much better evaluation outcomes than random or across-the-board evaluation
- *Weigh the Cost* – Some training might be relatively straightforward, and results are immediately apparent even without a Level 4 assessment. Results of other programs might be extremely difficult (and costly) to validate using a Level 4 approach. Do a cost-benefit assessment first, before ploughing full steam ahead with a Level 4 evaluation
- *Have Realistic Expectations* – Some training results cannot be validated through empirical data because the outcomes might be too subjective in nature. In such cases, where conclusive proof of results is not available, one should simply be content with evidence that the program was a success

Using these broad principles, trainers can put together a very effective framework to measure Level 4 evaluation outcomes.

Sports people need to continually practice their sport and be monitored by their coach, or they risk growing "stale." Similarly, trainees from a learning program must continually demonstrate their training has taken roots by exhibiting sustained predetermined behavioral changes in the workforce or community. Therefore, Level 4 evaluations must be designed to monitor those behavioral changes over the long term. Some ways to accomplish this include:

- Sending out post-training surveys to capture feedback from trainees as well as others who are impacted by the training
- Putting in place a long-term program of ongoing, sequenced training and coaching that reinforces key points of the training
- Conducting follow-up needs assessments to determine if any gaps are still apparent between training delivered and actual results achieved
- Verifying post-training metrics (scrap, absenteeism, quality, output, dropout rate) against pre-training metrics; and
- Conducting interviews with trainees and others that may be impacted by or have influence upon the training outcomes (Supervisors, Managers, Customers, Teachers, Patients, etc.)

Return on Expectations

Financial professionals often tend to ask for proof of success in terms of Return on Equity (ROE), while learning professionals focus on Return on Expectations (ROE). While the Financial ROE might be straightforward to calculate, it may be more challenging to quantify a Return on Expectation. Therefore, to deliver proof that expectations of the training program have been met, it is imperative that designers and evaluators of training programs know precisely what those expectations are. To accomplish that objective, learning professionals must:

- Involve as broad a spectrum of stakeholders (Senior Managers, Line Managers, Supervisors, front-line workers, Community leaders, Teachers, etc.) as possible when designing training programs and evaluation metrics.
- Ask probing questions about what each stakeholder group expects to achieve from the program.
- Arrive at consensus about how each expectation will manifest itself in the trainee upon successful conclusion of a training initiative.
- Where possible, agree upon appropriate and measurable metrics that will validate the manifestation of those expectations.
- Where empirical data points (proof) are not practical to measure expectations, agree upon alternative metrics (evidence).

It is extremely difficult for a training program in and of itself to meet the expectations set out by stakeholders. Many external factors also play a role in determining whether training was successful. Therefore, learning professionals should manage those expectations by encouraging stakeholders to exert influence over other favorable factors (outside of the training environment) which will impact how a trainee delivers to those expectations. It is that kind of partnership between all stakeholders that will ultimately ensure that Returns on Expectations is met.

The best way to determine whether Financial ROE or expectation ROE has been met is to ask those impacted by the training—including the trainees themselves. To that goal, learning professionals, in consultation with other key stakeholders, should ask appropriate questions and analyze the feedback received.

Questions to ask include:

- To what extent did the training meet expectations?
- How did training have a visible impact on the trainee's job (lower rejects, less cancelled orders, fewer days off)?

- Was there a measurable improvement to the broader group (Department, Organization, and Community)?
- Is there a need for any change to the training program (curriculum, frequency, design process)?

While such questions might be used as a way to receive significant insight into the question, **"Did training deliver the expected results?"** if structured strategically, they can also shed light on other elements of the training program, such as the quality of inclusiveness (Stakeholder engagement, Partnerships with other groups, etc.) during the entire training initiative.

Return on Investment

Since Donald Kirkpatrick created his Four Levels of Evaluation, theorists including Kirkpatrick himself have modified the original version to better suit modern requirements. Jack Phillips added a fifth step to the already existing four levels of evaluation. His fifth level is known as Return-of-Investment, or ROI. It compares the monetary program benefits with the program costs. According to Phillips, ROI should be measured between three and twelve months after the training. The evaluation of ROI is, in essence, a conversion of the Level 4 results into the monetary value and comparison of the monetary value with the cost of the training. When calculating ROI, you must keep in mind the analysis, design, development, implementation, and evaluation costs as well as acquisition and overhead costs. Interviews with supervisors and managers can provide an estimate for ROI calculations. In some cases, however, you may have to review extant data to get more accurate results. However, as with any business venture, eLearning projects need to show that they deliver real benefit to an organization. If they can't demonstrate such value, then they are likely to not attract champions and sponsors within the company. And without a strong champion, the program is not likely to take off.

The benefit of an eLearning program for any organization is measured in terms of the Return On Investment (ROI) that it delivers. As the name suggests, it is a measurable unit that represents an excess of value received (Return) over the cost (Investment) incurred for the program. A successful program will deliver greater returns than costs. The question, however, is how does one go about measuring eLearning ROI?

There are a few key factors that must be taken into consideration when calculating eLearning ROI.

1. The Investment (or Cost): This component of the ROI calculation seeks to address the question "What will it cost me to put eLearning in place?" Here, the term "cost" includes:

- **Personnel** – Calculate the cost of people (both internal and external consultants) that will be needed to build the program. Personnel costs may seem straightforward to identify and track, but sometimes they tend to get obfuscated, especially when existing staff are pulled into an eLearning team while also playing other (non-eLearning) roles. Project direction, development, management and administration costs also need to be factored into the equation.

- **ELearning Technology** – ELearning is largely a technology driven initiative. When calculating the cost for technology, organizations must consider what new technologies (Application tools, Virtual Classrooms, Learning Management Systems, Remote Learning infrastructure, etc.) are needed, as well as the cost of changing any existing technology (existing desktops, networking systems, replacing existing laptops/tablet devices) that may not support the new system. Often, organizations need to tailor newly acquired technology to assimilate it into the company's existing IT infrastructure. While such configuration is normally part of acquisition cost, there may be a sizable cost associated with it that is not covered under the initial acquisition.

- **ELearning Content** – Major costs should also include content development (in case unique content needs to be created), or off-the-shelf content acquisition costs. Additionally, where pre-packaged eLearning content does not easily integrate into an organization's existing learning environment, other modification and customization costs may be required.

- **Hidden Costs** – There are always costs associated with transitioning from an existing (conventional) learning environment into an eLearning model. Personnel disruptions, resource reallocations, existing project deferrals, (short term) team realignments, all of these costs are not readily visible. ELearning entails making a cultural change within an organization, and since human beings are "change resistant creatures," there is bound to be hidden costs associated with managing those changes.

2. The Return (or Benefit) – This component of the ROI calculation seeks to address the question "How will embracing eLearning help me?" And here, the term "benefit" includes:

- **Flexibility** – ELearning offers individuals and groups of learners the flexibility to learn anywhere and anytime. That means there is less likelihood that learners will shun embracing a learning opportunity, since they now have the option to learn at their own convenience. The benefit of flexibility can be measured in terms of cost. For instance, how many employees do not learn (how to follow a new process, or how to operate a new tool) because of a rigid learning schedule, and what does it cost the company as a result.

- **Less disruptive** – Along with this flexibility comes the promise of minimum disruption to an organization's "routine." Any disruption to an organization's standard operating procedures has a cost associated with it. For instance, orders might be delayed, schedules may be changed, inventory might not be updated—all because staff are in training. Companies could hire extra staff to pick up the slack, or pay employees overtime to complete their usual tasks after hours. That, however, adds to costs too. If courses can be delivered with little or no disruption to an employee's regular work schedule—for instance learning via mobile devices, or while at a gym or on a train—then the disruptive cost of learning will be reduced.
- **Personalized learning** – Even within classrooms of apparently homogenous learning groups there will be "outliers" who impede the learning pace of the entire group. Such interruptions do have a cost, even though it's hard to quantify exactly. With eLearning, individuals can learn at their own speed, thereby making personalized learning more efficient in delivering content effectively.
- **Travel** – Training-related travel costs are the biggest reason large corporations embrace eLearning. These costs are a major component of any ROI calculation. ELearning can dramatically reduce such costs, thereby delivering additional returns.

In conclusion, it is important to understand that all eLearning programs must be measured in terms of ROI. Not only that eLearning specialists should consider the investments such as personnel, technology, content, and hidden costs, but they should also look at benefits associated with eLearning. By accurately calculating the cost of a training program, eLearning professionals will be able to easily justify the investment in the program and decide if eLearning is ultimately a viable solution.

Use the following formula to calculate ROI:

$$ROI\% = \frac{Benefits - Costs\ of\ Training}{Costs\ of\ Training} \times 100$$

Marina Arshavskiy

Big Data in ELearning

ELearning has experienced a lot of momentum, largely as a result of a number of technological breakthroughs. Newer eLearning authoring tools have been developed, and more sophisticated Learning Management Systems have been deployed. ELearning course developers are also using new multimedia approaches for course delivery, as well as leveraging social media platforms and other online forums to disseminate information about eLearning, as well as to deliver the courses themselves. All of that results in a lot of data!

In today's digital age, almost every interaction we have with another individual, company, or service providing system generates data. In the eLearning environment, that may include:

- Who is taking a course (demographics—age, sex, geographic location, educational and professional background, etc.).
- Information about how a learner first "discovered" a particular eLearning program (advertisements, social media, corporate websites, referral programs, etc.).
- Data about the types of devices used to log on to a particular course (desktops, smartphones, tablets, etc.).
- The types of browsers and operating systems that the eLearning system interacts with; and
- Progress, assessments, and feedback received from the learner.

From an eLearning context, all data generated as a result of various eLearning interactions, not just the volume, but also the diversity of it, is called Big Data.

The role of Big Data in eLearning is as similar as sensitive intelligence gathering is to a successful military operation. All of the developments discussed earlier (new tools, new delivery mechanisms, new Learning Management Systems) are data-driven, and produce their own sets of data. Moreover, just as success for military leaders depends on analyzing and deciphering the intelligence gathered, so too can eLearning administrators and developers learn much from the Big Data they accumulate.

More specifically, amongst a host of others, Big Data's role in eLearning is to:

- Shed valuable insight into learning gaps across organizations,
- Identify preferred methods of pursuing eLearning by individuals and groups of employees,
- Highlight the strengths and weaknesses in an organization's eLearning strategy; and

- Provide clues on how to individualize and personalize specific eLearning experiences to provide best results for learners.

So, how specifically would you, as an eLearning professional, benefit from analyzing Big Data?

First, Big Data analysis can help you identify which courses, modules, or segments of a course are the most popular amongst your audience. Additionally, by looking at Big Data, you could pinpoint structural issues with your course design: Why do 96% of eLearners abandon a particular scenario-based exercise halfway through?

Deployment also plays a major role in Big Data as you may get invaluable insight on whether particular deployment strategies are worth the time and effort. For example, you may discover that only 1% of learners are using a Windows-based platform, with 93% learning from Android-based systems and 6% using iOS. Should you then continue to support a multiple OS deployment strategy?

Big Data can offer design-tweaking clues for you to consider in your next course update/refresh cycle. If, in the last five years, none of the employees have ever used the "Download and print" option of the Corporate Expense Policy course, then, you probably should not spend time and money updating that segment of the course feature.

Lastly, Big Data is almost instantaneous—you get it immediately upon each interaction. As a result, you could start parsing the data after each batch of learners has finished the course, as opposed to waiting several months before planning your next refresher cycle.

Without the use of Big Data, these benefits may be time-consuming to accomplish, and could be rather cumbersome to achieve.

A profound impact of Big Data will be on how future eLearning content is designed, delivered, and monitored. Some of the more discernible impacts include:

- Decision-making on what authoring tools and Learning Management Systems (LMSs) a company should use
- Selecting the most effective delivery mechanism—corporate learning sites, social media platforms, or individual downloadable modules
- Data-driven course personalization
- Influencing budget allocations for specific eLearning strategies
- Analysis of individual and group behavior as they interact with a course

All of these insights will help eLearning professionals build bodies of knowledge that will shape the future of eLearning. To take full advantage of Big Data in an eLearning environment, course sponsors, developers, and eLearning professionals must effectively manage and analyze the data. Here are a few best practices to help you get started on that front:

- **Data Objectives** – Start out by defining clear-cut goals and objectives for why you are collecting the data, and what you intend to accomplish from analyzing it. For instance, "Employee Skills Improvement" should be supported by the types of skills that need improvement, and measurable metrics of what "improvement" means.

- **Data Assimilation** – As indicated earlier, Big Data has multiple sources (authoring tools, Learning Management Systems, social media platforms, corporate eLearning sites). Make sure you cast a broad net and gather all of that data instead of being selective in what you harvest.

- **Data Rationalization** – Not all of the harvested data (the make/model of the device used; the version of the OS; the ID of a corporate terminal used to access the course) will be "actionable" from an eLearning stand point. Rationalize (parse) your data based on the analysis goals and objectives set out in Step 1.

- **Data Prioritization** – Sometimes, you may end up having several priorities (skills improvement; course popularity, etc.). Prioritize your data elements based on the importance of the analysis you wish to conduct.

- **Data Metrics** – Of course, Big Data does not always come in structured packages. You must use appropriate metrics to get Big Data to reveal its secrets. Some metrics might include: Learner Progress/Completion; Proficiency levels; Ratings and Evaluations; Relative Rankings and Return on Investment.

- **Data Analysis Tools** – It is now time to use some tools to conduct your analysis. Most often, your corporate Learning Management System will include a set of big data analysis tools as well. If you do not have built-in analytics within your Learning Management System, you may need to tap into third party tools like Google Analytics to see how learners interact with your online courses.

- **Data Protection** – The most important aspect of managing vast amounts of Big Data is security. Because of its sensitivity, ensure your eLearning data is well protected, possibly through data encryption—especially if it is being stored outside the corporate environment in the Cloud.

Now that your data is assimilated, rationalized, and analyzed, you need to take steps to act on the resulting analysis. Use your findings to tweak, update or revamp your eLearning strategy, and to make individual courses more effective.

Test Your Knowledge

1. Evaluation ensures that training courses improve _____, which is the ultimate goal of all training programs.
   - A. productivity
   - B. performance
   - C. quiz scores
   - D. engagement

2. To conduct a Formative evaluation, what must instructional designers ask themselves during the Analysis phase of ADDIE to ensure that they are on the right track?
   - A. Is this a training problem? What must learners be able to do to ensure the desired change in performance?
   - B. What must participants learn that will enable them to fulfill the goal? Are all objectives measurable and observable?
   - C. What activities and interactions will result in the required performance?
   - D. Have learners become performers?

3. Formative evaluation typically occurs _____, while Summative evaluation takes place _____.
   - A. during design / before implementation
   - B. after analysis / during implementation
   - C. after development / before implementation
   - D. during development / after implementation

4. The first level in the Kirkpatrick model is _____ and asks the learner what they think about the course's content and presentation methods immediately after it has taken place.
   - A. Results
   - B. Reaction
   - C. Behavior
   - D. Learning

5. The second level in the Kirkpatrick model is _____ and assesses the extent to which learners gained knowledge and skills from the training.
   - A. Results
   - B. Reaction
   - C. Behavior
   - D. Learning

6. The third level in the Kirkpatrick model is _____ and measures whether learners applied the knowledge and skills gained in the training to their jobs.
    A. Results
    B. Reaction
    C. Behavior
    D. Learning

7. The fourth level in the Kirkpatrick model is _____ and measures whether the learner's performance improved as a result of the training course and whether the organization benefited from that improvement.
    A. Results
    B. Reaction
    C. Behavior
    D. Learning

8. A fifth level known as _____ was added to the Kirkpatrick model and should be measured _____ after the training.
    A. ACT / 3-12 months
    B. ROI / 6-9 months
    C. ROI / 3-12 months
    D. ACT / 6-9 months

Exercise 14

How are you going to evaluate your course? What methods are you going to use to evaluate learners' reaction, learning, behavior, and results? How are you going to measure ROI and collect data?

Chapter 16: Assessments

This chapter will cover:

- Reasons for including assessments in eLearning courses
- Validity and reliability of assessment items
- Writing effective assessment items
- Types of assessment questions
- Scoring assessments
- Providing corrective feedback
- Intrinsic vs. extrinsic feedback

Assessments

At this stage, you would have conducted the necessary analysis, written learning objectives for the course, created storyboards, and even identified opportunities for interactivity, games, and simulations. The next step is to create effective assessment methods. Assessments allow both learners and their management to see whether they mastered the knowledge and skills presented in the course.

Below are some of the major reasons for including assessments in your training. Assessments help to:

- draw attention to the most important elements in the content of the course;
- determine the effectiveness of the course;
- measure the extent to which learners have mastered course objectives;
- reinforce learning through corrective feedback;
- identify learners' strengths and weaknesses; and
- keep track of learners' progress.

Effective test questions must cover the objectives of the course; in addition, they must

- be valid and reliable;
- have correctly written stems;
- include appropriate distractors; and
- provide constructive feedback.

The assessment instrument you select should be appropriate to the specific situation. When creating assessment items, concentrate on the learners' ability to apply content rather than their ability to recall facts. While recall questions are much easier to construct, they are not nearly as effective as questions that allow learners to analyze and apply what they have learned in the lesson. In addition, recall questions typically promote lower-order learning while assessment items geared toward application and analysis promote higher-order learning. Although memorizing facts and obtaining passive knowledge are important parts of learning, true learning and the ability to perform tasks come from higher-order learning. Learning is a process of acquiring new knowledge and skills and transferring them to the next level, known as application. The goal of training courses should be to promote higher-order learning through proper activities, hands-on exercises, and assessments that allow learners to analyze and apply new information.

Validity and Reliability of Assessment Items

Validity refers to the extent to which the assessment instruments measure the outcomes they are intended to measure. To ensure validity, assessment questions should be clearly written and easy to understand. If, for example, learners misinterpret the intended meaning of a test question, the results would no longer be valid. When writing test questions, the goal is to accurately assess the knowledge and skills specified in the learning objectives. To improve validity, you should write assessment items that focus on the application of knowledge rather than just comprehension level. As you create assessment instruments, consider having professional colleagues review them. Then, if necessary, revise your questions based on the reviewers' feedback.

Reliability refers to the ability of the measured items to produce consistent results over a period of time. While test validity determines whether the assessment accurately measures what it is intended to measure, test reliability determines how frequently it succeeds in doing so. Providing clear and specific instructions for each assessment item can significantly improve its validity. To increase reliability, tests should not be too short in length as short tests can influence the overall results whereas longer tests will not affect the results as much. However, since the primary goal of assessments is to measure learning objectives, the nature of these objectives may influence the duration of a test.

Therefore, the number of assessment items included in the test and thus the reliability of that assessment strongly depends on learning objectives.

When it comes to the multiple choice questions, which typically consist of a stem, correct answer choice and incorrect options known as distractors, creating reliable items can be especially challenging. Distractors should still make sense, but at the same time, they must be decidedly incorrect.

You should also keep in mind that the difficulty level of all test questions should not be the same. Otherwise, the reliability of your items will significantly decrease.

Writing Effective Assessment Items

There are three major types of assessment items. They are:

Diagnostic assessments – Also known as pretests. Some of the reasons for conducting diagnostic assessments include:

- finding out how much learners already know about a given topic;
- delivering various versions or levels of a course to the needs of learners based on their performance in such tests;

- allowing learners to test out if they already possess adequate knowledge of the content to be presented in the course; and
- helping to shape learners' expectations about the course coverage.

Formative assessments – Include questions after each topic or module, and allow measurement of learners' understanding of each unit of content.

Summative assessments – Also known as post-tests. They are given at the end of a training session to check learners' understanding of the overall content.

The most common types of assessment questions are:
- multiple choice
- true/false
- fill-in-the-blank
- matching
- free responses/short answers/essays

Multiple Choice Questions

Multiple choice questions are probably the most popular type of assessment in eLearning. These questions require learners to choose the best response from several options. When creating multiple choice questions, you should indicate in the instructions area the number of possible correct responses. This step will avoid confusion among learners. Multiple choice questions are composed of three parts:
- question stems,
- correct answer or answers,
- distractors.

You should create your assessment items in such a way that learners only have to read the stem once to begin formulating their answers. Stems can include either complete direct questions such as, *"What is Instructional Design?"* or statement completions items such as, *"Instructional Design is...."* The second type requires that the correct answers are inserted into the blank to complete the statement. When writing question stems, you should try to keep them short and, if possible, choose complete direct questions over statement completion items. Longer stems can be easily misinterpreted. Therefore, the results gathered from such questions will not be accurate indicators of learning, and the question itself will not be reliable. If the question is in the incomplete statement format, the stem must end with a word common to all answer options so that each option flows logically from it. The following example illustrates this concept.

Example:

The role of an instructional designer is to design:

a. graphics

b. courses

c. houses

d. clothes

Instead of repeating the word "design" in each option, it was included in the question stem. While most incomplete question stems should have a verb, you should consider the grammatical structure of both stems and answer options when constructing your assessments.

Another suggestion for ensuring the clarity of questions or statement stems is to avoid negatives. Oftentimes, learners overlook the word "not" and, as a result, choose an incorrect response. Rewording negative question stems will make assessment items more reliable. If the stem cannot be reworded, bolding, underlining, or capitalizing the negatives will draw the learners' attention to these negatives and help them concentrate on the actual question. It is also suggested to add negatives at the end of the question stem and use capital letters to bring attention to them. The example below illustrates this concept.

Example:

All of the following are Gagné's Events of Instruction EXCEPT:

The stems should be written in a way that does not automatically reveal the correct response to any of the questions on the assessment. This can be accomplished by including only the information needed to answer each specific question and avoiding information that can be used to answer another question on the test. For example, using the same word in both the stem and the option can easily reveal the correct response. Another way to avoid the unintentional revelation of correct responses is to eliminate such grammatical cues as a/an. This can be done by including both options in the stem. The example below illustrates this concept.

Example:

A/An_____ about instructional design is now available on the Amazon Kindle.

a. eBook

b. Report

If, on the other hand, the stem had included only "an" instead of "a/an," the learner would be able to easily guess the correct response.

While correctly written stems are crucial for developing reliable test questions, it is equally important to choose appropriate distractors for each item. You should include no more than five answer choices in each question that is one correct answer and three or four distractors. Unless it is a multiple-answer question, there should only be one correct response. While all other options are distractors, they should still be plausible, meaning that they should make perfect sense in the context of the question. The best way to come up with distractors for assessment questions is to think of common errors that learners make and turn these errors into distractors. The following example illustrates this concept.

Example:

According to Robert Gagné's Nine Events of Instruction, *the first step in creating an effective lesson is:*

A. Gaining learners' attention

B. Analyzing learners' current performance

C. Stimulating recall of prior knowledge

D. Eliciting performance

While this question makes perfect sense and the correct answer choice is clearly A, the first distractor is not plausible because analyzing learners' performance is not part of Gagné's *Nine Events of Instruction*.

All the answer choices included in the question should be consistent in terms of content, form, and grammatical structure. In other words, all options should be logically derived from the stem so that test-takers would not be able to guess the correct answer based on the fact that the other options do not flow logically or grammatically from the stem. Additionally, all answer choices should be either nouns, verbs, or adjectives, not a mixture of three depending on the sentence construction and its relationship to the answer options provided. Otherwise, the item will appear confusing and may unintentionally reveal the correct response. Keeping both the correct response and distractors similar in length will also prevent learners from guessing the correct answer.

Many assessments use qualifiers such as "always" and "never" as well as absolutes such as "all of the above" or "none of the above." While it is tempting to include these phrases in your distracters, they make the options too easy, as they are often the correct response. The same principle applies to the "Both A and B are correct" option.

If learners do not know the answers to the questions, they often use guesswork. When learners do not know which option to pick, they frequently select option "B" as their answer. The reason for this is that when instructional designers create questions, they often make "B" the correct response. To improve reliability of the assessment, you should consider varying the placement of correct responses.

True/False Questions

True/false questions typically measure understanding of facts such as names, dates, and definitions. This type of question requires learners to choose between the two options, leaving them with a 50/50 chance of guessing the correct response. True/false questions are also difficult to construct without making the correct response too obvious. The main downside to this type of question, however, is that it only assesses learning at the knowledge level. If, however, you want to test at the application level, these items will not give adequate and reliable results. To avoid confusion, only include one idea in each statement. Just like with multiple choice items, true/false questions should be clearly worded and should not include negatives, broad statements, qualifiers, and absolutes.

Fill-in-the-Blank Questions

Fill-in-the-blank questions are also known as completion items. This type of question requires learners to finish a sentence by filling the correct word or phrase in a blank. While fill-in-the-blank questions are beneficial to learners, they are difficult to construct as they must be written in a way that significantly reduces guessing the correct response.

Matching Questions

The matching type of assessment consists of a list of questions or statements and a list of responses. Learners should find a match or association between each question and response. This type of exercise can be very effective because it can cover a lot of content at the same time and test learners' understanding of the material at the application level. However, constructing matching exercises can be challenging. While all of the options should be plausible, there should be only one correct answer choice. In addition, when constructing matching exercises, ensuring that both columns or lists are similar in content is important. A good practice is having the questions/statements on the left side as a numbered list and answer choices on the right side as a lettered list. Another practice is to include more answer choices than questions. Otherwise, learners will easily respond to the last question using the process of elimination.

Free response/Short answer/Essay Questions

While free response questions are less commonly used compared to multiple choice, true/false, and fill-in-the-blank assessment items, there are many benefits associated with this type of question. Free response questions require learners to understand the content in order to answer the question. It is nearly impossible for learners to answer this type of question correctly by guessing or eliminating incorrect responses. In addition, free response questions require a higher level of thinking, analyzing, and logically presenting information. At the same time, because instructional designers do not have to worry about plausible distractors, free response questions are easier to construct compared to other question types. For learners, these questions help put their newly acquired knowledge in perspective. For instance, instructional designers can present realistic scenarios that enable learners to apply what they have learned in the course to solve a problem. However, free response questions should be used sparingly as they can be difficult to score. In synchronous eLearning courses, trainers can grade questions or provide corrective feedback to each participant, but grading free response questions in asynchronous eLearning is impossible. Therefore, the only way to provide constructive feedback is by restating the points that learners should have covered in their responses.

Since online learning often separates instructors from learners across time and distance, we rely on evaluations—in the form of tests, quizzes and assessments—to judge each learner's successful comprehension of the content (and to judge how well the course designers presented their information).

But what makes a good test question? Is it meant to challenge a learner? Should it stump as many learners as possible? If every learner answers a question correctly, does that mean your question is too easy, or is it a perfect example of an effective test question?

To find out, let's begin by reminding ourselves why we test our learners in the first place. As a general rule, a good question tests the six levels of intellectual understanding, as espoused in Bloom's Taxonomy:

- Knowledge
- Comprehension
- Application
- Analysis
- Synthesis
- Evaluation

Going further, the Cornell University's Center for Teaching Excellence provides a great summary of the characteristics of what a "good question" is:

- **Intention** – Did the question assess what you intended to assess?
- **Demonstration** – Did learners demonstrate that they learned what they needed to learn?
- **Progress** – Were learners able to show progress in their learning?
- **Motivation** – Did the question help motivate learners to further their academic pursuits of the subject matter?
- **Distinction** – Did the question help distinguish "learners" from "non-learners"?

Notice that these guidelines have nothing to do with the structure of the question itself. Whether your questions involve True/False answers, Multiple Choice, Matching items, Fill-in-the-Blanks, or Essay responses; good questions must demonstrate all of the traits above.

At the heart of any good question is an understanding of the learning outcomes that the questions are seeking to measure. Before you develop your question bank, revisit the objectives of the course to ensure your questions are built with those objectives in mind.

For example, if the objective of a course is to ensure that learners are capable of executing the basic functions of trigonometry, you might begin to formulate your final exam by first listing all the necessary functions you would expect a learner to be able to execute by the end of your course. This will give you a checklist of "must-have" test questions, and provide a structure for the progression of the test.

For a more subjective topic, like political theory, you might first list all the key concepts you would expect the learners to be able to explain by the end of your course, as well as the critical thinking skills you would expect them to be able to employ. Then, you could devise an exam which includes all the necessary topics while simultaneously testing the learners' cognitive functions in their explanation of those terms.

From there, you can decide which question formats best serve those purposes. While choosing from a series of Multiple Choice or True/False answers may be sufficient to prove a learner's familiarity with glossary terms or the basic comprehension of functions, those formats also allow for "educated guesses," which may not be enough to prove a learner truly understands the underlying concepts. Thus, you should also include Essay, Fill-in-the-Blank, and other open-ended question formats that require a learner not just to deduce (or guess) the correct answer but to apply their knowledge and rhetorical reasoning—or, in the case of mathematics, to prove they can actually perform the computations effectively.

How hard should a test be? Experts vary on their responses to this question, but the general consensus seems to be: harder is better, with a caveat. Learners who feel "put on the spot" or otherwise expected to achieve errorless results in a difficult situation are reportedly more likely to retain the correct information afterward, even if they make mistakes. The caveat? For this approach to work best, learners must also have the opportunity to review their responses and understand what they got wrong. (Understanding why an answer is wrong also helps with retention.)

However, it is critical to note that a question's difficulty should be derived from the challenge it presents, not from any complexity in the way it is phrased. As an incident in the UK proved, learners of all ages can feel "demoralized" if they struggle to even understand the questions on a test.

Thus, if you are presenting questions in such a manner that your learners will barely be able to answer them—whether by writing them for an advanced reading level or by purposely writing them to be obtuse—you are not truly testing your learners' knowledge; you are making them jump through needless hoops which may result in lower scores and a dislike of the material simply for the sake of appearing "challenging."

Not sure if your test is too hard? Ask a beta tester in your target audience to take it before you administer it to your class. For example, a grad student or teacher's aide in the field should have no real trouble passing a test for undergrads, nor should a senior manager in a department that is receiving employee training in a specific topic. If they do, you may want to step your difficulty level down a notch or two. After all, a test that no one passes means it might be you, and not your learners, who need a refresher.

To Score or Not to Score

There is no one correct answer to whether or not instructional designers should score assessments. Most people, however, prefer to see how well they did on the test. Scores motivate them to learn and master the content. However, some learners are afraid of failure and tend to avoid taking scored assessments. There are also learners who feel that scored tests are a pedagogical approach to learning not suitable for adult learners who simply need guidance to achieve better performance results, not scores. In spite of negative attitudes toward scores, scored assessments provide information to management about learners' progress and determine whether the learner is ready to move on to the next, more advanced level. When it comes to assessments, you should consider the nature and requirements of each training course as well as the organizational culture to determine whether the lesson will benefit from scored assessments. Whenever possible, involve stakeholders in the decision making process as they are typically more familiar with organizational culture and values than you are.

Corrective Feedback

"If you don't know what went wrong…how will you fix it?" is an often repeated mantra. This applies to feedback about a specific initiative being reviewed, and is equally relevant to eLearning environments, where the provider of feedback and its recipient are often physically distant from each other. Here is the challenge, however: How do eLearning designers provide corrective feedback in a setting where they have not met or physically interacted with the learners? Providing corrective feedback is imperative as it allows learners to progress toward their goal and tells them whether they have mastered the content from the course. Feedback also shows learners the parts of the course that need to be revisited or reviewed. When providing feedback to learners, you need to ensure that the overall tone is friendly and supportive even if the question was answered incorrectly. The goal of corrective feedback is not to embarrass or scold learners, but to provide remediation and promote learning.

Before we delve into the "how," let's pause and think about "why" corrective feedback is important. Adult learners participate in eLearning courses to obtain new knowledge and skills. However, the following questions often come to mind:

- What if the learners were not able to fully grasp the course content?
- What if their approach to taking the course was not conducive to distance learning?
- What if there was a lack of understanding of the initial content, which they then carried through the entire course, thereby defeating the objectives of the course?

With a formal corrective feedback mechanism in place, all of these issues would be addressed appropriately, ensuring that the learner can then take remedial action to fully benefit from the instruction.

However, corrective feedback is not just a one-way street:

- How will course designers know what they are lacking in course delivery?
- What alternative (other than filling out an end-of-course survey) do learners have if they need additional assistance with the content of the course?
- How can the training be improved if there is no feedback from learners about the challenge areas of the course?

Corrective feedback is therefore essential for both the instructional designers and learners.

Some of the approaches that are generally recommended as part of a formal corrective feedback process include:

- **The "feedback sandwich" approach** – This is the approach where feedback providers start with positive comments about the participants' performance, sandwich negative feedback, and then, close with positive comments at the end.
- **The "chronological feedback" approach** – In this approach instructors enumerate their good and bad observations in chronological order, enabling learners to get a sequential picture of how they fared throughout the course.
- **The "clinical education" approach** – This is more of a learner-centered method for delivering corrective feedback that uses a conversational technique to produce goals and action plans as a result of the feedback provided.

Depending on the type of course, the complexity of content, and the level of maturity of the audience, eLearning course designers may opt for one, or a combination, of these corrective feedback approaches.

Proponents and opponents of each of these corrective feedback approaches abound, and each of these methods has its pros and cons. It is recommended to keep the following best practices in mind:

- Corrective feedback should not wait until the end of the course. Instead, it must be provided regularly to be effective.
- Feedback should not focus solely on the "corrective" aspect. It should be balanced, also highlighting what went well.
- Before starting a feedback session, ensure that you understand exactly what you want to achieve from it.
- If this is purely an online feedback session, offer opportunities for the learners (via free-text form fields, drop-down lists, and check-box responses) to provide their own assessment of the course, even if that includes criticism of the content or design.
- Rather than highlighting the negatives ("You did not respond fully to…"), try to suggest how things could be improved ("Next time, try to elaborate…" or "Perhaps you could have done…"), and lastly,
- Always conclude with a positive reinforcement.

Each learner reacts differently to corrective feedback. Some may take it as a slight on their abilities; others receive it positively. Therefore, it is essential to avoid making the feedback "personal," and always offer alternatives. Be specific about what needs to be changed, and avoid criticism without having specific examples of what is wrong. Finally, always summarize corrective action needed, preferably with a timeline for improvement.

While templates and online forms are great corrective tools for quantitative feedback, text-based feedback (emails, brief reports, text messages, tweets) works well for more descriptive corrective recommendations.

Once you know what learners feel is good, bad, or indifferent about the course, you can begin making improvements. To help this process go smoothly, follow these four steps:

Step 1: Archive – Make sure you create a chronological archive of all the feedback you received from the very first iteration of the course, right to the most recent version.

Step 2: Organize – Arrange all comments/suggestions according to focus area: User Interface; Graphics; Assessments; etc. This will allow you to apply your time and resources more effectively when improving the next version of the course.

Step 3: Prioritize – Arrange all of the feedback in each focus area in terms of criticality. For instance, any flaws that impede the objective quality of the learning itself—such as factual errors, typographical omissions, or grammatical mistakes—should be a much higher priority focus than any subjective suggestions like aesthetics, color theory, font choice, module length, etc.

Step 4: Review – It is always a good practice to not only review feedback from the most recent iteration of a course, but to go back several versions to see if the same (or similar) feedback keeps repeating itself. For instance, repeated spelling mistake complaints might mean there is a systemic editorial issue that needs to be addressed, while repeated complaints about the course's length might mean that learners are understanding its core principles much faster than you might expect.

Using past feedback to improve your future courses is an iterative process that should never stop. By seeking, analyzing, and applying such feedback in a structured way, you will develop a reliable process of continuous improvement that your future learners will appreciate.

Most feedback statements should be composed of the following four parts:

1. *Acknowledgment of learners' response.* For example: *"That's correct"* or *"Sorry, that's incorrect."*
2. *Statement of the correct response.* For example: *"The correct answer is 'True.'"* Note that this statement should only be

included if the learner chose the incorrect response.

3. *Repetition of the correct response.* Instead of saying *"The correct answer is B,"* consider repeating the entire statement. For example: *"The correct answer is B. Instructional designers create prototypes during the development phase of the ADDIE model..."*

4. *Explanation of why the response is correct.* For example: *"...because prototypes are typically developed after conducting thorough needs analysis and writing learning objectives."*

To offer further remediation for incorrect responses, the course can branch back to the sections that provide information for the question that was answered incorrectly.

Intrinsic and Extrinsic Feedback

The feedback that learners receive can be either intrinsic or extrinsic. *Intrinsic feedback* is an indirect type of feedback. It immediately lets learners know they made a mistake and allows them to make adjustments based on that feedback. An example of intrinsic feedback is showing a person shaking head whenever the learner answers incorrectly.

Extrinsic feedback, on the other hand, is a direct type of feedback that comments on the learner's performance in a straightforward way. For example:

"That's correct" or *"No, that's incorrect."*

The type of course, presentation methods, and assessment instruments chosen determine the type of feedback you provide. For example, while extrinsic feedback may be a good choice for multiple choice questions, it may not work well for a game. When learners play a game, they do not want to be interrupted; therefore, intrinsic feedback will guide their learning and provide information on how their response should be adjusted.

Test Your Knowledge

1. Assessments help to determine the effectiveness of the course as well as the learner's mastery of the content. They can also:
    A. Draw attention to the most important elements in the content.
    B. Make the learner jump through extra hoops to earn a certification.
    C. Legitimize the overall training course.
    D. Gauge how many learners make it to the end of the course.

2. When writing assessment questions, it is important to concentrate on the learner's ability to:
    A. Analyze and apply the content being taught.
    B. Memorize and recall every fact.
    C. Read and write.
    D. Memorize and recall almost every fact.

3. The _____ of assessment questions is gauged by how clearly they are written and whether they measure the outcomes they are intended to measure.
    A. audacity
    B. reliability
    C. legibility
    D. validity

4. Test _____ determines how frequently and consistently an exam is successful in accurately measuring the intended metrics.
    A. audacity
    B. reliability
    C. legibility
    D. validity

5. In a single-select multiple choice question, such as this one, with four possible answers, how many distractors will you be presented with?
    A. One
    B. Two
    C. Three
    D. Four

6. The Three Major Types of Assessments are:
   A. Diagnostic Assessments, Assumptive Assessments, Formal Assessments
   B. Didactic Assessments, Summative Assessments, Formal Assessments
   C. Diagnostic Assessments, Summative Assessments, Formative Assessments
   D. Didactic Assessments, Assumptive Assessments, Formative Assessments

7. All of the following are typical uses for the Diagnostic Assessment EXCEPT:
   A. As a pretest, finding out how much learners already know about a given topic.
   B. Delivering various versions of a course based on learner's performance.
   C. Evaluating the efficacy of the content during a Beta test of a course.
   D. Allowing learners to test out if they already have adequate knowledge of the topic.

8. Which of these assessment types are also known as Post-tests, typically given at the conclusion of the entire training course?
   A. Diagnostic Assessment
   B. Summative Assessment
   C. Formative Assessment
   D. Cumulative Assessment

9. When writing multiple choice questions, it is always a best practice to:
   A. Intentionally confuse the learner by writing confusing question stems.
   B. Indicate a false number of correct responses in the instruction area.
   C. Intentionally confuse the learner by writing misleading correct answers.
   D. Indicate the number of correct responses in the instruction area.

10. Qualifiers such as "Always" or absolutes such as "All of the above" or "Both A and B" should not be used because:
    A. Learners know that they are often the correct responses.
    B. They can lead to cognitive overload.
    C. Learners know that they are often the incorrect responses.
    D. They can be easily misinterpreted by the learner.

11. True/False questions should be used only:
    A. If you have run out of ideas to construct multiple choice questions.
    B. If you need to capture the learner's opinion on a specific topic.
    C. If the intention is to check the learner's knowledge of certain facts.
    D. If the LMS you are using limits you to two possible answers per question.

12. Matching questions can be very _____ because they can cover _____.
    A. effective / a lot of content at the same time
    B. ineffective / a lot of content at the same time
    C. effective / all of the topics in a whole course in detail
    D. ineffective / only a finite amount of material

13. Free response questions are:
    A. Harder to construct because they must be carefully crafted.
    B. Easier for the learner to answer because the question stem gives a lot of the answer away.
    C. Easier to construct because there are no distractors to produce.
    D. Easier to implement because they do not require someone to score them.

14. Why might an instructional designer decide not to score an assessment?
    A. They ran out of time to test the SCORM integration for their eLearning course to send results to the LMS.
    B. Some learners feel intimidated by scored assessments and are afraid of failure.
    C. Management can feel hesitant because they would rather not see how their teams are performing.
    D. Building a scored assessment takes a lot more work and is often not worth the reward.

15. The goal of corrective feedback is to:
    A. Embarrass the learner for incorrect answers.
    B. Tell the learner if they have mastered the content.
    C. Scold the learner for mastering the content.
    D. Share a learner's performance on social media.

16. What factor(s) should an instructional designer use to determine whether to use intrinsic or extrinsic feedback as part of their assessment design?
    A. The type of course, presentation methods and assessment instruments chosen.
    B. The type of learner that will be taking this course.
    C. The requirements put forth by the stakeholder.
    D. The requirements as mutually agreed upon during the learning analysis phase.

Exercise 15

Decide on the assessment instruments you are going to use to test your learners. Think about how you are going to ensure the validity and reliability of your assessment. Then, create one effective assessment item and the appropriate corrective feedback for it.

Part III - Interactive Elements in the ELearning Course

"Tell me and I forget, teach me and I may remember, involve me and I learn."
Benjamin Franklin

Chapter 17: Interactivity in ELearning

This chapter will cover:

- The role of interactivity in eLearning
- The four levels of interactivity
- Navigation and layout
- Experiential learning
- Augmented learning

Case Study

To make training easier to access, Petrol Oil Company needed to translate its instructor-led PowerPoint course on best practices in petroleum engineering to the eLearning format. When the instructional designer assigned to the project met with the engineer SMEs, however, she had a lot of skepticism.

"This information is very technical and boring," one of them said. "I guess I don't see the point to make it a flashy web course."

"I'm sure we can do it. We might even make the course better. With eLearning, we'll get the chance to use interactive elements that can make your material more interesting and presentable."

"If you say so," the SME said. "I'll be honest with you, most of us consider this training the most boring parts of the job."

Determined to change that, the instructional designer got to work.

With some help and clarification from her SMEs, she set about identifying areas of the course content that could benefit from interactivity. Most of it was indeed very technical, but with an eye to what would benefit from graphics, she came up with several ideas for interactive diagrams that would help the learner visualize how different aspects of the content worked together.

Looking through the sections of the course that emphasized problem solving, she came up with several tricky situations that would require critical thinking from the learner and translated them into short branching scenarios.

Finally, she made sure the course had just enough visual appeal, games, simulations, and demonstrations to inspire motivation (but not so much that it would distract from the content). The result was a course that was highly technical, but fresh and engaging.

The best way to lose your learners is to offer them a click-and-read course with lots of text on the pages. Adding interactivity to courses can help you avoid this problem. Interactivity is an exercise or activity that allows the learner to become more involved with the content by discovering information and checking knowledge through assessments, simulations, and games as opposed to simply reading text on the computer screen. To avoid text-heavy pages, you can add popup text boxes. Expandable charts, graphs, tables, and animations that appear in small chunks can also help you avoid having a large amount of text on the screen.

An interaction can be a scenario where the learner is presented with a problem that needs to be worked out to achieve a certain outcome. It can also take the form of a role-play, content revelation after selecting a specific object, or a game that puts learners in a realistic setting and allows them to explore, try, succeed, and fail in a safe environment.

For example, if you are developing a new eLearning course for legal assistants, it may include some videos that present relevant information as well as some *clicking on the objects to reveal information activities.* Then, to test learners' understanding, you can add a game where future legal assistants would have to make decisions and answer questions related to certain on-the-job situations in a virtual world environment. If they answer incorrectly, the game would bring them to the remediation page. The game could also address possible consequences if people get that same question wrong in real life. While the game would illustrate situations legal assistants may come across at their job, no one will judge them for selecting incorrect responses. When learners actively perform tasks rather than passively sit and read or listen to something, they tend to retain more information. Additionally, when learners learn new material through trial and error, they are less likely to make the same mistake again. Remember, learners do not want to take courses that contain screen after screen of information. They do not want to read textbooks. All they want is to take a course that will help them address their current problems by providing relevant information in the most interactive and engaging manner. Instead of having learners go through bulleted lists, instructional designers should put them in realistic situations and force them to learn by making decisions.

Interactivity allows learners to become more involved with the content. The goal of any interaction is to process, encode, and store the material in memory. Most instructional designers sprinkle in one interaction for every 10 to 15 minutes of learning. It is important to keep the type of content in mind when deciding on the amount of interactivity. If the content is dry and boring, adding more interactions may spice it up and make the lesson more exciting and motivational.

Most eLearning courses can be classified according to four levels of interactivity:

Level 1 – Passive Interactions. Involve very limited interactivity such as assessment at the end of the lesson or module. The content is mostly linear and static. In this level, learners do not have control over the course. They can only passively sit and either read or watch the lesson. This type of eLearning is inexpensive compared to the other types and can be effective when communicating simple concepts and facts. However, passive courses are not very motivational for learners.

Level 2 – Limited Interactions. Give learners more control over the sequence of a course. The course may contain some multiple choice questions, hyperlinks to additional resources, simple activities such as matching and drag-and-drop, audio, and video. This type of eLearning can be effective when teaching facts or systematic procedures.

Level 3 – Complex Interactions. Give learners even more control of the course. The course may include animations, complex simulations, and scenarios. Most eLearning lessons fit into this category because this level of interactivity finds a balance between reasonable development time and active learning. This type of eLearning can be used to improve proficiency, to learn physical or mental skills, or to solve problems.

Level 4 – Real-Time Interactions. Involve all the elements of Levels 1, 2, and 3, plus very complex content, serious games, and 3D simulations. This level of interactivity often uses avatars, custom videos, and interactive objects. Real-time interactions can be used to have learners solve problems or apply their knowledge to real life situations. Even though real-time interactions are highly effective and motivational, they are very time consuming and expensive to develop.

Many factors can influence instructional designers' decisions to select one level of interactivity over the other. Some of these factors are target audience, budget, content, and available resources. You should know most courses that involve complex and real-time interactions are not 508-compliant. Therefore, if your eLearning course has to meet accessibility requirements, the choices will be limited to Level 1 and 2 interactions.

Experiential Learning

Experiential learning is a process that allows learners to develop knowledge and skills from their own experience rather than from formal training courses. Experiential learning encompasses a variety of interactive and participative hands-on activities. This type of learning is much more effective than traditional learning approaches.

Before we look at the ways to apply experiential leaning to eLearning design, let's go back to history. Way back in 350 BCE, Aristotle, a Greek philosopher, thinker, mathematician, astrologer, historian and analyst, wrote: ***"...for the things we have to learn before we can do them, we learn by doing them."***

Even prior to that, the Chinese philosopher, Confucius, wrote:
I hear and I forget
I see and I remember
I do, and I understand!

Based on that, one might say that Confucius and Aristotle planted the seeds of Experiential Learning as it is formally called today. Until those fundamental principles of Experiential Learning were articulated and understood, learning environments were confined to didactic and rote styles, where learners had more of a passive role to play in their education. Perhaps a more "modern" definition of what Experiential Learning is all about comes from The Association to Advance Collegiate Schools of Business (AACSB). The AACSB Task Force, in their 1989 report, defined Experiential Learning as a *"...curriculum-related endeavor which is interactive and is characterized by variability and uncertainty"*

Five Critical Elements of Experiential Learning

If you carefully analyze the above definition, you will notice several key elements that a curriculum must embrace to meet the criteria of being called "experiential":

1. Participative – Unlike one-way rote or didactic learning, Experiential Learning is all about participation and two-way learning experiences, where learners and other stakeholders actively engage in learning experiences.

2. Interactive – While most learning styles (even rote and didactic) require interaction between instructors and learners, Experiential Learning stresses other interactions too—learner to learner, learner to environment, and learner to outsider (clients, civic leaders, community members etc.). In other words, Experiential Learning experiences take learners beyond the classroom and ventures out into the real world.

3. Multi-dimensional – Not only does Experiential Learning tap the behavioral dimensions of learners, but also their affective and cognitive dimensions.

4. Variability and Uncertainty – While "rote based" learners are unprepared to deal with anything other than the prescribed syllabus, Experiential Learning curriculum is deliberately structured to add uncertainty and variability into the learning environment. Under the instructor's guidance, learners are taught to deal with situations that they are unfamiliar with.

5. Feedback – Experiential Learning relies heavily on feedback loops, both from learners about their experiences, and from instructors about their views of the process.

The world today is much more complex and integrated than that which produced legendary minds like Confucius and Aristotle. The pace at which environments and knowledge change is far greater than what we have witnessed before in history. The need for "outside the box" thinking, and thinking "on one's feet" is even more important today than it was historically.

The only way that learners can survive and thrive in a dynamic and constantly evolving environment is by learning to quickly adapt to change. It is only through Experiential Learning characteristics that, when weaved into learning curricula, learners will be better prepared to face the complexities of the modern world.

There are two different schools of experiential learning—David Kolb's and Carl Rogers'. Let's learn about them in detail.

Kolb and Experiential Learning

According to the psychologist David Kolb, Experiential Learning is **"...a process whereby knowledge is created through the transformation of experience."** This was a radical switch from previously held beliefs of cognitive theorists (emphasis on mental processes) and behavioral theorists (largely ignoring subjective experiences in learning).

Kolb believed that learning was a more holistic experience than simply a function of the cognitive or behavioral elements. In addition to these two, Kolb's theory recognizes that other factors, including emotions and environmental conditions, greatly influence learning outcomes.

Kolb's theory of Experiential Learning is based on four factors: *Concrete Experience, Abstract Conceptualization, Reflective Observations*, and *Active Experimentation*. According to Kolb, these four elements form a cycle or process through which learners are able to observe, understand, grasp, practice (experiment) and learn.

Carl Rogers and Experiential Learning

Psychologist Carl Rogers advocated his own theory of Experiential Learning, which is grounded in several core principles:

1. Learning is accelerated when the learner is interested in the subject matter.
2. Where the subject matter is perceived as threatening to the learner (e.g., the need to change his/her behavior or attitude about strongly held perceptions), learning is accelerated if external (threatening) factors are eliminated or reduced.
3. Learning that has been self-initiated by the learner will prove to be more effective than learning that is forced, without choice of the learner.

According to Rogers, there are two distinct types of learning: *Significant (Experiential)* and *Meaningless (Cognitive)*. Rogers opined that true learning only takes place when there is confrontation between personal, social or practical challenges and the learner or the subject matter being studied.

At its very basic level, Experiential Learning seeks to foster learning as a byproduct of learners' experiences. People can read all the books about venturing into space, but it is only an astronaut who has actually traveled into space and really knows what space travel is all about. You do things. You fail at them. You understand why you failed. Then, you experiment again...and succeed!

Experiential Learning works by designing curriculum seeking to:

- Mimic (as closely as possible) real-world experiences
- Structure and monitor those experiences
- Ensure that there is planned and deliberate "deviation" from the base curriculum, and
- Provide ample opportunity for hands-on doing, experimenting and simulation

Using all of these elements produces a powerful learning experience that cannot be replicated by rote or other styles of learning. So, is there any "real life" application to Experiential Learning, and can we apply eLearning principles to facilitate it? The answer is a definite "YES." Given everything discussed above about Experiential Learning, here are two situations where ELearning and Experiential Learning can be combined:

Situation 1

In days of yore, future physicians and surgeons relied on cadavers to hone their skills, and practiced under strict supervision of senior surgeons/tutors in a hospital or clinic. Today, we can design comprehensive eLearning programs to simulate all the skills and knowledge needed by medical practitioners in an operating room. Medical "complications" can be introduced into the setting, and learners can be forced to interact with their environment, and think creatively to resolve the challenges posed.

Situation 2

Learning complex concepts like Trigonometry, Algebra, or Calculus is not very easy without extensive help, especially for adult learners. ELearning can change all that! By creating interactive learning content, and offering skills tests, online assignments and quizzes, and self-assessment modules, learners can experiment with multiple solutions while they understand the underlying principles of the subject.

In both situations, eLearning and Experiential Learning are a perfect fit. ELearning does not require learners to be co-located with instructors. Learning can be performed at the learner's pace by doing, failing, observing (videos, graphics, audio, etc.) and then practicing. A varying degree of variability and uncertainty can be introduced in course content. Learners can pace their learning based on the skills they learned previously (using a modular approach). Learning happens in a structured manner, yet "uncertainty" is part of that structure. There is a comprehensive mechanism of monitoring, tracking, and feedback built using eLearning techniques.

Marina Arshavskiy

Augmented Learning: An Argument for Its Use

While the concept of "on demand" eLearning is not new to instructional designers, the use of Augmented Learning (or AL) is fast catching currency within learning content creation circles. Augmented learning is a technique that helps instructional designers adapt learning environments to a particular learner. However, it is not necessarily a replacement for conventional eLearning content design. The idea behind augmented learning is to create supplemental learning modules using rich media content that simulates and interacts with learners to further reinforce specific learning concepts.

One example of AL would be where instructional designers have created core content using text, graphics, and other online content to indoctrinate new nurses at a children's hospital. Embedded within each module of the indoctrination course, say as a popup or sidebar, could be supplemental training material that augments some of the core content the nurses have already been exposed to, such as *"Click here to watch an emergency resuscitation procedure now."*

Here are some key ideas behind augmented learning:

- Moving learners away from a culture of memorization, rote, and "cramming."
- Encouraging "on demand" learning, as opposed to learning before the actual need to apply the new content arises.
- Producing short, interactive, digestible learning pieces to reinforce lengthier core training materials.
- Being aware that, to use augmented learning successfully, instructional content must be context-sensitive—making learning examples and simulated exercises more relevant to a specific learner and their environment, as opposed to producing generic content.

While just-in-time learning does bridge the gap between traditional classroom teaching and online learning, augmented learning fosters a culture of personalized, continuous learning to target specific areas of an individual's learning needs.

When it comes to augmented learning, instructional designers build content by taking learning context (a particular situation, place, or learner) into consideration. Then, using eLearning tools, content creators can superimpose specific learning material into core teaching content.

Nowadays, online learners are not restricted to soaking up instructional content behind a desk, or in their home offices. They may choose to learn while at the gym using their smart phones, during lunch breaks using their tablets, or while on vacation using a laptop computer. A key element for successful augmented learning is, therefore, in its delivery.

The idea is that augmented content should be highly "responsive" in its construction, having the ability to dynamically "scale" to any device used for its delivery, whether a laptop, desktop, or any other mobile or static device.

Navigation

ELearning courses can be either *linear* or *non-linear*. Linear courses are set up in a way where learners must go through the entire section before they can move to the next one. Linear courses require learners to complete the entire training. Typically, all mandatory courses including compliance-training have linear navigation. Non-linear navigation, also known as branched navigation, allows learners to jump from one section to the next in any desired order.

There are some pitfalls and benefits to each type of navigation. Even though linear navigation is a good way to make learners go through the entire training, many learners find it boring and ineffective. Additionally, because the navigation is locked, learners cannot go back and review those sections that were not clear to them. As a result, their level of understanding and retention goes down. Moreover, according to adult learning principles, adults learn better when they can make their own decisions; therefore, locking navigation will not motivate them to take the course. Non-linear navigation, however, permits learners to go through the course in any order that they want, allowing them to skip or review sections. This, however, can be problematic because learners often treat such courses as "click through," which results in minimal understanding, retention, and application of the material. In contrast, with non-linear courses, learners have an option to go back and review any section that they want and therefore increase their retention rate.

While there is no single best answer as to what type of navigation is better, it is suggested that you treat each course separately and design navigation based on course content and requirements. Using non-linear navigation whenever possible and motivating learners to complete the entire course by offering vivid and interactive presentation is more effective than having learners go through the course in a linear manner. During the analysis phase, explain all the benefits and pitfalls of linear and non-linear navigation to the client to ensure the end-result matches the stakeholder's vision.

Test Your Knowledge

1. All of the following are examples of interactivity in eLearning modules EXCEPT:
    A. Simulations and games
    B. Audio narration
    C. Popup text boxes
    D. Expandable content

2. Which of the following is an example of an eLearning interaction? (Choose all that apply)
    A. A Scenario-based game
    B. A narrated slide
    C. A click-to-reveal box
    D. An embedded video

3. ELearning interactivity can be extremely effective because it promotes:
    A. Passive learning
    B. Passive listening
    C. Active learning
    D. Active listening

4. It is a best practice to incorporate one interaction for every _____ of learning.
    A. 1 minute
    B. 2-3 minutes
    C. 5-10 minutes
    D. 10-15 minutes

5. Which level of interactivity is characterized by having limited interactivity, linear static content, and comparatively low production cost?
    A. Level 1 – Passive Interactions
    B. Level 2 – Limited Interactions
    C. Level 3 – Complex Interactions
    D. Level 4 – Real-Time Interactions

6. An eLearning course classified as having 'Complex Interactions' (Level 3) typically includes what type of elements?
    A. 3D simulations and graphics
    B. Animations, complex simulations and scenarios
    C. Simple interactions and limited animations
    D. Voiceover and hosted videos

7. If your eLearning course has to meet accessibility requirements, which interactivity level(s) will you be limited to?
    A. Level 1
    B. Level 2
    C. Levels 1 and 2
    D. All levels except 4

8. Typically, all compliance courses have _____ navigation.
    A. linear
    B. self-guided
    C. branched
    D. non-linear

9. Non-linear navigation:
    A. Forces the learner to go through an entire section before they can move on to the next one.
    B. Is a good way to make learners go through the entire training.
    C. Typically does not allow the learner to go back through previous sections.
    D. Permits learners to go through the course in any order they want.

Exercise 16

Think about the look and feel of your course. Will it be linear or non-linear? Now, based on what you know about your course, decide on the level if interactivity you will include, and state your reasons for choosing one over the other.

Chapter 18: Simulations and Games

This chapter will cover:

- The difference between games and simulations
- Types of learning games
- Elements of learning games
- Creating a story for the learning game
- Games as assessments
- Structure of the game
- Virtual Worlds
- Avatars
- Storytelling and scenario-based learning
- Choosing a game for the eLearning course

Regardless of our age, playing with simulators (e.g. stock market investment, driving or flight simulators) and games (Starcraft, Hearts of Iron, World of Warcraft) always puts us on the path to learning and experiencing new things. That is because if our objective is to "win" the game, then we need to explore and learn the "system" to beat it. That is exactly what Game-Based Learning (GBL) is all about. In this chapter, we will talk about the types of game-based learning as well as the benefits of simulations and games.

Today, many instructional designers use simulations and games in their training courses because they believe games help learners understand and retain the content. However, to create a learning experience, you should be familiar with different types of games as well as the process of effective game design.

Gamification is the process of changing the dynamics of any activity by incorporating several game elements. This technique has gained popularity in various fields because of its effectiveness in increasing productivity, speed, and learning. The field of eLearning also tapped into the use of gamification to enhance the efficacy of eLearning courses and materials. However, not all companies have extra money to spend on gamification features, which can get very expensive.

Types of Learning Games

So, what is a learning game? The learning game is an activity inserted into any eLearning course with the goal of improving the learning process and motivating the learner to complete the course.

Many different types of game-based learning have evolved over the years, each having a different audience and its own unique objective. Here are some alternate gaming styles to consider when designing game-based learning content:

- **Flash Cards, Game Show Competitions** – These are best suited for memorization-based or drill-based applications.
- **Role-Plays, Quests** – These work well when the learning objective is to encourage imitation, reinforce continuous practice, and emphasize increasingly challenging content.
- **Strategy, Adventure** – When the objective is to foster decision-making abilities, or sharpen choice-making and quizzing skills, these types of games are the best way to go.
- **Multi-Player Gaming** – These types of games are best suited when fostering collaboration and teamwork is the ultimate learning objective.

- **Open-Ended Simulation** – For teaching experimentation and logic, exposing learners to games and simulations that are open-ended (no single right/wrong answer) is the best way to go.
- **Timed Games, Reflex Testing** – When the objective is to foster quick thinking and thinking "out of the box," then these types of games are ideal.

Even though the above list classifies each type of game as being the best for specific learning objectives, there is no rule that says game-based learning design cannot mix and match several of these elements into a single course. For instance, role-playing games can easily be based on open-ended simulation techniques.

Experienced instructional designers know that true learning is not about memorizing or learning by rote. The right type of simulations and games can challenge and engage a learner into comprehending and then practicing new skills. Some of the immediate benefits of well-designed learning games include:

- **Active engagement** – Unlike traditional lectures or hands-on training, games push the learner to get actively involved in the learning process.
- **Adaptability** – Lectures do not offer "try, fail, learn" experiences. With simulations, learners will learn to adapt their skills to the real world.
- **Self-pace** – The pace of most traditional learning is set by the educator; not so with games and simulations. Learners tailor the pace of the game to match their temperament.
- **Feedback** – Miss a beat in a game, and you immediately get a "buzz" or "demerits" or lose points. If you do poorly on a traditional test, it may be days before you know how you fared.
- **Standardization** – When it comes to hands-on training, it is extremely difficult to assess all learners in a standardized way. Subjectivity invariably creeps in. With simulated learning, the rules are applied equally to all participants, allowing for better learner-to-learner assessments.
- **Cost-effectiveness** – As opposed to organizing instructor-led or workshop-type learning, simulations are much more cost-effective and broadly distributable.

Ways to Build Blocks for Game-Based Learning

One of America's most celebrated educators, James Paul Gee, in his classical book *What Video Games Have to Teach Us About Learning and Literacy*, has advocated a set of 36 learning principles that designers of game-based eLearning content should adhere to. Here are a few ways that instructional designers can incorporate "gamification" into eLearning content while still holding true to Gee's eLearning principles:

- **Defined goals** – Remember that the goals of "gamification" are to harmonize the goals of the game with those of learning. When you start putting together gaming content, know exactly what you want the player to learn as they play the game.
- **Personalization** – Not every learner learns the same way. When designing game-based eLearning content, instructional designers must provide for customized learning experiences (fonts, colors, cast of characters, sounds, "quest" objectives, etc.) to reflect each "player's" preferences.
- **Gradual progression** – The idea behind this design concept is that learning games should allow players to gradually progress into higher, and more complex, levels of learning. If level 1 (i.e. module 1) is extremely complex, a game player will immediately lose interest for progressing to the next level (module).
- **Accomplishment** – Gamification of learning is all about reinforcing self-accomplishment amongst learners. Each time a learner clears a simulated hurdle, there must be recognition of accomplishments.
- **Illustrated progress** – This is a corollary to gradual progression, in that games must visually illustrate (through scores, points, accumulated treasure, etc.) the progress gamers make from completing each module/level. Seeing progress in real-time helps keep players motivated to continue playing.

As eLearning gamification slowly becomes an industry on its own, many vendors are now providing advanced gamification services. Vendors offer intricate eLearning module designs, integration to various communication software (Skype, chatrooms, etc.), and even personalized cloud-based storage for users. Needless to say, many third-party vendors capitalize on their advanced programming know-how to provide gamification services that cost way more than what one spends on traditional eLearning.

However, the truth is that eLearning gamification does not have to be costly. By keeping the basic principles behind gamification in mind, one can gamify eLearning without having to spend too much money. Let's take a look at some of the best low-cost gamification strategies:

- **Simple over sophisticated user interface (UI)** – Many vendors who offer expensive gamification services often have extremely sophisticated user interfaces (UI). However, a good-looking UI is not the primary concern for learners. To avoid spending more than necessary, it is best to stick to simple, easy to use UIs. A heavy and complicated visual design can cause distractions. By choosing user-friendly UIs, you can cut the cost by up to 50% without compromising the effectiveness of your materials. Streamlined UIs also tend to be simpler on the administrator's side.

- **Features** – Another misconception about low-cost gamification vendors is that they do not provide quality features. There is absolutely no truth in that. When it comes to features, uniqueness, and usability are more important than quantity. One does not need multiple features that serve the same purpose. Instead, focus on getting one unique feature that is highly effective and versatile. For example, separate features for chat and voice communication can slow the system down. It is better to get a single instant messaging feature that allows efficient and fast person to person sharing.

- **Social media integration over mobile integration** – One of the most brilliant solutions to low-cost gamification is social media integration as it provides an alternate UI for learning. Twitter, Facebook, and other social networking sites allow maximum user interaction. Some of these sites also allow file sharing and video calls to save storage. The best part about social media integration is that even those instructional designers who are not too tech-savvy can easily integrate various social media platforms themselves. Mobile integration can be costly; thus, one way to channel announcements, leaderboards, bulletins, etc., is through social media—which is already mobile-integrated.

- **Self-help guides over live/video training** – Think carefully whether you truly need to have live training or use up precious storage space through video tutorials. In many instances, the same content can be easily delivered through infographic guides and FAQ pages.

- **Scheduled versus real-time performance analysis** – Performance analysis is a standard feature provided by many vendors. What sets expensive vendors apart is that some of them have real-time performance analysis systems that allow users to check their progress immediately after completing tasks. While instant feedback is important in eLearning, it may get costly. Additionally, real-time performance reports are much cheaper and equally appreciated by the learners.

- **Design your own assessment tools** – Many people who are new to eLearning often think that the content is the only major thing that determines cost of their eLearning product. However, that is not always the case. Some vendors actually charge additional payment just for formulating and implementing assessment tools. To avoid spending more money than necessary, consider developing challenging assessments yourself.

- **Be strict with standard features** – Standard features include curriculum paths, batch uploads, reports, and calendars. When going for low-cost gamification, it is best to ensure that the standards are well-delivered and without compromise. Focus on a few highly efficient features that really add value to learning—not on the UI's appearance.

While eLearning is an effective teaching method, lack of interaction is one of the biggest challenges instructional designers face when developing online courses. This is where gamification comes into play. Gamification adds fun to eLearning modules while also helping learners absorb the material. Here are some tips that you will find useful when adding gaming elements to your courses.

- **Apply realism to your games** – A good example of this is a realistic and fun game for teaching McDonald's trainees how to improve their customer service. The game is set in a virtual restaurant. It has appealing stories and characters that stimulate emotional engagement. The "customers" behave as if they were real people. The trainees are being timed during exercises and are encouraged to continue practicing until they completely satisfy the customers.

- **Story-driven games must have branching scenarios** – Applying branching scenarios to eLearning modules is another technique that helps learners identify the content they need to focus on and concentrate just on information that is relevant to them. The best example for this concept is an interactive game that takes learners on an exciting trip in the annals of history to solve various mysteries. As the players unlock each mystery, they are being transported to different scenes that are also comprised of different levels. After completing one level, learners earn bonus points and move on to the next scene. Another interesting game element is a dynamic map, which helps players pinpoint the current and previous stage they are in. There is also instant feedback after solving a mystery.

- **Take advantage of the native features of a mobile device** – Using the native features of a mobile device can help trainees improve their motor skills and reflexes. For example, in a crisis simulator, players need to perform basic responses for cardiac arrest, choking, and other emergency situations. For the tablet version, players need to "pump" their devices to check if their timing is correct for CPR. On desktop computers, you will use the keyboard keys to accomplish each task. With this method, trainees can easily monitor their progress and get a hands-on experience with the concepts they learn. There is also an option to share your scores on social media for a little bit of competitive gameplay.

- **Accompany your module with a physical board game** – Even though your eLearning module is digital, you can still use a physical board game to improve learner engagement. This method is effective if you want your learners to interact with their peers. A good example of this is a dynamic game where learners try to answer questions about various subjects using an app for recording and sharing their scores on social media, but they also rely on the physical playing board and question cards to see their progress and determine their next task.

As you can see, there are many ways to improve learners' engagement. To create effective educational games, however, instructional designers need to conduct thorough needs analysis and familiarize themselves with learners' behavior, their reasons for taking the course, demographic makeup, the device used for taking the course, but, most importantly, instructional designers should carefully analyze learners' current vs desired knowledge of the subject covered in the game.

Now that you have a good understanding about gamification principles and techniques, let's talk about some of the popular games in eLearning that you can apply to your courses.

- *Casual games*
- *Serious games*
- *Advergames*
- *Simulation games*
- *Assessment games*

Casual games

Casual games engage learners in a fun way. The purpose of such games is to reinforce the learning objectives through play. Some of the casual games include drag and drop, sequencing, and matching. These games can be easily created with a rapid eLearning tool and do not require any programming or technical skills.

Serious games

Serious games are typically simulations with other elements of game design. The intention of serious games is to improve a specific aspect of learning. Serious games are very popular in health care, military training, and in corporate education. The main goal of serious games is to achieve measurable and sustainable changes in learners' performance or behavior.

Advergames

Advergames include elements of both casual and serious games. These games are often used for advertisement and marketing purposes. Many times, they are designed in such a way that players do not even realize there is an advertisement involved.

Simulations

Simulations or branching scenarios are typically scenarios that allow learners to go through situations they will most likely encounter in real life. Simulations expose learners to many different choices they have to make and continue to the next step based on the decisions they make. Branching scenarios can either be a part of a serious game or a standalone activity in the eLearning course.

There are many ways to create educational simulations that are both engaging and result-oriented. However, developing these simulations can be very expensive and resource consuming. Therefore, instructional designers should strategically analyze all goals and objectives prior to getting involved in the design process.

Here are some suggestions on how you can create educational simulations quickly and effectively.

- **Introductions Matter** – Rather than separate the introduction and the main body of the simulation, effective simulation models integrate them into the core content, allowing learners to quickly delve into the intros, and then, get to the substance of the game. By doing so, instructional designers familiarize their learners with the look and feel, and overall mechanics (background, themes, navigation, feedback/messaging) of the simulation early on, thereby shortening the learning curve.

- **Pay Attention to Learning Objectives and Outcomes** – When designers get deeply entrenched with the excitement of the simulation, they often forget to pay attention to creating effective learning objectives. Most tools allow ISD professionals to define multiple goals (Targeted Skills Improvements, Enhancing Product Knowledge, etc.) in a snap. Doing this early in the design process will help with defining and compiling relevant core content for the simulation.

- **Clear Rules of The Game** – Before launching into the simulations, adult learners often want to know how they will be evaluated, and in what ways they can engage with the simulation model to ensure success. It is important that eLearning creators take some time to set clear and well-defined "engagement rules" before starting to build core content.

- **Relating to Your Audience** – Before piling up core content, designers should familiarize themselves with the simulation tools they are using. One element that can quickly be configured, and has a powerful impact on learner engagement, is the background and environmental settings for simulated scenes. Consider developing stories that learners can easily relate to, and have them participate in interactions that they will most likely experience on the job.

- **Choice of Characters** – While creating characters/avatars requires knowledge of graphic design or significant investment in hiring a professional designer, there are ways to create meaningful simulations without spending too much money. For example, there are sites with free images that can be modified, cut, or cropped using PowerPoint and other free graphic design and editing tools available on the market. These characters can then be animated using any free animation tool, (if a paid tool is not available to you) such as Caligari.

Assessments

As instructional designers look for new and engaging ways to present content, many of them want to test learners' knowledge without adding traditional true/false and multiple-choice types of questions. Instead, they hide tests behind a "game skin." Some examples of games used purely for assessment purposes are Snakes and Ladders, Hangman, and popular game show variations. While these games are fun to play, they are neither engaging nor task-oriented. The sole purpose of such games is to test the content using a different approach.

Game Structure

Many people think that eLearning gamification means incorporating actual games in virtual courses. Although games do complete the gamification process, eLearning gamification is not limited to including actual games. In fact, gamification of any activity only needs to include the crucial game elements that target the skills discussed in the specific course.

The simplest way to approach the learning game design is to mimic the elements found in typical video games. The elements of a good game include the following:

Narrative – This is the key to successful gamification. Not only that narratives tell stories, but they also offer real life examples that help learners understand main concepts that games are trying to teach. The art of storytelling is the main challenge that instructional designers face here. Not only that they need to think of a plot relevant to what is being taught, but they also have to incorporate protagonists and antagonists to ensure proper flow of the game.

Rules – This is an important element of any game. Rules add structure as well as a sense of expectation. If learners do not know the rules, they will not know how to play the game and will soon become frustrated and disinterested.

Score – This element adds excitement and forces learners to continue with the game. Players want to know if they are winning or losing.

Strategy – This element allows players to manipulate the game to maximize their score. Giving learners rewards and bonus points for completing a level or achieving certain milestones are ways to add strategy to the game design.

Message – This element is responsible for communicating the objectives and goals of a lesson. Hide your messages in the game and allow players to discover them as they go.

Interactivity and Discovery – We all know that games are about actively doing something. To keep learners engaged, instructional designers should know how to incorporate discovery and exploration elements. One way to do that is to have learners hunt for a treasure, or ask them to put the steps of a linear process in order. Always be sure that your games stimulate mental and physical processes.

Time constraints and Competition – Most games use time constraints to pressure people to think quickly and develop a sense of competition. When creating a learning game, instructional designers should incorporate a timer, so that learners know that there is a time limit to complete the game.

Challenge – You should aim to provide clear goals and feedback to engage learners in the game. It is important to make sure the goals are immediate. In other words, learners are much more likely to succeed if they know that they will achieve their goal instantly rather than a few days after playing the game. In addition to clear goals and appropriate feedback, learners should experience a certain degree of curiosity or surprise. You should give them control by providing enough but not too many options. If exposed to many choices, learners may become frustrated and refuse to continue exploring the game.

Risk – This is a very important part of game design, especially when it comes to serious games. Learners want to have a sense of risk. Design your games to make the failure possible but avoidable and ensure that, regardless of how players move, failure is not their final result.

Levels and Titles – This element allows you to split the course into sections providing learners with the opportunity to move on to Level 2 after completing Level 1. As learners move through the levels, their titles can change from Novice to Expert. Assigning levels and titles will motivate learners to complete the course.

Feedback and Rewards – This is an important motivational element in any game. As learners progress through the course, they expect appropriate motivational feedback. Just like with assessments, providing timely feedback is a crucial component of gamification. Your feedback does not necessarily have to be verbal or written. Instead, if the learners are doing well, allow them to proceed to the next level. You may also give rewards in a form of points or badges or simply show a progress bar. Corrective feedback can be either direct or indirect. "Great job! You are well on your way to becoming a superstar" is an example of a direct type of feedback while assigning scores is an indirect type of feedback. Regardless of the type of feedback provided, it should not interrupt the flow of the game.

The game elements mentioned above encourage adult learners to utilize their skills in solving a problem. Unlike traditional eLearning techniques, eLearning gamification transforms the learner from a passive absorber of information to an active participant in creating strategic solutions. Gamification increases engagement and motivates learner to think out of the box.

Always keep in mind that learning games should align with your objectives and be based on a relevant, interesting, and meaningful story. To add a motivational factor to the story, the game can have learners go on a journey, discover a secret, or conquer the opponent. While being creative can add a spark to the plot, the story should not be unreasonably complex. Otherwise, the game will increase the extraneous load. The following questions should help you plan your learning game.

- Who are the characters?
- What are the genders, ages, and physical characteristics of characters?
- What happens to the characters in the game?
- How does that affect the players in the game?
- What learning objectives will the story cover?
- What content should the story cover?
- What will motivate learners to continue playing?
- What type of feedback will be provided?
- When would the learners win and when would they lose the game?
- What will happen at the beginning, in the middle, and at the end of the story?
- Where does the story take place?

The success of any learning game depends on instructional sequencing and methods as well as on the plot and motivational factors included in the game.

Virtual Worlds

Instructional designers often search for ways to gamify their eLearning courses quickly and efficiently without hiring professional developers and graphic artists. We all know that gamification can get expensive! So, what can you do if your client wants to get an engaging product and, at the same time, does not want to pay a fortune? Luckily, there is a rapid solution that can make everyone happy. Virtual Worlds have been around for quite some time now and many designers have been successfully incorporating them in their eLearning lessons. With Virtual Worlds, the sky is the limit. There are many avatars and settings you can choose from. All you have to do is choose a Virtual World you want, find the characters that best meet your needs, find settings, and create your story around your settings. One of the best features of Virtual Worlds is that you can maneuver your camera very quickly to capture your characters at different angles. You can easily change and capture emotions and even change settings at any time you want. Some Virtual Worlds allow you to record short videos and voiceovers. If you were to hire a professional graphic designer, not only that you would spend a lot of money to complete all the scenes and angles to make your game interactive, engaging, and professional, but you would also spend a lot of time on all the prep work including describing every scene and characters involved in these scenes.

So, what do you need to gamify your course using Virtual Worlds? First, you need to have a completed script, and have a good idea about what you want to portray in your game. Think about the setting of your game and the characters that will be involved. Then, do your research about the pros and cons of each Virtual World, and choose the one that best meets your needs. Once you select your desired Virtual World, you will have to add your characters and settings. Then, capture the scenes with your camera and do screen captures. That is all it takes to create an eLearning game!

While it is certainly possible to create your entire course in the Virtual World environment, not all instructional designers choose to go that route. Instead, they may decide to develop a short simulation or quiz using Virtual Worlds.

In summary, Virtual Worlds are immersive 3D online environments where users can interact with any other users and characters. In a Virtual World, learners can experiment, plan, solve problems, negotiate, collaborate, evaluate, learn from mistakes, and take risks while learning new skills. The environment of Virtual World is three-dimensional, which allows users to choose an "avatar." While there are many virtual worlds, some of the most popular are Second Life, Active Worlds, and There.

Many instructional designers like to include Virtual Worlds in their courses for the collaboration purpose. They also design their lectures, demonstrations, simulations, and experiences in the Virtual World environment. Additionally, Virtual Worlds work well for distance learning where trainers can post slides, audio, video presentations, and even self-paced tutorials. Virtual Worlds are a good platform for group projects. Designing one requires a lot of planning and understanding of how these environments work.

In Virtual Worlds, you can create both synchronous and asynchronous learning experiences. The first step in designing the 3D environment is ensuring that learners are comfortable with the Virtual World, keeping in mind that different people learn differently depending on their background, experience, personal preference, and motivation. While some people will immerse themselves almost immediately in this 3D environment, others will need months to become comfortable and be able to fully concentrate on the learning experience.

Avatars

An avatar is a graphical representation of a character. Avatars are an effective way to engage learners. They often provide feedback and remediation to learners. In addition, avatars can ask questions and lead discussions, helping learners progress. The avatar can act as an instructor or a learning mate depending on the purpose of the game. As you plan the game, you should think about the role the avatar will play and how it will support learners.

Storytelling and Scenario-based Learning

Storytelling is a learning tool that teaches, motivates, and entertains at the same time. Well-crafted stories provide learners with necessary facts using realistic situations and at the same time evoke an emotional response. As a result, learners can easily relate to the content, better retain it, and transfer their new skills to the job.

Some of the reasons to add stories to the eLearning courses include helping learners to

- memorize facts,
- relate to an incident, or
- reflect on a situation.

Stories should contain the following elements:
- Setting – Where the story takes place
- Characters – The actors in the story
- Problem – The purpose of the story
- Development – Outcomes of correct and incorrect performance
- Climax – Lessons learned from the outcomes
- Ending – Conclusion, summary, or review of the key points

You can present stories using text, audio, or video elements, but you do not have to construct the stories yourself. Instead, consider delegating this task to Subject Matter Experts (SMEs) and have them provide stories related to the content. To help SMEs come up with relevant stories, you can ask related questions such as, "Think about a time when…", or "What happened when…"

There are multiple ways to incorporate stories into eLearning courses. The most commonly used approach is making them part of a learning scenario. Typical learning scenarios include a realistic situation or story followed by questions that require learners to react to the story. In addition, storytelling can complement courses that include social learning elements in them. For instance, you can create a story and ask questions based on it. Then, have learners react or respond to the questions in the social media environment.

Scenario-based learning, also known as problem-based learning, seeks to elevate the learner's training outcomes from merely comprehension to analysis, synthesis, and application. Obtaining a real skill truly happens once the learner is able to use information to make decisions and correctly perform an objective.

It is important that instructional designers keep their scenarios as realistic as possible. The most well-written scenario will fall flat for learners if it involves walking through a situation that he or she will never encounter in the real world. Talking with subject matter experts to obtain examples of true situations in the workplace is one way to determine appropriate scenarios. Even more helpful is to interview the employees who are in the same job as learners, and discuss the problems they encounter on the job. Basing scenarios on real issues will help learners engage in training and, as a result, retain more information.

Scenario-based learning can be used in both eLearning and instructor-led training. There are benefits and pitfalls to both. Scenarios in eLearning can be highly controlled—no one can go off-script. There is a set number of "paths" the learner can potentially explore. Additionally, an avatar can give specific feedback based on each choice. Learners can feel free to explore every possible avenue, and even choose an incorrect step on purpose just to see what happens. While scenario-based learning is a great way to make eLearning more engaging and useful to the learner in general, it may feel simplistic within the parameters of an eLearning course. For example, potential responses may seem obvious, and they may not actually capture the choice a learner would make given the freedom to say or do anything. To ensure that eLearning scenarios are truly valuable, instructional designers should create the most realistic scenario possible, and capture all potential paths that learners could take. Working closely with the SMEs is one of the most critical steps in designing these interactions.

On the other hand, scenario-based learning in an instructor-led setting can be a great way to really see where participants go wrong, and correct them along the way. Live and timely feedback is invaluable to learners as they practice their new skills. However, constraints of the live classroom may hinder employees from acting as they actually would in their workplace. Oftentimes, participants are shy in front of a group, or do not want to lose face by making a wrong choice, or only observe and never participate at all. Learners may hesitate to learn through trial and error, and may feel uncomfortable to make mistakes and learn how to self-correct. Creating a "safe" and comfortable environment is crucial to the success of scenario-based learning. Therefore, in many instances, instructional designers should consider a blended learning approach, and translate their classroom scenarios to the virtual environment.

Choosing a Game for Your ELearning Course

Most of the time the type of game selected for the course will depend on the content and objectives associated with it. However, before making the decision to add a game to the course, you must determine its overall purpose. If the game does not communicate an instructional message or motivate learners, then it most likely lacks any instructional value. In addition, because game development requires significant time and resources, you must consider the shelf life of the information and skills in the game. While it may be worthwhile dedicating resources to create games for mostly static content, if the information is constantly changing and updating, it may not be worth the investment.

The large variety of learning games makes the process of picking the appropriate one challenging. To decide which game suits the needs of your specific course, you should answer the following questions:

- Who is the target audience?
- What is the learning objective?
- How will this objective be evaluated?
- What type of content will be included in the game?
- What are the intended results?

Test Your Knowledge

1. Learning games are:
    A. Seen by many as a distraction from the core purpose of building effective learning content.
    B. Activities which are done outside of the eLearning course to reinforce the content that was presented.
    C. Activities inserted into eLearning courses to improve the learning process.
    D. Often used in place of a formal assessment, especially to obtain certification.

2. All of the following are benefits of learning games EXCEPT:
    A. Improvement in learner understanding.
    B. Practice and application of the content being learned.
    C. Inexpensive to develop and maintain.
    D. Increased learner motivation to complete the course.

3. Games such as drag and drop, or sequencing and matching, reinforce the learning through fun play, and are referred to as:
    A. Serious games
    B. Advergames
    C. Simulation games
    D. Casual games

4. The main goal of _____ games is to achieve measurable and sustainable changes in learners' performance or behavior by using simulations combined with other elements.
    A. serious
    B. simulation
    C. casual
    D. assessment

5. Otherwise known as "branching scenarios," this type of game allows learners to go through situations they will most likely encounter in real life:
    A. Serious
    B. Simulation
    C. Casual
    D. Assessment

6. Rules, Rewards, Feedback and Strategy are just some of the:
   - A. Elements of adult education
   - B. Elements of a good eLearning module
   - C. Elements of a good assessment
   - D. Elements of a good game

7. This element adds a level of excitement to the learning experience and include things like badges and points.
   - A. Rewards
   - B. Score
   - C. Strategy
   - D. Levels

8. The game element of "Message" allows for:
   - A. The incorporation of subliminal messages into the training content.
   - B. The communication of the lesson's objectives and goals throughout the game.
   - C. Learners to incorporate user-generated content back into the training.
   - D. Instructional designers to hide Easter eggs into the content.

9. Designing your games to make failure possible, but avoidable is a great way of incorporating _____ into your learning game design.
   - A. rewards
   - B. strategy
   - C. risk
   - D. challenge

10. Providing the learner with a congratulatory message in the game is an example of _____ feedback.
   - A. indirect
   - B. direct
   - C. intrinsic
   - D. extrinsic

11. Presenting the learner with their score throughout the game is an example of _____ feedback.
    A. indirect
    B. direct
    C. intrinsic
    D. extrinsic

12. Second Life and Active Worlds are examples of _____, where learners can _____.
    A. Learning Communities / self-study using other peoples' resources
    B. Learning Communities / collaborate with others and learn
    C. Virtual Worlds / experience the content using virtual reality glasses
    D. Virtual Worlds / collaborate with other users and learn new information

13. In virtual worlds, you can create _____ learning experiences.
    A. neither synchronous nor asynchronous
    B. synchronous
    C. asynchronous
    D. both synchronous and asynchronous

14. All of the following are correct statements about avatars EXCEPT:
    A. Avatars can be used to provide feedback and remediation to learners.
    B. Avatars can be virtually controlled in synchronous learning environments.
    C. Avatars can ask questions and lead discussions.
    D. Avatars can act as instructors or learning mates.

15. _____ is/are a great way to connect emotionally with the learner while presenting necessary facts using realistic situations.
    A. Script writing
    B. Interactive games
    C. Storytelling
    D. Jokes

Exercise 17

Decide whether your eLearning course will include
games, simulations, or scenarios. Then, using the
guidelines from this chapter, outline their essential
elements and write a script capturing all of these
elements.

Chapter 19: ELearning Tools

This chapter will cover:

- Adobe eLearning Suite authoring tools
- Rapid eLearning tool
- Screencasting and screenshot capturing
- Interactivity development tools, and
- Choosing the right tool for your needs

Case Study

Swiftfoot Software Company traditionally used Lectora for its training needs. It was affordable, straightforward and had all the features necessary for simulations. However, as the company's technical portfolio expanded, they found themselves needing more in-depth training, and greater capacity for interactivity than Lectora could provide. They asked one of their instructional designers to guide them down the tool selection process.

After doing some research, the instructional designer came up with a rubric, which he presented at a meeting. He displayed a table with each authoring tool and its features on the board, and asked the team a series of questions.

The first consideration was delivery methods. Did the tool cover the delivery methods they wanted to use? The team decided they could tailor the delivery method to the project, but carefully considered the platforms their learners were likely to use.

The second consideration was tracking data. The team decided they wanted to conduct a wide variety of data tracking and narrowed down the tools to the ones with detailed tracking abilities.

Finally, the instructional designer asked them to consider what level of interactivity the courses would need. The important thing is not to just leap to the tool with the most features, he said, but to really think about what would benefit the courses. What kinds of interactivity was important? The team decided on some essentials: simulations, interactive graphics, and embedded videos. Ultimately, the team decided that Captivate met their requirements.

There are many different eLearning authoring tools on the market that help instructional designers assemble their courses. Authoring tools are software used to build eLearning courses. These tools allow for the developing, editing, testing, and arranging of eLearning experiences. Authoring tools range from basic applications that have almost no learning curve to sophisticated software programs that involve coding. Earlier, when we talked about rapid eLearning design and custom eLearning design, we concluded that you should use rapid authoring tools whenever possible. Rapid authoring tools can save time, money, and resources while allowing you to produce highly effective learning experiences. Authoring tools vary in price and complexity.

Adobe eLearning Suite software is a toolbox for creating eLearning courses. These programs allow developers to create fully SCORM-compliant simulations, demonstrations, rich animation, and digital imaging. Adobe eLearning Suite includes the following software:

Adobe Captivate for creating software demonstrations, simulations, branched scenarios, randomized quizzes, screencasts, and podcasts

Adobe Flash for authoring vector graphics, animation, games, and Rich Internet Applications (RIAs) which can be viewed, played, and executed in Adobe Flash Player

Adobe Dreamweaver for website development

Adobe Photoshop for editing graphics

Adobe Acrobat for viewing, creating, printing, and managing PDF files

Adobe Presenter for creating professional-quality videos and converting courses into interactive eLearning presentations

Adobe Audition for audio recording, editing, mixing, restoration and effects

Because there is programming involved, eLearning Suite allows ISD professionals to create almost anything they can possibly think of. However, course development with these tools is quite expensive and time consuming.

Nowadays, more and more instructional designers lean toward rapid eLearning tools. It is nearly impossible to cover all of them in just one chapter; therefore, we will focus on the most popular programs on the market.

There are three types of rapid eLearning authoring tools. They include *PowerPoint plugin authoring tools*, *desktop authoring tools,* and *cloud-based authoring tools*.

Articulate 360 is one of the most popular eLearning tools on the market. It is an annual subscription that includes everything instructional designers and eLearning developers need. This is a multi-toolkit that puts together a suite of nine tools to provide the most comprehensive solutions to eLearning design. It is comprised of Studio 360 as a PPT add-in, the standalone Storyline360, and the Rise web service for mobile-ready courses. Articulate 360 has an extensive asset library (over 1.5 million in total assets) composed of characters, icons, templates, photos, and videos. It also has live online training to walk designers through the various features of the program. Additionally, there is a project review application that allows you to "test" your design with subject matter experts before going live.

PowerPoint Plugin Authoring Tools

The PowerPoint plugin authoring tools use PowerPoint as the authoring environment. However, in addition to all the bells and whistles that PowerPoint offers, these tools allow instructional designers to add interactivities and assessments. Since most people are familiar with PowerPoint, they find these tools easy to use. iSpring Suite is one example of a PowerPoint plugin tool and is one of the most popular rapid eLearning tools on the market. This tool is easy to use and the learning curve is minimal. It also has a considerable compilation of eLearning assets. You can create interactive modules with iSpring's quizzmaker, video and audio editor, and conversation simulator.

ELearning programs created using iSpring Suite automatically adapt to mobile devices as necessary. There is no need for developers to manually configure complex interactive elements when iSpring is used to create online learning materials.

Desktop Authoring Tools

Desktop authoring tools are installed on the desktop. These tools offer more flexibility to eLearning designers, but at the same time, there is a learning curve. Some of the most popular desktop authoring tools are Adobe Captivate, and Lectora.

Adobe Captivate

Even though Adobe Captivate is part of the eLearning Suite, it is still considered a rapid eLearning tool. With Captivate, you can create multimedia presentations in the form of movies. Captivate enables you to create step-by-step tutorials and animated help file enhancements. Usually, Captivate presentations contain mouse cursor movements with accompanying captioned text. They may also include multimedia elements, such as voiceovers and music. In more advanced applications, Captivate can be set up to prompt the learner for input. Captivate also allows you to record software demonstrations and simulations as well as to create presentations, quizzes, and screencasts. The new version of Captivate comes with a suite of characters and pre-programmed interactions that can be easily customized to meet the needs of each individual course.

The latest version of Captivate introduced the smart positioning feature for increased responsiveness of online learning modules. You can also add responsive motion effects to your page elements, and preview them by simply hovering over the objects.

Captivate allows you to create various simulation modes labeled as: *See* for demonstrations, *Try* for "hands-on" training, and *Test* for assessment. Among the other features of Captivate are geolocation, multilingual support, LMS preview, and diverse distribution possibilities.

Lectora

Lectora is a very powerful rapid eLearning tool by Trivantis. Because it is capable of producing high quality interactions and because there is a higher learning curve than with other rapid eLearning tools, some people do not consider Lectora a rapid authoring tool. However, once you learn how to use it, you can begin developing high-level eLearning courses very quickly. Lectora comes with image, audio, and video editing tools. This software allows you to create true/false, multiple choice, matching, hot spot, drag and drop, essay, and short answer assessments. With Lectora, you can create interactive learning objects such as mouse overs to engage learners with onscreen activities. Moreover, the tool allows designers to create branched learning scenarios. More advanced users of Lectora can add external elements as well as incorporate additional code to create custom applications.

The makers of this tool are reputed to be the ones who first published in HTML. One of Lectora's key features is their Responsive Course Design, which basically involves a more fluid grid layout designed as desktop first, and then adjusted for other devices using the inheritance model. In the prebuilt themes and layouts, the adjustments for cross-device moving and resizing is automatic, and you do not have to manually "edit" each screen.

Lectora gives you more control over how your content appears across devices. The design of your courses can allow for the detection of the type of device and the orientation in which the learners are viewing your materials. As such, you can choose to design your content for optimal learning. You can have several images lined up as static content or as .gif images for desktop use, for instance, and then turn them into flip-through cards or images for tablet use.

Cloud-based Tools

Cloud-based tools are tools that eLearning developers can access over the internet via a secure hosted system. The main benefits of these tools is that they do not require IT configurations, special set-ups, or licenses. Many eLearning developers turn to these tools because they allow collaboration with colleagues, and can be accessed anywhere. CourseArc is one example of a Cloud-based eLearning authoring tool.

CourseArc

Ease of use and built-in features are this tool's best characteristics. It is 100% cloud-based, so there is no need to download anything or to use plug-ins. There are a number of templates and pre-set building blocks that make it easy for instructional designers to create eLearning materials without hiring expensive developers or graphic artists.

CourseArc allows you to embed videos from YouTube and Vimeo to enrich your content and provide more learning materials to your learners. It also allows you to add interactive features like drag and drop and inline quizzes for more interactivity.

Built-in analytics are incorporated into the design as well, so that you can monitor performance and track progress. You can have dashboard stats as well as detailed reports on responses and scores from your learners. Another great thing about this tool is that it is not only compliant with industry standards, but also with provisions that support full accessibility for individuals with disabilities for Section 508 compliance.

This tool comes with great support for high quality instruction as well as responsive support services. This means that you will not be left hanging if you have concerns or need clarification on using CourseArc's features.

Other Tools to Consider

In addition to the eLearning Suite and rapid eLearning tools, there are other software programs that do not belong in either of these categories, as they are not authoring tools. However, familiarizing yourself with these programs can be extremely advantageous for creating powerful eLearning content.

Camtasia

Camtasia Studio from TechSmith is a video-based screen capturing software program. The software is installed on the computer, so the screen captures are directly recorded in a digital video format with high quality audio. Camtasia can be customized to capture the entire screen, a specific window, or a user-defined region. Screen capture videos can be recorded with or without voice narration and annotated after recording. With Camtasia, you can create demonstrations, website tours, narrated PowerPoint presentations, and explanations of lecture notes. Camtasia also allows the production of podcasts and vodcasts.

This tool features the Camtasia Recorder for audio video capture and the Camtasia Editor for multimedia authoring. This tool is considered to be a powerful toolset when it comes to video production. You can work with HD production settings and navigate your way through this tool's user-friendly interface.

Some of the most prominent features of Camtasia are the quizzing feature, the Hotspots that learners can "click" for more information, and the Smartfocus for key frames and additional close captions.

SnagIt

SnagIt is another software from TechSmith. This screen-capturing tool allows instructional designers to create highly engaging images, presentation videos, tutorials, and training documents. SnagIt is especially useful for developing technical training.

Raptivity

Raptivity is a tool that lets eLearning designers create a wide range of learning interactions that they can publish as .swf files. These interactions can be used as standalone learning objects or you can insert them into learning programs developed in tools such as Articulate, Lectora, or Captivate. Raptivity provides a pre-built library of more than 225 rapidly customizable interaction models including 3D, games, videos, scenario-based simulations, branching simulations, interactive diagrams, surveys, puzzles, animations, and many more. These interactions are based on the best practices in instructional design. The tool allows instructional designers to select the learning theory they want to use to create their training, such as Bloom's Taxonomy, Gagné's Nine Events, or Keller's ARCS model. Once selected, Raptivity suggests a number of interactions for each step of the learning theory. With this option, even novice instructional designers can create instructionally sound eLearning courses. More experienced ISD specialists do not have to select learning interactions by learning theory and can simply browse by type of interaction instead.

This tool can be used on its own or in tandem with other authoring tools. It features customizable interactions as well as device responsive frames. You can use Raptivity to create interactions in HTML5 and Flash formats, and either add them to your eLearning course or string them together to come up with learning modules. The tool offers multi-language support as well as expert support. Raptivity-created learning materials are SCORM-compliant.

Selecting the Right Tool

Before making a decision about the appropriate development tool, you should take budget, learning curve, and content requirements into consideration. Even though one tool may be perfect for creating simulations, it may not work for software demonstrations. It is suggested that instructional designers add as many eLearning tools to their arsenal as possible and use each one based on the needs and requirements of each course they develop.

The following questions should help you pick the eLearning tools that best suit your needs.

What type of eLearning are you creating: synchronous or asynchronous? Does your course have social learning components such as wikis or forums?

- What type of media will your course have?
- What is the level of interactivity in your course?
- Do you need a specific output file format?
- How much money can you spend on the authoring tool?
- Does your course have to be Section 508-compliant?

When it comes to deciding which eLearning tool to use, you need to take into consideration your eLearning and training objectives, learning curve, as well as your budget.

Additionally, you should always keep your learners in mind and consider their needs as you think about the features to look for in your eLearning tool.

Test Your Knowledge

1. Adobe Captivate, Flash, Dreamweaver and Photoshop are among a collection of software tools for eLearning called the:
   A. Adobe eLearning Suite
   B. Adobe Learning Suite
   C. Adobe Learning Collection
   D. Adobe eLearning Collection

2. What are the three types of rapid eLearning authoring tools(Choose all that apply)?
   A. PowerPoint plugin tools
   B. Desktop authoring tools
   C. Mobile authoring tools
   D. Cloud-based authoring tools

3. Articulate 360, one of the most popular rapid eLearning tools on the market, is an example of a:
   A. PowerPoint plugin tool
   B. desktop authoring tool
   C. mobile authoring tool
   D. cloud-based authoring tool

4. Tools like Lectora and Captivate are examples of _____ which are _____.
   A. desktop authoring tools / the easiest type of rapid eLearning tool
   B. cloud-based authoring tools / flexible, but not as easy to learn
   C. desktop authoring tools / flexible, but not as easy to learn
   D. cloud-based authoring Tools / the easiest type of rapid eLearning tool

5. Some people do not consider Lectora to be a rapid eLearning tool because:
   A. It has a higher learning curve than other tools and produces high quality interactions.
   B. It does not produce eLearning courses but authors excellent video courses.
   C. It does not have nearly the amount of capability of some of the other rapid eLearning tools on the market.
   D. It is incredibly easy to use for a tool that produces such high quality interactions.

6. All of the following statements about cloud-based tools are correct

257

EXCEPT:
- A. Cloud-based tools allow instructional designers with limited technical skills to create great-looking courses and assessments.
- B. Cloud-based tools are hosted over the internet via a secure hosted system and can be accessed anywhere via the internet.
- C. Cloud-based tools allow instructional designers to upload content and organize it into a course.
- D. Cloud-based tools are hosted on a local computer and can only be accessed from that one computer.

7. Camtasia Studio is a tool used for:
- A. Video-based screen capturing
- B. Rapid eLearning development
- C. Audio recording
- D. Photo-based screen capturing

8. It is suggested that instructional designers acquire as many eLearning tools as they can and:
- A. Use only one or two of their favorites.
- B. Use each one based on the needs and the requirements of the course they are developing.
- C. Use every tool for every course they are developing to enhance the interactivity found within each module.
- D. Use only one primary tool as bringing too many tools into active practice can cause technical issues.

Exercise 18

Based on what you know about the timeframe and budget for your project, select the tools that best suit your needs. Explain your decision.

Chapter 20: Video in ELearning

This chapter will cover:

- When to include video in the eLearning course
- Three types of videos in eLearning
- Selecting your talent
- Screencasts in eLearning

Case Study

Petrol Oil Company needed new and improved sexual harassment training. The problem was the material: it was incredibly tricky to teach how nuanced some cases of sexual harassment could be. The legal definitions were easy enough to convey, but teaching learners how to think in terms of broader, and perhaps more subtle forms of sexual harassment was much harder.

Exploring his options, the instructional designer assigned to the project reached a conclusion: instead of teaching abstract facts, he was going to show the learner what some of these knotty situations looked like. Otherwise, the course would be full of dry legalese that might not make any sense to the learners.

Trying out written scenarios and case studies, the instructional designer soon discovered these nuances were too hard to show through text alone. Videos, he thought, could demonstrate realistic scenarios that would illustrate problematic situations to the learners.

It took some time for him to convince his manager that videos were worth the extra cost, but by emphasizing their realism and pointing out that videos tended to be naturally engaging, the instructional designer finally persuaded the supervisor.

The next step was to integrate videos well into the course. The instructional designer did not want the learners to become passive recipients of information—he wanted them to use the videos to understand the material. So, he crafted each video to highlight a specific concept and created a series of activities and assessments that would get the learner to think critically about what they had seen. The course became a highly effective tool to teach a sensitive and controversial subject.

Adding videos to your eLearning courses can either benefit or hinder the learning process. Prior to including a video recording in the course, you should review objectives to see if they lend themselves to video. Just like anything else in the course, videos must have a goal. All videos included in eLearning need a hook. They must be interesting, engaging, and educational at the same time. Commercials only have couple of seconds to get people's attention. They are short and to the point. This is exactly what all eLearning videos should be like. They should include important information and avoid superficial and irrelevant content. Long videos tend to be boring and take a lot of time to load. Instructional designers should always let the learners know that the program is loading; otherwise, learners will get frustrated and exit the course.

There are many types of videos that can be used in eLearning. However, most instructional designers use *short video clips*, *talking heads*, or *scenarios.*

- *Short video clips* – These are video clips from YouTube or any other source that are relevant to the content. Instructional designers should keep in mind that most courses benefit from short videos of no more than five minutes. If the video is longer, breaking it into a number of shorter chunks needs to be considered. This can be done by pausing after each clip to ask questions or presenting opportunities for learners to actively interact with the content instead of passively watch a video.

- *Talking heads* – The main problem with talking heads is that they often appear uninteresting and dull. Therefore, in general, it is recommended to avoid this type of video in eLearning. However, there are certain situations when a talking head video can be beneficial. For instance, your talking head can briefly introduce the course, or serve as a guide and appear for a brief period of time to guide or coach learners, then disappear from the scene and reappear when necessary.

- *Scenarios* – Video scenarios are a perfect way to assess learning. One way to add scenarios to courses is to have learners watch a role-play or a situation that illustrates certain points from the course. Then, ask learners what they would do in this situation, or have them identify what went wrong. Using scenarios to get learners' attention at the beginning of the course and building the entire lesson based on that scenario is also a common practice.

Producing ELearning Videos

To effectively convey learning messages, eLearning videos must be done in a professional way. Hiring a professional videographer can be very expensive, so if money is an issue, you should consider self-producing your video.

The camera is the most important piece of equipment for shooting videos. There are many options to choose from, starting from the webcam built into the laptop to the expensive professional cameras. While the camera selected will mainly depend on your budget, the following questions should be considered:

- What resolution do you need? The options are 480i, 720p, and 1080i. Remember, higher resolution equals higher quality.
- What kind of zoom do you want? The answer to this question depends on your budget. While optical zoom costs more than digital zoom, the video quality with optical zoom will be much better than with digital zoom.

- What kinds of controls do you want? There are manual and automatic controls.
- What battery life are you looking for?
- Do you need a night vision?
- What kind of lighting do you need? There are built-in and external lighting options.

Once the camera and script are ready for the shoot, you can choose actors and assign roles to them. Hiring professional actors is rather expensive, but it will give the most professional results. If the budget for the project is low, using people on your team or other volunteers should be considered. Presenters who are not professional actors may feel uncomfortable being on camera. Leaving plenty of time for rehearsal is the best way to bring their comfort level up. As eLearning professionals guide actors through production, they should pay attention to their tone of voice, facial expressions, speech rate, and gestures as well as their attire and overall appearance. The way of acting and presenting in front of camera should fit the subject matter as well as the target audience for the course. The presentation should not be offensive in any way.

Obviously, it is unrealistic to ask the talent to memorize the script. This is where a teleprompter comes handy. The teleprompter is a device that displays the script to allow presenters concentrate on their delivery rather than the material they present. Reading from a teleprompter, however, requires practice. The goal is to sound as natural as possible. Learners should not notice that the presenter is reading. Rehearsals and practice should help actors achieve the most natural result.

When it comes to video development, file size becomes a major issue. This is especially true if the video is high quality. To keep file sizes under control, instructional designers should consider splitting them into smaller segments and compressing as much as possible. Uploading a video on YouTube and taking it down will automatically compress it.

Even if you are fully satisfied with the video and believe it fits the lesson well, it is still a good idea to receive client's approval before implementing it into the course.

Some studies claim the adult attention span has become shorter than that of a goldfish, which is only about eight seconds long. Whether or not this measurement is accurate, the message is that the ability to stay actively focused on anything is a challenge for most learners. If you add typical distractions of daily life, such as emails dinging, chat windows popping up, and colleagues stopping by to chat, your training is up against some serious competition!

Video-based learning has the potential to make your training products memorable and engaging. However, in order to reap the benefits of this type of learning, videos must be short and interactive.

So, what are some things that you can do to make your training videos captivating?

First, you should combat the learner's short attention span by "chunking" videos into small pieces, rather than putting multiple topics into one long segment. Asking your learner to watch a video for two minutes is much more doable than having the learners invest more than ten minutes of their time. Putting each learning objective into a discrete video segment allows the learner to take a break without missing any of the content.

Video-based learning demands high quality—anything that is not polished will distract the learner. When recording professional actors, videographers must ensure that the person is well-lit, the sound quality is high, and the environment is free of any background distractions. Choosing the right talent is also important to making your video appear polished. Even someone who is typically animated and outgoing may shrink up in front of the camera. Give your actor time to acclimate to the setting, practice, and watch back the performance to liven up their delivery of the material.

As you create your instructional videos, be sure to add elements of interactivity. For example, you may have the learner watch a clip, and then answer a question or complete a simulation based on the video segment. Simulations are especially useful if the video features a process or is very technical in nature. Going into the system and applying the skill they just watched in the video will help learners internalize the content and, as a result, transfer that new skill to the job.

In post-production of a video, be aware of how you arrange the screen's "real estate." A white background with limited text and graphics will keep the learner focused. Overpopulating your screen with animations and text is distracting to the learner. Consider the way text is presented on screen versus how it is spoken in your voiceover narration. If the text does not sync with what is being said, the learner's mind is pulled in too many directions to focus on the point.

Lastly, take time to do your research and plan your video shoot. Watch videos on YouTube to determine the most appropriate style for your specific content. For example, while "talking heads" or "motion graphics" may work just fine for some types of content, other videos may benefit from role plays, avatars, and on-screen interactions. Regardless of the type of video you will be creating, always survey the setting you will produce your video in, and do a test shot to ensure it is not too noisy or dark. Then, storyboard in detail all actions, and how you want to integrate text and animations on the screen.

Remember, while video-based learning is much more effective than the click-through courses, producing truly valuable video requires much more planning than developing click-and-read eLearning materials; therefore, instructional designers should consider building extra time during the design and development phases to ensure accuracy, relevancy, and quality of the training experience.

A study investigating the effectiveness of two teaching approaches, illustrated text-based versus video-based, concluded the following: "Video-based eLearning is superior to illustrated text-based eLearning when teaching certain practical skills."

The explosive popularity of Massive Open Online Courses (MOOCs) has further stressed one key fact: If instructional designers want to engage learners in a way that produces a high percentage of content absorption, then video-based eLearning is the way to do it, especially when teaching practical, hands-on courses.

Here are some best practices that eLearning content creators should follow when producing video-based course materials.

1. Movement over Static – The psychology of learners is such that if they are left staring at static images for too long, their attention tends to "drift," especially if the presenter is not engaging enough. If video courses are based on highly static content—such as flow charts, maps, or symbols—then some level of interactivity should be added to spice things up! For example, instructional designers may add quiz questions or gamification elements after each video segment.

It is suggested that rather than converting boring static PowerPoint slides or stock photos into videos, course designers should consider creating graphics with movement, or videos of the instructor drawing the sketch on a digital screen – like Khan-style video courses.

2. Keep It Short – Empirical studies suggest that shorter length videos are more likely to be watched in their entirety, allowing learners to digest a particular thought, idea, or concept in a single sitting. These same studies also show that learners who sit through lengthier learning video sessions are more likely to do poorly on post-video quizzes and tests. Research on video-based learning indicates that the ideal length of a video clip is no longer than six minutes. Anything longer than that will lead to learners' disengagement.

3. Use Mixed Media – Many practical eLearning courses (Engineering, IT, Clinical Studies) are based on massive doses of slides, diagrams, and tables. If a video continually presents this content to the audience, learners' motivation will immediately drop. According to research, if the presentation is slide-heavy, it is best to intersperse slide-based videos with a "talking head" of an avatar or presenter.

4. Go Informal – Many videos are filmed inside professional studios or in drab classroom settings. Research suggests that such videos are not only more costly to make, but often bore learners into disengagement. Consider filming in an informal setting. For instance, a real manager's office may be a perfect place to film a course on performance improvement. It is great to produce shock-giving videos to get learners' attention. However, keeping learners engaged for a longer time is another challenge. Using highly enthusiastic presenters in eLearning videos will "transfer" some of the speakers' energy to the learners.

Screencasts in ELearning

Screencasts are the recordings of a computer screen converted into a movie. Even though screencasting is a relatively new addition to eLearning, it is becoming increasingly popular for the development of software and information technology-related training courses. Training that includes demonstrations of the use of online tools such as websites or catalogues can also benefit from screencasts.

When it comes to designing screencasts, you should treat them as videos. There are both free and paid tools for creating screencasts. *Camtasia Studio* and *Adobe Captivate* are the most popular commercial tools for recording screens. *Screenr* and *Jing* are among the most commonly used, free, screencasting tools that have similar features to Camtasia and Captivate. The drawback to most free tools is that later editing of recordings is not possible; therefore, every time you make a mistake, you will have to go back to the beginning and rerecord the entire presentation. Commercial tools, on the other hand, allow for editing out any mistakes made during recording. In addition, both Camtasia and Captivate are desktop tools, meaning the screencasts can be saved to the desktop as opposed to having to publish them online as is the case with free, non-commercial tools.

Because screencasts are typically used for tutorials that teach how to use tools or programs, it is especially important that they cover all the steps. Oftentimes, Subject Matter Experts (SMEs) are so familiar with the topic and have used the tool so many times they omit small steps important for learners seeing the program or tool for the first time. Therefore, after receiving the script for a screencast from an SME, you should ask for access to the tool they are doing the screencast on, and walk through the steps. As you review the script, note any inconsistencies or missing steps, and discuss them during the meeting with your SME. If the SME refuses to provide access to the tool or if there are privacy concerns, schedule a time to follow the navigational process in the SME's presence. Before recording the final version, you should walk through the steps in the script as many times as possible. This will help you catch problems early in the process, before editing and embedding the screencast into your eLearning course.

Also, prior to recording the screencast, it is necessary to ensure the desktop that will be recorded is clean and all documents, websites, and other windows are closed. Once the screencast has been recorded, video editors should go in and remove dead space and Personally Identifiable Information (PII) such as names, addresses, and social security numbers. In addition, they can add voiceovers and transitions, as well as highlight and zoom-in features.

When recording voiceovers for screencasts, there are several things to keep in mind. First, even though it is possible to record audio using screencasting tools, the quality of the voiceover will not be the best. Therefore, if the project's budget allows for the use of professional audio recording services, use them. Otherwise, self-recording audio with a good quality microphone, editing it, and then importing into the screencast should be considered.

When recording audio for screencasts, the talent should read as slowly as possible. If the narrator's pace is fast, it will be hard to match the voiceovers with screen recordings. In addition, fast-paced narration makes it difficult for learners to follow the screencasts. In the next chapter, we will cover audio and voiceover recording in detail.

Test Your Knowledge

1. Videos which are _____ should be _____.
   - A. shot using a webcam / less than five minutes in length due to poor quality
   - B. intended for us in an eLearning course / as long as possible to include every detail
   - C. five minutes in length or longer / broken into shorter chunks
   - D. shorter than five minutes in length / combined to ensure continuity

2. Talking Head videos should generally be avoided EXCEPT:
   - A. For a brief course intro or coaching.
   - B. For a lecture-based course.
   - C. For a software tour or simulation.
   - D. For assessment feedback.

3. Using videos for scenarios or role plays within a course:
   - A. Tends to be a distraction from the core learning objectives.
   - B. Is a great way to replace expensive interactive elements.
   - C. Tends to give away the answers to assessment questions.
   - D. Is a great way to illustrate certain points and elicit feedback.

4. Camera selection is critical to:
   - A. Your decision on which videographer to hire.
   - B. Your decision on how many videos to produce for your course.
   - C. Ensuring that your self-produced videos are of good quality.
   - D. Ensuring that your video and audio sync flawlessly together.

5. When researching a camera's zoom features, remember that while it costs more, _____ results in better video quality than _____.
   - A. optical zoom / digital zoom
   - B. digital zoom / optical zoom
   - C. analog zoom / digital zoom
   - D. digital zoom / analog zoom

6. Using a teleprompter requires:
   A. Practice, as it can be hard to sound natural while reading the script.
   B. Very expensive optical equipment so that your talent can clearly read the script.
   C. The use of specialized tools to properly sync the audio and video together.
   D. The re-write of the script so that it fits within the teleprompter's screen.

7. When guiding actors through production, pay attention to all of these factors EXCEPT:
   A. Tone of voice and speech rate
   B. Facial expressions
   C. Geographic location
   D. Attire and appearance

8. Screencasts are great for:
   A. Learners to submit proof that they have finished the course.
   B. Providing your learners with a "talking head" within a course.
   C. Accessibility as it allows people with visual disabilities to hear what is on the screen.
   D. Demonstrating how to use online tools, software, or websites.

9. Prior to recording screencasts, it is best practice to do all of the following EXCEPT:
   A. Review the screencast steps with your SME.
   B. Gain access to the tool which needs to be recorded.
   C. Ensure that the desktop to be recorded is clean and all windows are closed.
   D. Leave personally identifying information in place as it can be edited out later.

Exercise 19

Based on the topic of your course, do you think it will be beneficial to include videos and screencasts? If so, are you going to record your own video or hire a professional? Explain your reasoning.

Chapter 21: Audio in ELearning

This chapter will cover:

- Role of audio in eLearning
- Recording audio narration
- Quality of audio
- Equipment needed for audio recording
- Voice-over narration

Marina Arshavskiy

Audio is a critical element in the eLearning course. The quality of audio narration should be clear, easy to understand, and free of any ambient noise that distracts from the learning process. Professional recording studios have walls that absorb all the noise. Therefore, the quality of the recording done in a studio with an audio engineer is much higher than a self-recorded audio. However, professional recordings are very expensive. If the budget for your project is low or if the course is intended for a small audience, it may not be practical to record a professional quality audio narration. Currently, most rapid eLearning tools allow to record and edit audio quickly and easily without the need for more expensive editing tools. While the quality of such recordings will be nowhere near professional, it will be decent enough for most eLearning courses.

Audio is a powerful way to convey information and subtext at the same time. In fact, a speaker's voice can provide memorable cues that help learners retain and retrieve the information later. Other benefits of audio-enhanced lessons include:

- **Context through Vocal Inflection** – Even brilliantly written and artfully designed text and graphics may not be able to convey the essence of a concept or theory the same way spoken words can. For example, if you have ever read a transcript and then watched that same interview, you know how little context from body language and vocal inflection makes it onto the page. By differing your tone and varying your speech pattern, you can provide additional context to the subject matter through vocal inflection—something that even the most effective slide decks cannot accomplish!

- **Critical Thinking** – Text can be authoritative by nature, while listening to a speaker encourages learners to process not just the content (what's being said) but also the context (how it's being said, and what it implies).

- **Learner's Emotions** – Listeners are more apt to connect with a voice—especially if it is clear, articulate, and convincing—than they are to form an emotional response to reading text. As mentioned, these emotions can also be a critical component of recall and retention.

- **Accessibility** – Learners who are visually-impaired or who have special needs can often access audio lessons much more easily than text. However, be sure to also include a text transcript of your audio assets so learners with reduced hearing can read any information they might not be able to hear easily.

Finally, some content is naturally better-suited for audio learning than it is for text-based teaching methods. For instance, training on language skills, interpersonal communication, and other subjects where vocabulary, pronunciation, and the nuances of language play a key role are best accomplished via audio-based or audio-enhanced lessons.

Investing in a good quality microphone is necessary for obtaining optimum quality of audio. When recording narration for eLearning courses, it is best to use a *unidirectional microphone* because it does not pick up distractions from other directions, only recording the sounds coming from the narrator. If the lesson includes a scenario where voices and sounds come from various directions, the *omnidirectional microphone* is recommended. Regardless of the quality of a microphone, it is always wise to start the recording session with a sound check. Usually microphones pick up all kinds of noise; therefore, narrators should avoid turning pages as they are reading. The best way to do this is to break the script in a way that does not require the narrator to turn pages in the middle of a paragraph. Advising talent to pause before turning the page is another common practice that allows instructional designers or media specialists to easily edit out the noise.

Recording audio in-house is often associated with ambient noise, which adds distraction to the learning experience. The environment where voiceovers are recorded should be as quiet as possible. This can partially be accomplished by unplugging all machines and putting a Do Not Disturb sign on your door. Moreover, using a small room or a sound booth can eliminate a lot of the noise.

Incorporating audio into the eLearning course is a science in itself. The most popular type of audio used in eLearning courses is known as **voiceover narration**. This type of narration is typically added to slides, interactions, or quizzes. Just like with any other media in the course, the length of the audio should be as short as possible. Otherwise, learners will not be able to maintain their concentration. It is best to describe each scene in less than 60 seconds, and whenever possible, keep the descriptions under 20 seconds in length.

Many instructional designers avoid adding audio to their courses because they are concerned that learners will not be able to read the text on the screen and listen to the narration at the same time. Not only are their concerns valid, they also have scientific proof behind them. Even though providing the same information in different modes may seem appealing as it addresses multiple learning styles, according to Ruth Clark, learning is actually suppressed when screens are explained by combining narration and text.

So, how can you accommodate visual learners without displaying text on the screen? First, unless it is a podcast, the screen should have some graphics on it. To add text, ISD specialists can simply summarize narration or add only key words to each screen. If the client wants to have both on-screen text and audio, the request can be accommodated by giving an option to turn the audio off. Offering the opportunity to take the course without audio is a good instructional practice in any situation as it allows learners to take the course in public places without disturbing other people.

Test Your Knowledge

1. When recording audio narration, it is best to use a _____ microphone because it does not add distractions from other directions.
   - A. omnidirectional
   - B. unidirectional
   - C. bidirectional
   - D. polar

2. It is always wise to start a recording session with:
   - A. A sound check
   - B. A throw-away take
   - C. A pot of coffee
   - D. A new microphone

3. The environment where voiceovers are recorded should always be:
   - A. A space with ambient sounds
   - B. A recording studio
   - C. As loud as possible
   - D. As quiet as possible

4. Offering your learner the opportunity to take a course without audio:
   - A. Will negatively impact the learner's ability to retain information.
   - B. Has negative effects, especially for visual learners.
   - C. Is a good instructional practice in any situation.
   - D. Can be a great way to check if your course meets accessibility standards.

Exercise 20

Now think about the audio for your course. Will you include voiceovers? If so, are you going to record your own narration or hire a professional narrator? Explain your decision.

Chapter 22: Graphics in ELearning

This chapter will cover:

- Benefits of adding graphics to eLearning courses
- Types of visuals
- Seven types of graphics for eLearning
- Ruth Clark's visual design model

Case Study

The training team at Paean Insurance Company did not know what was wrong. Their HIPAA training was not getting good results, and they had worked hard to create a course that was as engaging as possible, featuring plenty of animations, video and graphics. The visuals were sleek and modern, the course was fully narrated, and there were plenty of interactive activities—yet the learners were not performing well on tests, and the evaluations feedback had many comments saying they felt underprepared.

Bringing in a consultant to evaluate the course, the training team was shocked to learn that the graphics needed to be redone. "But graphics lead to better learning transfer," the team lead told the consultant when she heard the news.

The consultant shook his head. "They do, but only when they're presented in an effective way. Right now, you've got too many irrelevant graphics."

He explained that when selecting graphics for a course, the graphics must be relevant to the content. If the graphics are tangential in any way, they will serve as a distraction. He pointed out a slide where the text was covering HIPAA terminology, and the image was a generic picture of two people in the office.

"Chances are, your learners are overwhelmed, and confused" he said.

With the consultant's help, the team streamlined the course down to the graphics that truly contributed to the course content.

The main job of an instructional designer is to design instructionally sound courses. In most cases, ISD specialists are not expected to also be professional graphic artists. However, to make your lessons more visually appealing to learners, you should be aware of basic graphic design principles.

Without a doubt, graphics play a significant role in designing eLearning courses. Visually appealing courses draw learners' attention. No one wants to take training where they have to read page after page of text. Additionally, visual learners find graphics beneficial for understanding, analyzing, and processing information. However, simply adding images to your eLearning will not enhance it in any way. It is important that the graphic used in the course is relevant and appropriate to the topic.

There are different types of visuals that can be included such as: clip art, photographs, cartoons, animations, and 3D images. Consistency plays an important role when it comes to selecting visuals. For example, using cartoonish drawings when most other photos are realistic should be avoided. Otherwise, the overall course design will appear inconsistent.

According to Ruth Clark and Chopeta Lyons, there are seven types of graphics for eLearning:

Decorative graphics – Even though this type of graphic looks appealing, it does not add any instructional value. Instructional designers use these graphics on book and course covers. Overall, decorative visuals should be avoided as much as possible.

Mnemonic graphics – This type of graphic is used to represent factual information. You can use mnemonic graphics to help learners retrieve facts from memory by looking at images that represent these facts.

Representational graphics – This type of graphic is used to represent on-screen text. In other words, learners should be able to understand what the text is about just by looking at the graphics. You can use representational graphics to convey information to the learner.

Organizational graphics – This type of graphic is used to help learners organize the information provided in the eLearning course. Charts and graphs are the best examples of organizational graphics. You can use organizational graphics for comparing and contrasting information as well as for helping learners organize the knowledge they already have and the knowledge they are obtaining from the course.

Relational graphics – This type of graphic is used to show the quantitative relationship of variables. Two examples of relational graphics are pie charts and line graphs. You can use relational graphics when you want learners to see the relationship between the numbers presented in the content.

Transformational graphics – This type of graphic is used to show changes over time. Examples of transformational graphics include timelines and before and after images. You can use transformational graphics when you want to show how the objects are affected by a process.

Interpretative graphics – This type of graphic is used to illustrate abstract theories or principles. Examples of interpretative graphics are diagrams and animations. You can use interpretative graphics as simulations with series of animated images to show how something works.

Once the decision for the type of graphic is made, the next step is to choose the appropriate size and format. Even though high-resolution visuals look nice and crisp, they take a considerable amount of space. Furthermore, high-resolution graphics may take a long time to load, causing frustration for learners. By scaling small images up, graphics will appear pixilated. The best approach to resizing images is to start with the highest possible resolution and squeeze the graphic down as much as possible.

You now know that graphics can make our eLearning courses fun and engaging and, at the same time, relevant to the content. Designing effective graphic that really works is time and resource consuming, so let's take a look at some ways you can create effective eLearning graphics.

1. Crop existing stock photos – Using existing stock images can be a real time saver, but most of the stock images are simply boring. Furthermore, a lot of these images have been used and reused so many times that most of us are so tired of looking at them that we often ignore them to the point where these images become meaningless in the course. Luckily, there is a quick and easy fix for that. Consider cropping photos, so that you only leave the details that are truly pertinent to your message.

2. Recolor existing graphics – In addition to cropping photos, you may consider recoloring them. You do not have to recolor the entire photo, but may choose to change shades of certain colors or match the color scheme of your lesson. You can recolor any piece of graphic you created previously and want to reuse.

3. Change background of existing graphics – When you change the background of already existing graphic, it becomes a brand new graphic. You can completely remove it, match it to the existing color scheme of your lesson, or apply a new background that you think matches the point you are trying to make. For example, if you have an image of two people sitting at the desk in a classroom setting, but your course is geared toward business professionals, you may consider making the background of an image transparent, and applying the "business background" over top. You may also consider cropping the image so that the background (in our example, classroom) is removed, and pasting the people from the image on the "business background" that matches your content.

As you can see, you do not need to be a professional graphic designer to create new and stunning graphics for your eLearning courses, nor do you need to spend a fortune on your graphic design needs.

Ruth Clark and Chopeta Lyons' Visual Design Model

Ruth Clark, together with Chopeta Lyons, developed a Visual Design model. The aim of this model is to help instructional designers without graphic experience envision the appropriate art for their courses. The model consists of five phases and focuses mainly on planning graphics, not on the design and development of visuals. The five phases of the Visual Design Model are to:

- *Define Goals*
- *Define Context*
- *Design Visual Approach*
- *Identify Communication Function Needed to Match Content Types*
- *Apply Principles of Psychological Instructional Events*

Define Goals Phase – During this phase, you should define the instructional goal for a given project. Which graphics you choose for the course will depend on your goal. According to Ruth Clark, there are three possible instructional goals. They are to:

- inform or motivate learners;
- build procedural skills and teach content associated with these skills; and
- build problem-solving skills and teach content associated with these skills.

Define Context Phase – In this phase, you are responsible for identifying the target audience, delivery methods, the learning environment, and constraints. If learners are visually impaired or color blind, the message the graphic is trying to convey will be lost. Additionally, external factors such as poor lighting, low bandwidth, and a small budget can restrict the graphic design.

Design Visual Approach Phase – During this phase, you are responsible for assessing general requirements such as real estate, page orientation, and the colors of each graphic that will be included in the course.

Identify Communication Function Needed to Match Content Types Phase – In this phase, you identify graphics that will illustrate key instructional points. For example, if there are multiple types of content in the course, organizational visuals should be used. If your aim is to teach procedures, concepts, or facts, representational graphics should be considered. Transformational graphics, on the other hand, should help you teach processes and principles.

Apply Principles of Psychological Instructional Events – The final phase in planning graphics for your eLearning course. In this phase, you should review the graphics to ensure they meet the key instructional events, including gaining learners' attention, activating learners' prior knowledge, minimizing cognitive load, and maximizing learning transfer as well as building new mental models and supporting motivation.

Basics of Color Theory and Typography

The way your eLearning materials look and feel have an impact on their effectiveness. The combination of colors, font types, and images effect the way your learners go through your content and eventually the lessons. Your goal is to make your content more exciting, easier to understand, and more interesting to read.

A good combination of these elements helps you achieve your training goals. Conversely, a bad combination could make learners bored and disinterested. Needless to say, this results in bad performance and ineffective learning.

Using colors appropriately is a science in itself. If the colors in the course do not appeal emotionally to learners, their interest will immediately drop. When selecting graphics, it is important to consider the overall look and feel of the course. The color, quality, and shapes of the graphics should be very similar to the shell of the course. Otherwise, they will look out of place and distract learners. Understanding the basics of color theory can help you create better graphics. The color wheel organizes the *primary, secondary*, and *tertiary* colors. The primary colors are red, blue, and yellow. From these colors, secondary colors originate. They are green, orange, and purple. Finally, by mixing both primary and secondary colors, tertiary colors emerge. In addition to primary, secondary, and tertiary colors, the color wheel consists of different shades, including dark and light values.

When creating an eLearning course, moods that different colors convey should be considered. It is generally recommended to use passive colors such as blues and greens for the background. If certain information in your course needs to be emphasized, using yellow, red, or even purple is advisable. These are active colors and help learners pay closer attention to details.

Contrast also plays an important role in the look and feel of the course. When deciding on the color of the background and font, it is necessary to establish good contrast between the two. For example, learners should have no problem reading black text on a white background. However, if yellow font appears on the white background, the text will most likely be illegible.

The font used in the eLearning course has direct impact on how learners react to your training. Therefore, having a basic understanding of typography is essential for evoking positive emotions about the course. While creating contrast is important, too much contrast can be distracting to learners. Type is broken into the following categories:

- *Serif fonts* – Have a small line attached to the end of a stroke in a letter. Serif fonts include Times New Roman and Courier.
- *Sans-serif fonts* – Do not have serifs and are typically associated with a more modern look. Popular sans-serif fonts are Arial and Helvetica.
- *Script fonts* – Resemble handwritten letters. Some examples are Script MT Bold and Kunstler Script.

When choosing fonts for eLearning courses, it is best to stay within the same family and limit the course to three fonts.

Here are some important considerations when using color theory, typography, and images in your eLearning course design:

1. Keep it clean and simple – This does not mean that your design should be stark and boring. You can use bold colors like reds and oranges, avoid the clutter and pay attention to readability and ease of navigation.

Use color combinations that complement each other so that they are easy on the eyes. You can also use color to highlight certain types of information in your content. For instance, you can have chapter snippets or takeaways in bullet points in a reverse block using the darkest shade of either the main background color or a complementary color.

You would most likely have a lot of text in your learning materials. Use fonts that are easy to read and understand. San serif fonts in 14-point or 16-point are usually the preferred typeface for eLearning materials. Keep your columns at about 70 characters in width as this allows for ease of reading.

2. Use the right images – You do not need to bombard your learners with images all the time. The images are supposed to reinforce and support your content. As such, you have to limit your images to only those that are relevant to your content and are helpful to your learners.

Pay attention to the subject, colors, size, and placement of your images. They should not distract your learners from your content. Be consistent in the kind of images that you include in your eLearning design.

It is not only the physical size of your images that you have to consider. You also have to think about the file size as it may have an impact on the way your pages load. Among the most common file types that are used in eLearning modules are: jpg (Joint Photographers' Expert Group), .png (Portable Network Graphics), .bmp (Bitmap), .tiff (Tagged Image File Format), and .gif (Graphics Interchange Format).

- **JPG** – Images that can be saved in small files without affecting their quality. They retain their crisps and sharp quality and color range. With this image file type, you can have high quality images on your pages while keeping your file size within reasonable levels.

- **PNG** – Images of this file type are small in size, but are of high quality nonetheless. Use png images if you need to apply transparency to your design, such as when you need to "die-cut" an image to be superimposed over another image.

- **BMP** – This image file type is a rasterized file format which means that it is made up of pixels. Since bmp images cannot be compressed, you will end up with larger file sizes when using them.

- **TIFF** – This image file type is similar to both the png and bmp. This is also a lossless file type, so it can be compressed and uncompressed without sacrificing image quality.

- **GIF** – These images are usually the preferred format for animations. The downside to these images, however, is that they are of low resolution, and are only in 256-color formats. GIF files are normally used for charts and graphs.

3. Check for compatibility and interoperability – Your design should be versatile enough to appear as you intended across browsers and device types. Learners should see the same elements in the same quality regardless if they are using a laptop, a tablet, or a desktop computer.

There are online templates for module designs that you can use across devices. Many LMS vendors and SCORM compliance software suite suppliers often throw in these templates for their clients. While using these templates is helpful, you have to remember that you still have to put in the work to customize these templates to fit your training goals.

Eye appeal when it comes to eLearning modules is not all about the frills and embellishments. It is about combining colors, fonts, and images in a way that enhances learning. Your content should be visually arranged so that the various elements seamlessly lead your learners through the sections of your eLearning module.

It is also important for you to listen to what your learners are saying about your course design. Monitor how they are going through your site and take note of any hurdles that could be preventing them from moving at your expected pace.

Lastly, do not be afraid to make changes along the way. This, however, does not mean that you can make sudden and drastic changes. Proper planning from the initial stages of eLearning design is important so that you only have to make slight tweaks and adjustments after your eLearning modules go live.

Graphics included in your eLearning course should be 508-compliant. There are several ways to ensure that visuals meet the accessibility requirements. First, whenever possible, they should be described with alternative text. The goal of alternative text is to convey the same information as the image. Visually impaired learners use screen readers to receive the same information as learners without disabilities. Not all graphics can be described with alternative text, however. For instance, alternative text cannot be added to charts and graphs. Therefore, providing a text version of the information included in these visuals should be considered to address Section 508 requirements.

Test Your Knowledge

1. Visually appealing courses can help the effectiveness of an eLearning module in the following ways: (Choose all that apply).
   A. They help draw a learner's attention.
   B. They can give learners the impression that a lot of money was spent on creating the course.
   C. They benefit the understanding, analyzing and processing of information.
   D. They can distract learners from external stimulus.

2. Using a mix of realistic and cartoonish images:
   A. Is considered a best practice as it creates a sense of momentum for the learner.
   B. Can be a very effective means of keeping the learner entertained during training.
   C. Should be avoided as the course design will come across as inconsistent.
   D. Has the effect of occupying a learner's subconscious mind so that they can concentrate on learning.

3. Decorative graphics _____ because they _____.
   A. are very useful / help add polish to an eLearning course
   B. should be avoided / do not add any instructional value
   C. can be distracting / are so beautiful
   D. should be a part of every slide / can serve as "containers" for content

4. Examples of organizational graphics include:
   A. Flow charts
   B. Boxes and lines
   C. Charts and graphs
   D. Stock photos

5. Relational graphics show:
   A. The quantitative relationship of variables.
   B. The relationship between the learner and the information being presented.
   C. The difference between right and wrong assessment question answers.
   D. The relationship of data to text.

6. A timeline showing the gradual changes of something is an example of a:
    A. Transformational graphic
    B. Timeline graphic
    C. Transitional graphic
    D. Sequential graphic

7. The best practice for balancing file size with high quality images is to:
    A. Start with the highest resolution image possible and squeeze its file size down as much as possible.
    B. Start with the smallest size image possible and scale it up to fit the area where the photo is to be placed.
    C. Add the highest resolution images possible and hope the customer's bandwidth can handle the large file size.
    D. Add a "loading" graphic to each slide containing large images.

8. Of the following image file types, all are commonly used in eLearning courses EXCEPT:
    A. PNG
    B. JPG
    C. DOC
    D. GiF

9. If there is a need for transparent images, which image file type should be used?
    A. PNG
    B. JPG
    C. DOC
    D. GiF

10. If small file size is the biggest design criteria for images, which file type should be used?
    A. PNG
    B. JPG
    C. DOC
    D. GiF

11. "Alternative text" should be included so that _____ and should
_____.
    A. graphs and tables can be easily analyzed / be grammatically correct
    B. course images are 508 Compliant / convey the same information as the image
    C. courses can be completed using an eReader / be very specific and descriptive
    D. course images can be scaled down in size / provide additional context to the image

12. The five phases of the Visual Design Model:
    A. Focus on planning graphics, not on their design and development.
    B. Are especially helpful for experienced graphic artists.
    C. Focus on designing and developing graphics, not on planning them.
    D. Are designed to assist in the implementation of graphics into an eLearning module.

13. This phase of the Visual Design Model identifies the target audience, delivery methods, learning environments and constraints for graphics in an eLearning course:
    A. Define goals
    B. Define context
    C. Design visual approach
    D. Identify communication function needed to match content types
    E. Apply principles of psychological instructional events

14. The color wheel helps you to understand and utilize _____, and is made up of _____, secondary and tertiary colors.
    A. color theory / singular
    B. design theory / primary
    C. design theory / singular
    D. color theory / primary

Exercise 21

Think again about the "look and feel" of your course.
What will be the color scheme? Which fonts will you
use? What type of visuals are you going to include? What
is the purpose of your visuals?

Part IV - Advancing Your Skills

"You can't teach people everything they need to know. The best you can do is position them where they can find what they need to know when they need to know it."
Seymour Papert

Chapter 23: Working with Subject Matter Experts (SMEs)

This chapter will cover:

- Roles and responsibilities of Subject Matter Experts (SMEs) in course design
- Process for selecting information for the course
- Repurposing classroom materials
- Communication with the SMEs
- Collecting content from the SMEs

Case Study

The huge scope of the military simulation project that Advanced Media, Inc. was working on meant that there was near constant contact with the SMEs. Because military and government standards were so specific, everything from the look of the course to delivery methods needed their input, and the content, especially, was proving tricky. As the project was progressing onto the prototyping stages, the instructional designer was finding that the review process was slowing down. The SMEs did not quite understand what the instructional designers needed, and the instructional designers did not have their knowledge base of military protocol.

"Why don't we include them in the process more?" the instructional designer said to his team lead one day. "Right now, they're mostly doing review, but they would be an invaluable help when it comes to content development and production."

"It might be worth a shot," the lead said.

The instructional designer made a case to the SMEs for greater involvement, and, seeing the need for better communication themselves, the SMEs agreed. The instructional designer made a point of not just soliciting feedback, but also using SMEs in the content development process and even had them furnish content themselves, which he then made instructionally sound. Showing them the QA review process, he used SMEs as an extra set of eyes for quality control. Finally, when it came to script supervision for videos, he had an SME remain on set to ensure that everything looked realistic. By leveraging SMEs in the process, the instructional designer made the course better and the process more efficient.

Subject Matter Experts, or SMEs, are individuals who have knowledge about a specific area or topic. All people are Subject Matter Experts in one area or another. A teenager, for instance, can be an SME in social networking while a housewife can be an SME in raising children. SMEs play a vital role in course design and serve as knowledge sharers in the training world. Often, the success of the course depends on SMEs. To develop a good relationship with SMEs, you should understand their role in the design process. Since you will be working hand-in-hand with SMEs, developing a successful relationship is critical. SMEs will not only provide the content for the course but will also review the design documents and scripts as well as test media and assessments for accuracy.

Before you even begin gathering content from SMEs, you need to ensure that the SME is truly an expert in his or her field. Since most instructional designers are not familiar with the subject area for the eLearning course they are creating, the client is typically responsible for selecting the SMEs. During the project-planning phase, project managers will provide a description of what is expected from the SME in terms of expertise and experience. The project manager should describe in detail the SME's responsibilities, including expected meetings and document reviews. In the project plan, the project manager should document the risks associated with having an SME that does not meet the described requirements. This way, everything is documented on paper, and the client will take full responsibility for the quality of course content, missed deadlines, or any other consequences associated with the SME's poor performance.

Subject Matter Experts should be aware of all the expectations. All responsibilities should be clearly defined prior to the initial meeting. The role of an instructional designer is to design courses while the role of an SME is to provide expertise in a subject area. SMEs should not be expected to arrange content in order. Often, SMEs provide either too much or too little content, and it is your job, as an instructional designer, to include the right amount of material in the course. Some SMEs are so knowledgeable that they want to share everything they know, thinking that every piece of information is indispensable. To ensure that SMEs only provide relevant information, you should follow the two steps below:

1. Ensure the content provided by the SME meets the intended objectives.
2. If it does not, go back to the SME and ask relevant questions to get all the information needed to satisfy learning objectives.

If the content covers all the objectives, break the information into the following three categories: *must know*, *need-to-know*, and *nice-to know*. The must-know information is what the learner absolutely needs to know to obtain knowledge or learn the skill. The need-to-know information is not as essential as must-know but may clarify certain concepts for learners. The nice-to-know information, on the other hand, is not needed at all. It may be helpful to the learner, but achieving objectives and learning new skills is possible without being exposed to the nice-to-know material.

When working with SMEs, you should always ask for examples of the content. Many SMEs use their knowledge and skills every day. The content is common sense to them; therefore, they may forget to share elements or steps crucial to your learners. You should catch situations where elaboration and examples may be needed and ask SMEs to fill the gaps. If SMEs have a tendency to provide too much content, reminding them that the course is not infinite and that they should only include the most important information from their content should help them identify the must-know material. If SMEs have a difficult time organizing all the content they want to share, a mind map or a graphic organizer will help them consolidate their thoughts.

Use the checklist below to collect content for each learning objective from your SMEs.

- What information do learners need to know to meet the objective?
- What skills do learners need to perform to meet the objective?
- What images can help learners understand the content?
- What activities can help learners understand the content?
- What are some examples or scenarios that illustrate the content?

Oftentimes, SMEs teach the classroom version of the same course; therefore, they already have training materials prepared. While these materials can be adapted to the eLearning lesson, they will have to be modified or even reformatted to meet the requirements of the eLearning environment. Keep in mind that the SME's training materials were created for classroom training where the instructor teaches the course; therefore, they are most likely missing the information needed to understand the content without the instructor's presence. SMEs can help you fill the gaps where necessary. Utilizing already existing materials and repurposing them for eLearning can save a lot of time for both instructional designers and SMEs.

Effective communication plays a crucial role when dealing with SMEs. Just like everyone else, Subject Matter Experts have busy schedules. Sometimes, they are not even part of your team and have many other on-the-job responsibilities. You should ensure the SME's time is not wasted with multiple meetings and meaningless questions. Prior to the meeting with the SME, some preparation work must be done. The goal is to get quality content, not to waste the SME's time by asking rudimentary questions. Researching the topic before the meeting to become acquainted with basic concepts and terminology can help instructional designers achieve that goal.

Meetings with your SMEs will be much more productive if you inform them of the goals and objectives ahead of time. You can also prepare your questions and send them electronically to the SME. Then, if there are additional questions or content that requires clarification, you can schedule a phone call or a live-conference call to address the issues. This approach works well as it allows SMEs to provide answers to questions at their convenience without attending any prescheduled meetings. Letting SMEs know how much their time and dedication to the project are appreciated is also a good practice. You may even consider sending a glowing thank you note to your SMEs' supervisor.

Recording meetings and conversations can be a major time saver. Oftentimes, instructional designers take written notes and then forget what they mean or cannot make sense out of their writing. The recorded version of the meeting will save both you and the SME a lot of time as multiple phone calls and meetings will be avoided. Before recording a meeting, however, always obtain permission.

Because learning theories is instructional designers' second nature, many tend to mention them when talking to their SMEs. However, most of the time, SMEs are not familiar with instructional design theories and terminology. To avoid miscommunication, you should consider explaining terminology in layman words. For example, instead of saying WBT, it is best to say Web-Based Training, and instead of saying using Bloom's Taxonomy to write objectives, say, using measurable action verbs such as develop and complete to write objectives. Because most SMEs are not learning experts, they do not know much about creating instructionally sound courses. Therefore, in many instances, they want to include certain elements in their training that do not work from the instructional design standpoint. Providing reasons why SME's ideas are impractical may overcomplicate things. Instead, instructional designers should show examples of successful eLearning materials and use these examples to explain why the recommended approach works best.

While it is important to value the SME's time and efforts, it is equally important to stay on top of the deadlines. Even though the project may be important to you, it may be last on the SME's list. As an instructional designer, it is your responsibility to have the course ready on time; therefore, frequent reminders and follow up emails to your SMEs may be a necessary step to meet your deadlines.

Project Kickoff Meeting with SMEs – Template

1.   What is your experience with the subject matter?

   _____

   _____

   _____

   _____

   _____.

2.   Who is the target audience and what are their needs?

3.   What topics do you want to cover in the course?

4.   What are the most important things in your message that you want to leave in learners' minds?

5.   How long will the training be?

6.   What is your preferred communication method?

7.   How do you want to receive /provide feedback? (In-person, via track changes, using specific software)

   _____

8.   What is your availability? (Are you able to work on this project full time? If not, how many hours can you dedicate to this project?

9.   What is the deadline for this project?

10.   When are you available to start?

11.   Is there anything that may impact the project or our intended due date?

Test Your Knowledge

1. Which of the following would be considered a likely Subject Matter Expert (SME)?
    A. A pre-teen on investment properties.
    B. A tax advisor on mutual funds.
    C. A young child on college entry exams.
    D. A real estate agent on early childhood education.

2. Subject Matter Experts typically provide _____ information and it is your job to _____.
    A. too much / decide what information will be included
    B. too little / research the missing information
    C. too much / find another SME
    D. too little / find another SME

3. "Must-know" information is:
    A. Information that may clarify certain concepts for learners.
    B. Information that is not needed at all.
    C. Information that the learner absolutely needs to know.
    D. Information that the learner must know before taking this course.

4. A mind map or graphic organizer may help SMEs to:
    A. Provide you with content without needing an interview.
    B. Organize their thoughts.
    C. Decide whether they want to participate in this project.
    D. Do more work for you in advance.

5. SMEs who already have existing training materials:
    A. Save time for instructional designers as additional work has to be done to create the eLearning version of the course.
    B. Can simply be videotaped giving their normal lecture without any modifications necessary.
    C. Should be discredited as they likely have a jaded view of the topics to be covered.
    D. Can help by filling in the gaps when converting it to eLearning.

6. Meetings with SMEs will be much more productive if you:
   A. Inform them of the goals and objectives prior to the meeting.
   B. Do not inform them of the goals and objectives prior to the meeting.
   C. Do not set expectations on their role as to encourage free-form discussions.
   D. Inform them that they must do all of the instructional design work for you.

7. Using terms like Bloom's Taxonomy and WBT will:
   A. Prove your expertise in learning methodologies to the SMEs.
   B. Make for productive conversations as the SMEs you select should have some knowledge of learning theory.
   C. Impress the SMEs and make them trust your judgement on which content should and should not be included.
   D. Not be as productive as most SMEs are not eLearning experts.

Exercise 22

Think about the responsibilities of your SMEs. Will they solely be responsible for providing content, or will they also review the materials? Decide on the methods you will use to collect information from your SMEs. Then, make a list of questions you will ask your SMEs.

Chapter 24: ELearning Project Management

This chapter will cover:

- Role of instructional designer as project manager
- IPECC model for project management
- Project management tools

Case Study

When the previous Project Manager of Petrol Oil Company's HR training course quit the job, the team was quietly relieved. Though a competent Project Manager in many respects, her background was in marketing, not instructional design, and her unfamiliarity with the process had made projects more about meeting deadlines than making a solid working course. In their hunt for a new PM, the company's training team came up with a list of skills for their new project manager.

The first skill was knowledge of learning principles and concepts. The team felt that it was difficult to collaborate with PMs who did not understand their workflow, processes, and goals, or who needed to learn on the spot. If the PM did not know what each member of the team was doing and why, they would not be able to set budgets and milestones effectively.

The second skill was that the PM needed to be a good communicator. Because many clients at Petrol Oil Company were unfamiliar with the instructional design principles and techniques, the PM needed to be able to educate them on the processes the team chose, and explain the reasons why scope of work might need to be changed. Likewise, the PM should be able to talk to the team about client concerns, goals and perspectives. Strong soft skills would be necessary to balance client and team interests.

With these two principles in mind, the training team was able to confidently choose the right manager for the task.

Most instructional designers play many roles and wear multiple hats. Project management is often one of them. The key to successful project management is a well-managed process combined with supporting tools. Skilled project managers apply their knowledge, skills, tools, and techniques to meet project requirements. You should know how to manage eLearning projects to ensure on-time delivery and top quality outcomes. Moreover, effective project management will help you avoid communication problems with other team members and minimize other issues related to poor management.

All projects are unique and temporary in nature. One project may only consist of a few tasks and can be completed in less than a month, while another may have so many activities that project managers will easily lose track of them and take well over a year to complete. Regardless of the scope, all projects have a definite beginning and end. ELearning projects, however, are more difficult to manage than most other projects because they include both training and technology. Every project must plan for risks. Projects must be delivered on time, within cost and scope, and meet customer quality requirements. Because most eLearning projects are more complicated than traditional projects, there is more risk associated with them. Moreover, there are more time constraints as well as budget and communication problems.

The most commonly used model in project management is known as the IPECC model. It is used for all types of projects, not just eLearning ones. IPECC model stands for:

- *Initiating*
- *Planning*
- *Executing*
- *Controlling*
- *Closing*

Initiation Phase

During the *initiation phase*, project managers present their vision, state expectations, define goals and objectives, as well as the scope of the project. To fully understand the requirements and desired outcomes of the project, a business requirements analysis needs to be conducted. The following steps outline the scope of the analysis.

Step 1 – Identify the stakeholders and the target audience.

Step 2 – Gather requirements for the course from both stakeholders and your target audience.

Step 3 – Categorize requirements into the following four categories:

- *Functional Requirements* – Describe the end-user perspective
- *Operational Requirements* – Describe what needs to be done to keep the course functional over a period of time
- *Technical Requirements* – Describe the technical requirements needed to successfully implement the course
- *Transitional Requirements* – Describe the steps needed to be taken for the smooth implementation of the course

Step 4 – Analyze, prioritize, and record requirements.

Step 5 – Ensure that the requirements you collected reflect stakeholders' needs.

During the *initiation phase,* you will develop a project charter. The project charter is a document that serves as a contract between an eLearning project manager and the client. This document is the foundation of any project and should be written in the most comprehensive way possible. The project charter answers all questions associated with the project. The length usually depends on each project's complexity and scope. For example, a project charter intended for a twenty-minute linear course developed using a rapid eLearning tool can be as short as two pages. On the other hand, a project charter for a ten-hour non-linear course that consists of multiple interactions and serious games may take up to twenty pages. Most project charters include the following elements:

- Objectives
- Deliverables
- Success Metrics
- Major Risks
- Budget
- Project Team
- Timeline
- Key meetings
- Activities for the project

Another document created during the *initiation phase* is known as the preliminary project scope. Its purpose is to identify the project's objectives. Some of the elements included in this document are:

- Objectives
- Project requirements
- Boundaries
- Assumptions
- Constraints
- Milestones
- Project costs

Planning Phase

The *planning phase* is probably one of the most important phases in project management because it ensures that the project is delivered on time and within budget and scope. During this phase, project managers refine the scope, assemble their team, and identify specific tasks and activities that need to be completed. After gathering all the required information, they begin writing a project plan. A project plan is a living document. It reflects both changes and new additions. A detailed project plan includes the project charter and preliminary project scope documents. It also includes information about the stakeholders, project team, budget, and resources as well as milestones and deliverables.

Executing Phase

The *executing phase* deals with leading the team, solving problems that occur along the way, and doing all the other work required to deliver the eLearning project. In other words, this is the phase for carrying out the project plan. During the *executing phase*, project managers also ensure that all team members understand what is expected of them and produce quality work on time.

Controlling Phase

During the *controlling phase*, the project manager makes necessary corrections and adjustments to the schedule created earlier based on the problems that occurred in the previous three phases. During this time, the project manager monitors the scope, schedule, budget, and risks for the project.

Closing Phase

The fifth and final phase is known as *closing*. At this point, the project manager delivers the project to the client, ensuring that all deliverables meet the requirements. This is also the time to write an evaluation report documenting all the lessons learned during the project. Many project managers deliver their projects without ever evaluating them. Nonetheless, this step provides an opportunity to reflect on the project and learn from mistakes to avoid them in the future.

As instructional designers and eLearning project managers move through project management phases, they should remember to schedule frequent meetings with their stakeholders and regularly update them on the status of the project. This approach will not only help to build relationships with clients, but it will also catch problems early in the process, avoiding needless rework and saving valuable time for both project managers and their team members.

It is important to realize that the roles of both instructional designer and project manager are equally important for successful eLearning course design. Both have similar but slightly differing goals and objectives. Yet, both have many identical stages in their lifecycles. Bottom line: ID and PM are not necessarily replacements to each other, but rather both roles complement each other.

So, why do eLearning projects fail? Looking at the causes of failure of the most well intended eLearning projects, the top six reasons that eLearning projects fail include:

1. Lack of alignment to the organization's needs
2. Poor communication with stakeholders
3. Improper implementation
4. Inadequate organizational support
5. Insufficient post-implementation support, and

6. Incorrect choice of design and roll-out technology

However, when you delve deeper into the reasons why these causes were instrumental in derailing what looked like an otherwise "perfect" project, two roles appear to have significant responsibility and stand out quite starkly. Those are the roles of

1. The Instructional Designer (ID), and
2. The Project Manager (PM)

Therefore, to avoid failure, it is absolutely essential to understand, compare and contrast both roles.

An Instructional Design (ID) initiative is quiet often looked upon as a "project" or "sub project" within an organization's broader learning strategy. What this means is that, in addition to having all of the traditional elements that come with any ID venture, such as those included in the ADDIE (Analysis, Design, Development, Implementation, Evaluation) model, to be successful, ID initiatives must also include aspects of project management (PM). If you have never given a thought to this aspect of instructional design, you are probably wondering, **"So, do I now need to also hire a project manager for my upcoming ID initiative?"** Well, the answer is "It depends!" PM methodologies, like those espoused by PMBOK (Project Management Body of Knowledge) or PRINCE (Projects In Controlled Environments) often separate what they are developing (an eLearning Course, a Mobile App, a multi-storied building), managing and delivering, from discipline-specific methodologies (like ADDIE or SDLC (System Development Life Cycle)). However, there are many similarities in the roles that an instructional designer and a project manager play. For instance:

- Where an instructional designer might need to consider the needs analysis of the ID initiative, the PM looks at the project's concept.
- As part of ADDIE, the designer will get into learning objectives and outlining the curriculum, while the PM will similarly focus on defining and scoping the project.
- The instructional designer looks at authoring, coding and scripting as part of the Development phase of the course, while a PM will consider this to be part of a Detailed design phase of the project.

A closer look at the similarities between the two disciplines, ID and PM, then leads us to conclude that an instructional designer does, in fact, also wear a (partial!) PM's hat when carrying out his/her role. However, while PMs look at project sponsors, project charters and project budgets as within the purview of their role, the instructional designer has to worry about learning experiences, skills gaps and learning outcomes. While many companies might afford to hire dedicated PMs for ID initiatives, with some training, an instructional designer can very easily fulfill that role.

So, what does an instructional designer need to know about managing eLearning projects? Well, most of their knowledge from discipline-specific methodologies like ADDIE will be leveraged while playing the "eLearning project manager" role. Here is a high-level overview of how ID and PM roles complement each other in the successful design, development and roll out of any eLearning project.

Table 16 – PM vs ID Hats

The PM's Hat	The ID's Hat
Project Definition	• Conceptualize: Learning challenges needed to be addressed • Definition: What features and functionality to offer
Project Planning	Who does what, when?
Project Analysis/Design	Content collection, assessment, review, storyboard, instructional design
Project Management/Execution	• Review/approval of Scripts, GUI, Images Animation • Content development and course production • Courseware authoring • Content quality reviews • Instructor training • Pilot rollout • Content/Design refinement • Staged Rollout
Project Review	Post rollout review and feedback

To truly understand what it takes to be an effective ID project manager, you first need to understand that, as a PM, your role will be somewhat different from an "operational manager." While operational managers add value to the organization by focusing on process improvements and long-term operational efficiency, a PM's objectives are much shorter-term, and only span the life of an ID project. Once the project is completed, the PM's skills are no longer needed (at least not in terms of what the project required when it started). Therefore, to effectively manage an instructional design project the following skills are needed:

1. Instructional design knowledge – Having a good understanding of ID principles is a definite asset when managing an ID project

2. Working with Teams – The PMs role is not about "doing the job," but more about "getting the job done." As such, PMs need to be great team players

3. Leadership – A PM must be able to inspire the team to meet project objectives—timeliness, within budget, of high quality. PMs must also be adept at building consensus amongst the team, as well as between the team and external stakeholders. Most importantly, as part of the Leadership role, a PM is expected to master the art of conflict resolution when dealing with difficult people

4. Soft Skills – PMs do not just work with the team skills they are provided, but they also work to enhance those skills within the team. Listening to people, coaching them to improve performance and mentoring them to aspire to higher goals are all part of the skill set that an effective PM needs

There are three major goals that a project seeks to achieve. They include ensuring that the task is completed **On Time**, **Within Budget**, and delivers **Expected Quality** results. To accomplish that, the project team, and specifically the project manager, should focus on:

1. **Good time management practices** – This means monitoring critical tasks to ensure they are completed within agreed upon timeframes. More importantly, it also means accurately estimating the time required for the job

2. **Good asset management practices** – Whether it is a laptop or a tablet, or a high-definition projection system or specialized eLearning content development software. All project assets must be closely tracked and their usage monitored

3. **Effective communication** – It is estimated that 60% of project "issues" would never have existed had there been effective communication between conflicting parties. As a PM, you must know how to communicate effectively with all project stakeholders, both internally and externally.

4. **Team organization** – How teams are managed, how files are organized for quick and efficient retrieval, and how teams communicate and collaborate internally and externally as workgroups is something that will impact the three goals (Time, Budget, Quality) of the project.

Even though, it may seem like managing eLearning projects is a complex task, in reality, it is not overly complicated or undoable. However, to do it right, PMs must give due consideration to the following:

- Clearly understand the learning challenges within the organization
- Identify all key stakeholders as early as possible
- Get key sponsors onboard early on in the project's life cycle
- Define the desired outcomes (success/failure criteria) for the project in as much detail as possible, and get formal sign off on them
- Agree upon metrics for measuring project outcomes
- Identify and secure the right resources, people, technology, processes, for the project
- Initiate regular stakeholder communication
- Pay attention to organizing the project's library: Create common object repositories and manage /control them. Update the library with new and discard old versions. Manage course versions carefully
- Identify potential risks to the project and revisit them frequently
- Project Closeout: Build a project "Knowledge base" and "Lessons learned" repository with all pertinent information about the project for future PMs to refer to

A very crucial part of the eLearning project manager's responsibility is to produce and manage a variety of eLearning deliverables. Some of the key eLearning deliverables include:

- **Project Charter** – This document clearly outlines the project's scope, and defines the roles and responsibilities of major stakeholders
- **Course Design Document** – This is one of the more important deliverables for an ID project as it outlines in detail what the final course package will look like
- **Storyboard Templates** – Storyboards help everyone—the Project Sponsor, the Project Team, and Instructional Designers. Where possible, the use of templates also saves time, introduces standardization and ensures consistent quality of all storyboards
- **Scripts** – Instructors depend on these scripts to deliver the course. It is essential that the PM institutes processes to build, validate and control these scripts throughout the project, including updating and archiving them when necessary

- **GUIs and other graphics** – An instructional design project will not be completed without a slew of graphics and other animation objects. All of these are part of the final ID package.
- **Other assets** – Depending on the type of content being developed, the project may produce other deliverables, including Microsoft Word documents, Microsoft Project Plans, MS Power Points, Videos, Audio and Animation files.

It is the eLearning project manager's responsibility to institute adequate process to ensure that not only high quality deliverables are produced, but also to make sure they are managed throughout their individual lifecycles (Creation, Change, Updates, Version Revisions, Archival and Destruction/Deletion).

Project Management Tools

Example of a typical Gantt chart

		Task Name	Duration	Start
1		Project	19.47 days	5/6/2011
2		Start	0 day	5/6/2011
3		Task A	4 days	5/6/2011
4		Task B	5.3 days	5/6/2011
5		Task C	5.15 days	5/12/2011
6		Task D	6.32 days	5/12/2011
7		Task E	5.15 days	5/19/2011
8		Task F	4.5 days	5/20/2011
9		Task G	5.15 days	5/26/2011
10		Finish	0 day	6/2/2011

Example of a typical PERT chart

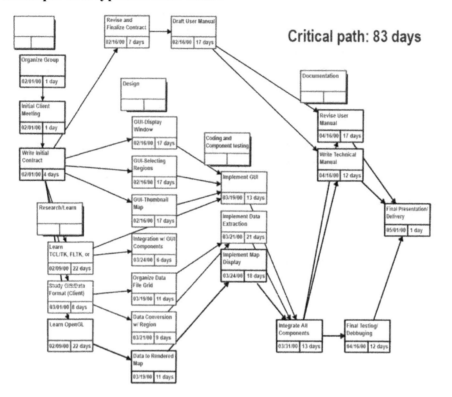

Critical path: 83 days

To successfully complete an eLearning project, it is important to stay on schedule. ELearning project managers have many responsibilities, so missing a deadline is easy. There are several tools that will help you deliver projects on time. The first one is a **Gantt chart**. A Gantt chart is a horizontal bar chart that enables project managers to organize the events identified during the planning phase. This chart allows project managers to visualize all the tasks as well as the costs associated with each event. On the Gantt chart, you can specify the time needed to complete each piece of the project by indicating the start and finish dates. Moreover, the chart summarizes the elements of the project. When project managers set up the Gantt chart for their project, they need to include the individuals responsible for each task, the amount of time they will need to complete each task, and the problems that may be encountered along the way. It is important to remember to update the Gantt chart whenever the deadline changes and as soon as each task is completed.

Even though the Gantt chart lists tasks, it does not provide an indication of the relationship between these tasks. This is where a PERT chart comes into play. A **PERT chart** is a project management tool used to schedule, organize, and coordinate tasks within the project. Many project managers prefer the PERT chart to the Gantt chart because it shows the relationship between tasks and therefore works better for more complex projects.

There are many different software programs that can be used to create both Gantt and PERT charts. However, the Microsoft Project is the most popular project management tool available on the market. This software program helps project managers develop a plan, assign resources to activities, track progress, manage the budget, and analyze workloads. If the project is relatively simple and does not have many activities, project managers may consider developing their charts in Excel.

Test Your Knowledge

1. ELearning projects are more difficult to manage and carry more risk because they involve:
   A. Both learning and technology
   B. Both child and adult learning theory
   C. Adult learning theory
   D. Technological challenges

2. The IPECC model is used:
   A. Primarily for curriculum development.
   B. Primarily for eLearning project development.
   C. For all types of projects, not just for eLearning.
   D. For all learning projects which necessitate multimedia development.

3. The Initiation Phase of the IPECC model includes:
   A. Conducting a Business Requirements Analysis to fully understand the requirements and the desired outcome of the project.
   B. Conducting a Business Requirements Analysis to ensure that stakeholders can prove the ROI of the course to be developed.
   C. Analyzing previous attempts at similar learning projects within the organization to identify potential pitfalls.
   D. Analyzing previous attempts at similar learning projects within the organization to identify the areas that worked well and repeat them.

4. The foundation of any project, this document serves as the contract between an eLearning project manager and the client.
   A. Project Plan
   B. Project Scope Document
   C. Business Requirements Analysis
   D. Project Charter

5. Refining scope, assembling a team, identifying specific tasks and writing a project plan are all aspects of the _____ phase of IPECC.
   A. Initiating
   B. Planning
   C. Executing
   D. Controlling

6. The Controlling Phase of IPECC is where:
    A. The project manager makes adjustments to the schedule based on any problems that occurred during the previous three phases.
    B. The bulk of the work in actually executing the project plan occurs, including the development of the content itself.
    C. The project is reevaluated based on alpha and beta testing of the course and stakeholder input.
    D. The project manager makes budgetary decisions based on how much the development of the project will cost.

7. A _____ is frequently used during project management to track and organize the events identified during the planning phase.
    A. bar graph
    B. project calendar
    C. Venn diagram
    D. Gantt chart

Exercise 23

Think about each phase of project management. What tasks are you going to complete in each phase to ensure the successful delivery of your project? Which project management tools will you use and why?

Chapter 25: ELearning Development – The Agile Way!

This chapter will cover:

- The Agile approach to eLearning design
- Writing effective user stories
- Agile roles and responsibilities
- Managing eLearning projects the Agile way.

Since the word "eLearning" was first used at a Computer Based Training (CBT) systems seminar back in 1999, a number of structured design methodologies (ADDIE, SAM) have been used to develop eLearning content. As far as methodologies go, you will be hard pressed to find two eLearning project managers (PMs) who agree upon which methodology is "right" and which is "wrong." The fact is that many of those "iterative" models, where content is developed using a cycle of repeated processes, have proved immensely resilient over the years in projects that produced high-quality content. However, now, there is a new popular kid in town.

To really understand what *Agile eLearning development* is all about, let's have a brief primer of what an existing iterative model—ADDIE—does. Developed in 1975, at the Florida State University primarily for IT project development, ADDIE produced eLearning content in distinct and iterative phases: Analysis, Design, Development, Implementation and Evaluation.

- Analysis are conducted to come up with course requirements
- The content is designed and passed to the developers
- Developers develop the content using appropriate eLearning software
- The developed course is implemented
- The course is evaluated by clients and users
- ...and if the changes are needed it goes back into the hands of the instructional designer.

Agile is associated with agility in developing content. It is designed to compress development time, usually associated with iterative processes, and takes a radically different approach to developing eLearning content. Simply put, Agile:

- Brings all the stakeholders together in a huddle...yes, INCLUDING the client/end user!
- They agree on small/discrete chunks of what the course should look like in a "scrum" (meeting) session
- That part of the puzzle is built in a "sprint" (iteration), with any issues/changes addressed quickly
- The team then moves on to the next segment of the course

Obviously, the above points do not justify what Agile actually is, and what it does. However, when compared to other iterative processes, Agile:

- *Engages* a broader cross-section of stakeholders earlier in the development process

- *Helps* the project team stay focused on developing eLearning courses and content, and NOT get distracted by the "process" of developing the course or content
- *Delivers* tangible/usable deliverables early in the process, at regular intervals, and addresses changes/defects quickly in the development process

No one is suggesting that the advent of Agile has made everything that eLearning PMs and Developers learned and did over the last decade obsolete. Quite the contrary! What Agile aims to do is take eLearning project development to the next natural level in its evolution. That means building (not fully replacing) upon the wealth of knowledge and experience of the existing body of knowledge.

ADDIE traces its roots to the 1950's **Waterfall** methodology of software design, where the development process gradually flows from one step to another, just like a waterfall. You cannot start step 2 until you are done with step 1, and so on.

As a result of new developments in how eLearning is viewed by training professionals, and significant enhancements in supporting IT and multi-media technologies, Agile methodologies have now sprung up. Agile eLearning design and development:

- Promotes a "parallel" way of developing courseware, as opposed to the serial Waterfall (ADDIE) approach
- Endorses the use of team-work as opposed to specialist roles (Designers, Developers etc.) that worked in insulation
- Infuses flexibility, speed and cooperation into the development process

The Agile approach, which is based on short iterative full-cycles that deliver usable components of the courseware, eliminates the biggest drawback to ADDIE, which is a time-consuming and often process-driven method of developing courseware. Agile methodologies, such as **Rapid Content Development (RCD)** and **Successive Approximation Model (SAM)** introduce a goal oriented, action-driven efforts that result in:

- More collaborative approach to eLearning content development
- A move to the "fail early, succeed earlier!" approach to content development—all issues are identified and fixed much earlier in the Agile approach than ADDIE
- The ability to reuse, recycle and reprocess previously developed content, saving lots of time and money for eLearning project sponsors

Agile not only speeds up courseware design and development, but also adds a dimension of better quality that is not possible with ADDIE. Moving away from the Waterfall and into Agile is definitely a windfall for eLearning projects.

When the ADDIE methodology is used to develop eLearning content, everyone knows that the course will take eight to ten (or however many) months to be developed. Agile, however, turns that concept on its head and says: Expect something every two weeks! How's that possible?

It is possible because of the way Agile approaches the development process:

- In short iterative cycles of two weeks (called Sprints), instead of one prolonged design, develop, test, and implement cycle
- By delivering small chunks of usable content frequently, rather than the entire course at the end of the project

Here are some Agile key steps to follow when developing eLearning courses.

1. Agile Teams: Build a team of self-organized, cross-functional people. Getting all the experts around the table early on is the key to successful Agile.

2. User Stories: Look at the content needs from a user perspective. The most popular way to do so is to use the following User Story template:

As a (*type of user:* Course Admin; Trainer; Learner);

I want to (*goal:* Add a Learner; Grade a test; Select a course);

so that I can (*reason:* Complete the registration process; Evaluate progress; Start a lesson)

3. Sprint Along: Once User Stories are documented, they can be grouped together into small development cycles of related content, and pushed out in iterations called Sprints. Each Sprint starts with a select number of User Stories (e.g. 7 User Stories about "How to Enroll in the Company's Benefits Program"), and ends with a complete chunk of content that addresses all those Stories.

4. Feedback: Each Sprint must culminate with a "Sprint Retrospective" review, where what worked and what did not work can be discussed candidly.

5. Manage Backlogs: At the heart of a successful Agile project is the successful management of User Story backlogs, both for the Sprint, and for the entire project (Product backlog).

Knowing what content (or which User Stories) should be developed for the entire course, and prioritizing which Sprint should contain which User Stories, is an essential part of the entire Agile development process.

A key difference between ADDIE and Agile is how teams work. Agile, unlike ADDIE, supports an open communication concept, where it is believed that ANYONE on the team can have a good idea, and EVERYONE should be heard.

While Agile has been proven to deliver higher-quality eLearning projects faster, thereby reducing both the time and the cost of developing courses, its benefits can only be reaped if Agile is done correctly. Here are a few best practices to follow when using Agile for eLearning project management and development.

1. Identify all of the impacted stakeholders and decision makers early on in the project, and invite them to your scrum sessions – Most eLearning projects fail because the right individuals and teams were not consulted at the outset.

2. Keep team sizes manageable – If you have five graphics designers, four content writers and seven web designers at a scrum, there is likelihood that the session will get bogged down in minutia, and end without reaching a conclusion.

3. Bring representative voices into the scrum – Each eLearning project is different, and every team will need to be organized differently. However, it is essential to have a cross section of representation on the team—even if that means nominating dissenters to scrum sessions.

4. Meet daily – Resist the temptation to cancel daily team meetings (scrums). These team meetings help to visualize and develop content, and quickly identify and address expectations.

5. Start iterations early – ELearning project sponsors are no different than those sponsoring any other type of project. They want to see REAL progress, FAST! While other iterative methodologies compelled them to wait for many months before a preview of what's to come, with Agile, you can start delivering iterations early.

6. Release frequently – Most Agile eLearning PMs make the mistake of delivering the initial release of the course early on in the project timeline, and then maintain a "long silence" before the next release. For best results, iterate regularly (one to four weeks) and release frequently (at least every two months).

7. Get trained – If you and the team are new to Agile, the best way to benefit from this relatively new methodology is to get professional help. The key role of Scrum Master must ideally be filled by someone who appreciates the essence of eLearning projects and can use Agile to break down barriers and remove impediments for the team.

8. Get coached – Most organizations adopting Agile for the first time will likely have existing eLearning PM who might feel threatened. Yet, if you wish to succeed in an Agile project, you must transition the role of the traditional PM to the Agile Coach—someone who can navigate the world of

Scrums and Iterations better than a (traditional) PM. In case you think of Agile as a radical replacement of the fundamental way of approaching the design and development of eLearning courses, you are wrong.

Successful implementation of Agile in eLearning projects does not mean all other fundamental eLearning design principles—identifying learning objectives, structuring the course, storyboarding, designing individual modules, building the user interface, creating content—will be compromised. On the contrary, Agile helps to bring all of these fundamental building blocks together, and manages the entire development process so the final product is delivered quickly and to the highest standards.

Agile Project Management

As you already know, Agile project management is an iterative method of managing the design and development activities for eLearning projects. The best part about Agile project management is that it embraces change even late in the development phase.

The main difference between Agile and traditional approaches is that Agile method reduces complexity of a project by specifying and managing small usable chunks of the project as opposed to managing the whole project at the same time. In the Agile method, team members handle most of the assignments, are responsible for managing their chunk of the project, and are accountable for quality control of their piece of the project.

To ensure success of any project, Agile project managers are responsible for managing the team's environment and encouraging decision making among team members. In other words, while the main role of a traditional project manager is to manage cost, time, and scope of the project, the main role of an Agile project manager is to act as a facilitator to empower the team to achieve results.

In conclusion, it is worth noting that Agile methodology does not work for all organizations. Just like with everything else, there is no one size fits all. However, the Agile approach has a lot of benefits that all organizations should consider. Some of these benefits are higher customer satisfaction, improved performance among team members, reduced risk of project failure, and better project quality.

Test Your Knowledge

1. Which of these Agile development terms refers to the iterative development phase where eLearning courses are built in segments?
   - A. Scrum
   - B. Sprint
   - C. SAM
   - D. Iteration

2. All of the following statements about Agile are true EXCEPT:
   - A. Agile engages more stakeholders early in the development process.
   - B. Agile delivers tangible and usable deliverables early in the process.
   - C. Agile fully replaces all of the concepts used in ADDIE.
   - D. Agile enables developers to address changes and defects quickly.

3. The role of a traditional eLearning project manager is to manage cost, time and scope of the project whereas the role of an Agile project manager is to:
   - A. Act as a mediator between teams working on different parts of the project.
   - B. Act as a facilitator and empower the team to achieve results.
   - C. Drive results through micro-management of tasks for each team.
   - D. Drive teams to achieve results by appointing leads for each functional section.

4. Successful implementations of Agile into eLearning projects typically means that fundamental learning design principles (identifying learning objectives, structuring the course, storyboarding, etc.) will:
   - A. Not be compromised, but rather strengthened.
   - B. Be compromised yet made up for by speedy development.
   - C. Not be compromised, but handed off to outsourced teams to manage.
   - D. Be compromised, yet made up for during final alpha/beta testing.

Exercise 24

Think about your project. Do you think it could benefit from the Agile development methodology? Why or why not? Which steps would you take to manage your project the Agile way?

Chapter 26: Job Aids

This chapter will cover:

- The role of job aids in eLearning courses
- Reasons to include job aids in your eLearning courses
- Types of job aids and appropriate use of each type
- Electronic Performance Support System (EPSS)

Case Study

The Vinter Restaurant Chain was considering developing a course to help its sales associates work on their upselling technique. Although they were a successful chain with a proven strategy toward sales, the merits of a course that went over tips, tricks, and best practices seemed unclear. Hoping to improve their sales even more, they hired an instructional design consultant to come onboard.

During the needs assessment, the instructional designer made a few visits to a restaurant to conduct observations, and noticed that many employees were already using these techniques. When he asked them about it, they said that discussions of best practices happened during their biweekly meetings, where they would often use role-plays to rehearse them.

The instructional designer considered ways to teach the material. Since the techniques were supposed to come up within the flow of conversation with the guests, the best option seemed to be to use scenarios. However, it seemed like the employees were already doing that with their instructor-led role-plays, he reasoned.

He finally decided to ask the employees directly what would be helpful. They mentioned that an image that showed a variety of different techniques would help—one that they could glance at in between tables, and which could remind them of the strategies available to them. Instead of a course, the instructional designer created easy reference cards and posters for each restaurant.

Even though the main role of an instructional designer is to design courses, what goes into the course is often a client's decision. Since most clients possess the content but do not know much about the learning theory, their content often includes a lot of unnecessary information. While stakeholders do not always want to hear an instructional designer's opinion about what should and should not be included in the course, ISD professionals can influence the presentation method of the content.

Typically, when teaching a process or practical skill, developing a **job aid** should be considered. Job aids are tools that allow individuals to access the information required to complete a task quickly and efficiently. They are also known as quick reference guides, checklists, and performance aids, which help individuals apply new skills to real-world problems without having to refer back to long training courses. This training tool covers only relevant information in the form of systematic instructions, worksheets, checklists, flowcharts, diagrams, and templates.

Regardless of the format chosen for the job aid, it should:

- include only the "must-know" content;
- utilize easy to understand short descriptive words; and
- incorporate simple, clear and illustrative graphics.

While it is not always possible to create job aids to meet the needs of all learning styles, the majority of learners benefit from visuals. You should consider including highlights, boxes, and arrows that emphasize the text. There is no standard size for a job aid—it can be just one page in length or fifty pages, depending on the content or procedure it is trying to convey.

There are many ways to make a job aid part of the eLearning course. It can be *embedded into the lesson, added as a Word or PDF attachment,* or *made available as a mobile* application. Each of these methods has its advantages and disadvantages, so just like with everything else in eLearning, the decision should be based on the content. For instance, if the information is related to the current video or activity in the course, embedding a job aid may be the best solution. If you want learners to be able to print a job aid and use it as a desk guide after the training, then adding it as a Word or PDF attachment may work best. If your goal is to provide learners with a reference they can access anytime and anywhere, your best bet is to create a mobile application. Sometimes, however, to accomplish the desired goal, you will have to select two or three options.

Most training courses contain so much information that it is impossible to retain all of it. In addition, people tend to forget information and lose skills when they do not use them on a regular basis. Job aids fill that gap while serving as reference, reminder, and refresher tools. When employees have a job aid in front of them, they can work faster as they do not have to stop and think of the next step. Job aids also work well in situations when certain tasks or skills are rarely used. They can help organizations keep the training costs down. If, for example, the organization has to train employees to follow a constantly changing procedure, it is better to create a job aid rather than a training course as it is much easier to replace a job aid than to rebuild the entire eLearning lesson.

You should consider adding a job aid as an attachment to eLearning courses if the intent is to:

- provide a quick overview of job tasks to new employees;
- teach complex, difficult to remember tasks that involve multiple steps and lengthy decisions;
- decrease informational overload from the training;
- help individuals make accurate decisions;
- reduce on-the job accidents;
- improve work quality;

- increase retention;
- promote transfer of training to the job; or
- deliver just-in-time information.

Once the job aid is complete, you can find someone who does not know anything about the procedure or skill and ask that person to review it to reveal problems, ambiguities, and missing steps.

Determine the Format of a Job Aid

Use Table 17 to determine the type of job aid that suits your content's specific needs.

Table 17 - Job Aids

Job Aid	Type of Task
Step-by-Step Instructions	• The task includes linear steps. • The task does not have any decisions associated with it.
Worksheets	• The task includes information that does not have an immediate application. • The task includes calculations.
Checklists	• The steps to complete the task do not have to be done in a linear order. • The task includes planning or inspecting something.
Flowcharts	• The task includes yes or no decisions that must be made in a specific order. • Each step in a task is associated with specific decision.
Diagrams	• The task illustrates a certain idea or concept. • The task explains how something works.
Templates	• The task includes creating a document, letter or report. • The task requires standardization; e.g., same style and structure

Use the following questions to ensure the effectiveness of the job aid:

- Did you gather the appropriate information such as sample documents, screenshots, and flow charts?
- What type of graphics would best illustrate the points/steps/procedures?
- What format would work best?
- What size and page layout are most appropriate?

Electronic Performance Support System

The *Electronic Performance Support System, or EPSS,* is any computer software program within a larger application that guides people through completing a task. It is an electronic job aid. The goal of EPSS is to provide the information or resources necessary to achieve performance requirements without training intervention or any other external support. Some of the reasons to consider EPSS include:

- a performance problem due to the lack of knowledge or skills; unavailable training for new employees;
- guidance to complete a complex task;
- infrequent performance of a task.

Whenever there is a performance issue related to knowledge or skill deficiency, consider developing a job aid. Even if the training is available, a job aid can increase retention, on-the-job learning transfer, and more importantly, improve performance.

As we all know, the main difference between *training* and *Performance Support* is that training is trying to fill the gap between the missing and the needed knowledge while the Performance Support tools provide on the job support when it is needed. Unlike training, which often includes some of the "nice to know" information, Performance Support tools offer "just enough" assistance to get the job done. Naturally, Performance Support can be either Electronic (EPSS) or Paper-based. Instructional designers have been developing quick reference guides and job aids to supplement their training courses for ages. Nowadays, most of us are used to having the information available to us when we need it at any time and place. This is where the Electronic Support System comes in handy. Many EPSSs offer a contextual, step-by-step, immediate solution to people's needs.

When instructional designers conduct their initial meeting with the client, they may discover that even though their client wants a formal training course, there is no real need to create one. Instead, a Performance Support System can resolve the client's issue. So, when would a Performance Support System be useful? Here are some of the situations when Performance Support can be used:

- If an organization lacks efficient procedures
- If procedures are frequently changing
- If accuracy is critical and mistakes are frequently made
- If a task is rarely performed
- If there are many steps in the process
- If the training budget is limited

In addition to everything listed above, how they can apply their formal training on the job. Since, even the best training course cannot make learners remember all the required information, a complete and concise job aid can help to embed the information into the learners' heads.

So, what are some ways you can integrate Performance Support into your eLearning course or even use it as a stand-alone tool for on-the job performance improvement? Of course, you can always develop a step-by-step, easy to follow job aid, you can also outline a task with appropriate decision-making criteria in the PDF file, or you can create a manual that people can keep at their desk and refer to it as needed. However, depending on your content, you may also take advantage of modern technology and create instructional videos or even record a podcast and make it available on iTunes. Another great way to incorporate Performance Support is to use the social network tools such as Facebook, Twitter, or even create a wiki page. In addition to improving organizational knowledge, the aforementioned approaches to Performance Support will greatly improve collaboration in your organization.

Test Your Knowledge

1. Also known as Quick Reference Guides, checklists and performance aids, job aids:
   A. Are one way to include all extra information provided by SMEs that was not incorporated into the eLearning course.
   B. Allow instructional designers to make sure the stakeholders' requirements are met without providing much value to the learner.
   C. Allow individuals to quickly access the information needed to complete a task efficiently.
   D. Are documents which instructional designers can use as an aid in designing eLearning courses.

2. All of the following statements regarding job aids are true EXCEPT:
   A. Job aids can be embedded into the lesson or made available as a mobile application.
   B. Job aids should be formatted using small font sizes to make room for all of the content.
   C. Job aids should include the "must know" content.
   D. Job aids should incorporate simple, clear and illustrative graphics.

3. Job aids can help organizations keep _____ down.
   A. attrition
   B. HR incidents
   C. hiring costs
   D. training costs

4. The Electronic Performance Support System (EPSS) is essentially:
   A. An electronic job aid.
   B. A device for delivering eLearning.
   C. A text delivery system for job aid information.
   D. An email delivery system for job aid information.

Exercise 25

Think about your topic and objectives and decide whether including a job aid in your eLearning course will be beneficial. If you decide to include a job aid, which format would you choose, and why?

Chapter 27: Web 2.0 and Mobile Learning

This chapter will cover:

- Web 2.0 technology and mobile learning solutions
- Incorporating social networking tools in eLearning
- Using podcasts and vodcasts in eLearning
- Designing courses and supplemental materials for social, and mobile learning.

Web 2.0

Case Study

As he thought about ways to translate his popular nutrition course to an online format, Dr. Hansen's biggest sticking point was the group discussions. He knew part of the reason his course had been so widely successful was because he was able to emphasize peer learning. In the on-campus course, he had students discuss course principles extensively and work on projects together, like creating nutrition profiles for a classmate. Through collaboration and conversation, students were given a sense of the relevance of their content, as well as the opportunity to immerse themselves in the material.

So, how could he translate those activities to an online format? In his last online course, Dr. Hansen had made extensive use of forums, but the students didn't visit them as often as he'd liked. Ideally, he thought, students would share thoughts with each other all the time, not just when they had a writing prompt or an assignment to complete.

Dr. Hansen came up with a few ideas. One was to move the discussions to a social media format. That way, the class' discussion forums were not removed from their daily interactions.

Next, he thought of ways to encourage students to do spontaneous research and discussion. He decided to reward sharing links and discussing them with some extra credit.

Finally, he decided to encourage the use of collaboration tools. With shared documents and file folders, the students would feel less isolated as they completed their tasks, and could learn from each other's studying process.

In today's internet-driven world, more and more knowledge workers prefer to have a say in how the company facilitates their learning. With so much of the world's workforce connected to *Social Media*, that is where most workers are turning to informally seek their knowledge.

According to a definition, **Web 2.0** is a term used to describe the second generation of the World Wide Web, focused on collaboration and information sharing. Some of the key characteristics of Web 2.0 are:

- applications that can be accessed from anywhere; and
- tools that encourage people to create, exchange, and share information

Web 2.0 technologies are comprised of *wikis, blogs, social networking tools, content hosting services*, and *podcasts*. In today's world of electronic communication, Web 2.0 greatly influences how people learn.

Social learning is a subset of eLearning. It refers to learning from and with other people using social media tools such as

- Facebook
- Twitter
- YouTube
- LinkedIn
- Blogs, and
- Wikis

This is the age of the "knowledge worker"—there's no question about it! Companies, both big and small, invest vastly in delivering workers the knowledge they require to do their jobs successfully. The more knowledge a worker assimilates, and the quicker they absorb it, the more competitive and profitable they will become for the company.

While companies spend a huge part of their personnel development budget on "formal" learning, such as training courses and workshops, a surprising number of learners that come out of those sessions are unprepared to put that learning into practice. However, once they are in the workforce, they use informal learning techniques, including:

- Observing other colleagues
- Asking senior employees
- Experimenting on their own, and
- Conducting additional research to fill in the gaps to perfect the skills they need in the real world.

This informal way of learning has been around for a while, where knowledge has been handed down from one generation to another. Even during the days of the Industrial Revolution, the Apprenticeship system was essentially an informal learning process that every supervisor and shop foreman underwent before they got to where they were.

Today's informal learning environment has many of the same characteristics as the system of the bygone ages. However, with the proliferation of the internet, learners are turning to social connections and tools to learn informally. The following are some ways that companies can leverage Social Media platforms in informal learning settings:

1. LinkedIn – This is a platform for aggregating professionals and peers, and then connecting with them through Social Media. Knowledge workers are much more likely to learn by interacting informally with their peers in such settings. Most professionals value tips/techniques and learning nuggets supplied informally by their peers more than those offered by a lecturer standing in front of a classroom.

2. Chat/Messaging – Formal courses will not provide answers to every work situation. Tools like Yahoo Messenger, MSN Messenger (Skype) and Google Talk (Hangouts) can become great informal learning resources for employees to use in order to get quick responses to desperately needed work-related questions. They are quicker than sending an email to a training officer, and more effective than a phone call to a supervisor.

3. YouTube – Most learning takes place by "seeing," and employers can take advantage of that by creating short videos about work-related situations, and posting them on YouTube for employees to access and learn. YouTube also hosts a wealth of instructional as well as "How To" videos that may apply to many organizational situations.

4. Facebook Groups – Almost two-thirds of the world's population is on Facebook, and that offers a unique opportunity to use this social platform as an incredible informal learning tool. While most employees "should" be using formal company platforms (like websites and email) to stay "plugged in" to major corporate developments, a surprising number of knowledge workers are more connected to Facebook. Setting up Facebook Groups, and using them to stimulate discussions and debates can be a great informal way to deliver much needed learning to broad and dispersed groups of employees.

5. Twitter – Tweeting has now become a standard way to provide instant updates and feedback on global events. Companies can use this medium effectively as an integrated informal learning tool, by providing ongoing commentary on important corporate initiatives. Tweets from known Subject Matter Experts (SMEs) will help new-comers in the field pick up invaluable insight on the situation in progress—more so than any formal classroom lecture can offer.

6. Blogs – Each time that a company releases a new product or service, it might be difficult (especially if the audience is global) to bring every employee into a classroom/training center to disseminate information to them. Blogs can not only be used effectively in such situations, but can also be configured to stimulate discussion, elicit feedback and provoke comments about them. Unlike a formal email system, feedback on blogs can also be anonymous, which can often be more meaningful than comments/feedback received through formal systems.

While some of these Social Media tools can be used to achieve multiple learning objectives, most are excellent at delivering specific informal learning experiences. YouTube, for instance, has a niche in delivering video content, while Messaging can be leveraged for rapid communication exchanges. Recognizing which tools to use, and what type of learning content to deploy using them is vital to successful use of Social Media in informal learning.

When it comes to ensuring effective informal learning, there are certain strategies that should be embraced by all organizations. However, there has to be a balance struck on how much latitude to give informal learners. Some points to consider when striking that balance include:

- **Standardization** – Recognize that not all learners will embrace the same set of Social Media tools as learning aids. Companies will need to introduce standards for their tools.
- **Expertise** – Realize that "expertise" offered via Social Media learning tools is often difficult (sometimes impossible) to verify.
- **Security** – If public domain Social Media learning tools are being made available to company employees, then security must be a concern that should be addressed.
- **Oversight** – Should there be oversight of an employee's access to such tools? Or, will the company go by the "honor system" and trust that employees will not abuse the use of these tools?

Building Social Media learning policies is the best way to proactively address all of the above concerns. However, the key to creating and implementing such policies is consultation. Without adequate consultation and buy-in from employees, companies have no hope of successfully integrating Social Media tools in support of informal learning.

Today, some organizations tend toward social learning tools more than others do. Additionally, many organizations run their own blogs and manage Facebook pages. The decision to incorporate these tools into the organization's learning environment mostly depends on their leaders' perspective and goes back to generational learning styles. Whereas younger generations tend to use social learning tools on a regular basis and even find them motivational because they allow to share knowledge with others who have similar interests, older generations remain wary of using these tools and may not see them as learning instruments.

Social learning tools allow learners to share the best practices and discuss solutions to problems with other professionals in their field. Some instructional designers incorporate social learning tools into their courses to establish a common ground among learners. For instance, they may post videos or blog articles with the information that they want their learners to become familiar with prior to the course. Instructional designers also use social learning tools to share links to additional resources either prior, during, or after the learning event. After watching a video or reading an article associated with the link, many people tend to comment and reflect on what they have seen or read. This often leads to multiple threads and knowledge sharing.

Wikis and Blogs

Wikis are collaboration websites on which anyone within the community of users can contribute to and edit the content. Most wikis are specific to the subject. Some companies use wikis to post their meeting notes or share valuable information about certain topics.

Blogs, on the other hand, are journals where people write their thoughts on a specific topic. As opposed to wikis, blogs are usually written and maintained by a single contributor and commented on by other visitors. Some instructional designers use blogs as part of their course design to post questions and assignments. When designing blended learning experiences, you can create wikis or blogs and have learners participate by contributing their opinions and reflecting on their learning.

In addition to wikis, blogs, and other social learning tools, instructional designers use *YouTube* to upload videos and have learners watch and comment on them prior to the learning event.

Mobile Learning

Mobile Learning, or *mLearning,* is another subset of eLearning that focuses on learning with mobile devices such as smartphones, tablets, and eBook readers. Mobile learning is convenient because people have instant access to mobile devices almost anywhere.

Mobile devices provide coaching, assessments, evaluations, on-the-job support, information, references, podcasts, forms, and checklists. In these ways, mLearning supports traditional learning modes as well as other eLearning modes and makes learning more portable and accessible. MLearning can reach a large number of people at the same time and provide them with just-in-time training. However, before delivering an eLearning course via mobile device, you should review learning objectives to ensure that the mLearning solution is truly needed.

Case Study

Because the learners were often away from the office and out in nature, designing the training course for the non-profit group Ecoquest was a tricky challenge. The course was designed to assist in the certification of employees as wilderness guides for elementary school children. While they were studying for certification, employees were often assisting certified guides or running errands for the hikes, and there was often little time to devote to training.

The instructional design consultant hired to create the coursework considered the problem. His needs assessment revealed that learners were in the office anywhere from zero to fifteen hours a week, and their schedules were unpredictable. Unless he was going to ask them to come into the office for mandated training, traditional approaches were not going to work, he realized.

Talking it over with his contact at the organization, it came up that the employees often used smartphones to track routes that help them identify flora and fauna in the area. Investigating the possibilities of Mobile Learning, the instructional designer found it had many applications—not just to people with technological limitations. Microlearning, repeatability, and learner preference were all relevant factors that would be helpful to his learners. Some team members did not have smartphones, but Ecoquest agreed to make accommodations for them.

The instructional designer ended up creating a fully-mobile course, segmented in such way that learners could go through it in bits and pieces in spare time. With glossaries, guidelines and maps, it would also serve as a reference after certification was complete.

Podcasting and Vodcasting

Case Study

When an instructional designer was tasked to teach cultural awareness to a team that was frequently traveling abroad, she knew she needed a way to supplement her training material with more information. She had already written an extensive eLearning course on French culture and general strategies for cultural awareness, but as the project had continued, the team was spending more and more time traveling to France. A common complaint was that although they were getting along with their French colleagues, the team felt "clueless." They wanted to know more about French culture to gain a better rapport with them.

At first, the instructional designer thought to make more training, but the organization decided there was not a budget for anything extensive. What is more, they did not want to take much time off work to help the team get trained in a potentially limitless subject. What I need, thought the instructional designer, is a convenient delivery method that is also cost-effective, and can give the learners the information they need.

After doing some research, the instructional designer was surprised to find out that podcasts were being used in training settings. Though it was not traditional, the more the instructional designer thought about it, the better suited podcasts seemed to be for what she needed. With minimal equipment, she could come up with episodes that covered small information bytes that could be listened to at anytime. If I get busy, she thought, the learners could even make an episode for me—which would help their retention. Her biweekly podcast became a favorite among the French liaison team.

Podcasting and *vodcasting* are types of mobile learning. Podcasts are audio recordings of a training program. Vodcasts are video-based podcasts. Podcasts can be listened or downloaded to hand-held devices such as iPods or mp3 players. Vodcasts, on the other hand, require a digital video player such as QuickTime or Windows Media Player. You can simply make audio files of your course lectures available for learners to download. To be more creative, you can also turn your content into a radio show, play, or journalistic investigation using an informal style and various voices. This will excite learners and possibly increase their retention level. In order for podcasts and vodcasts to enhance the learning experience, they should not be a substitute to complete courses, but rather an addition to them. Effective podcasts and vodcasts should not exceed 20 minutes and must follow the same ground rules for recording eLearning audio and video.

Convenience is the main benefit of podcasts and vodcasts. Learners can listen to the recordings when they work out in the gym, drive to work, or even cook dinner, and they do not have to be connected to the internet. Podcasts are inexpensive and can be created with a free software program for recording and editing audio.

Even though podcasts and vodcasts are convenient and can be a great enhancement to eLearning courses, they lack interactive elements and, therefore, do not appeal to all learners. For this reason, instructional designers should use podcasts as a supporting material that learners can explore on their own, not as a standalone course. If the content is not technical in nature, creating a podcast can be beneficial while more technical and difficult to understand content that requires visualization may need to be presented in a vodcast format. Before making the decision to add podcasts and vodcasts to the courses, ensuring that they align with learning goals and objectives is necessary. Otherwise, their instructional value will be lost.

Storytelling is one of the simplest yet most memorable and effective ways to present content. Build the presentation of new content upon content from previous episodes, and post all archived episodes, so that participants may go back to refresh their memory.

Think about some ways in which you can make use of many different voices. In podcasts, one person should never do all the talking. By using interviews, the hosts should be able to build their case and present a series of events that feel real. Contrast this method with the prospect of one narrator relaying information for an episode at a time—it would be difficult for listeners to stay engaged if they had to listen to the same voice all the time.

One best practice that helps to increase engagement among learners is building an online community of listeners. This community will enable learners to stay current, even when they are waiting for a new episode to come out. To increase the effectiveness of podcasts, instructional designers can create useful content or short posts of updates on the topic of the podcasts, add links to additional materials, design images/infographics, and even extra listening material. Adding an online space for podcast listeners to visit between presentations will give them more touch-points to connect with the material. Another benefit of adding a web component is that instructional designers will not need to talk through every piece of information in the podcast—some can be left for the learners to read on their own time. Message boards or other forms of live communication on the site allow users to explore their particular interests in the content in their own way.

Lastly, practice the art of podcasting. It is important that the recording space is free of background noise and distraction. Editing out mistakes is a good practice, but, keep in mind that, frequently, material sounds more natural if there are small hiccups. It is easier to listen to a real conversation than canned audio. Clearly, podcasts can significantly enhance eLearning courses; however, because they are not interactive in nature, it is best to use them as supporting material as opposed to stand-alone courses.

Designing for Social and Mobile Learning

Imagine for a moment that your organization has invested the necessary time and funds into creating the most cutting-edge training program possible. You have an easy to use Learning Management System (LMS); enough developers to create custom eLearning content, instructor-led training (ILT), ad-hoc training solutions; and access to research and reports to stay ahead of the needs of your organization, bringing just-in-time training to life. However, no matter what technology and resources used in the training, it must come to life for participants. This is where the social learning component comes into play.

Working with other learners adds another layer of learning, practice, and retention. Collaboration has been a cornerstone of formal education—the traditional classroom setting involves group work, team projects, and pairing up. However, once we leave traditional classrooms and enter the workforce, the social aspect of training and development often disappears from the learning experience.

So, what can instructional designers do to add social learning to their training courses? First, both the organization and stakeholders must accept that social learning is not a benefit, but rather a requirement for a successful training program. To receive clients' buy-in, instructional designers can share articles, blogs, and studies that reinforce the importance of social learning. Many organizations have a preconceived notion that the main benefit of eLearning is that it is available "anytime and anywhere." While this is a real benefit for cost-savings, it is important for stakeholders to understand that watching a training alone in a vacuum is not a meaningful experience for a learner. By adding a social component to the training, eLearning professionals will close that gap, ensure retention and on-the—job transfer of the information.

Adding social learning to existing training does not have to be time consuming or expensive. If, for example, a training course consists of eLearning modules, videos, and documents, eLearning professionals can easily add a discussion board or create a Facebook page dedicated to that particular class. This will give learners the opportunity to ask questions and comment on the content. Another way to incorporate the social learning aspect with traditional eLearning materials is through using a blended learning approach. While live social interactivity is ideal, it may not work for all learners, especially if their time zones are different. When scheduling a session where all learners can meet is not an option, instructional designers may consider giving learners access to a wiki or message board to post questions and share tips. Keep in mind though that message boards and wikis require a moderator who will actively monitor the discussion, and ensure that all questions and comments are addressed timely. In the most restrictive or tight-budgeted situation, a simple way to incorporate social learning is to begin email chains on a variety of topics the learner is trained on. Questions can be addressed by a wide audience with different backgrounds, lending experience and tips to everyone on the email chain.

The ISD principles and best practices for developing eLearning materials may not always apply to the design and development of mobile and social learning experiences. Since mobile devices are significantly smaller in size than computer screens, instructional designers should:

- keep the content short and simple of no more than five minutes in length;
- produce non-linear content;
- minimize interactivity whenever possible;
- use bullets to present information in a concise form; and
- avoid complex navigation.

Both social and mLearning are alternative delivery methods; therefore, it is best to use them as performance support tools that supplement training courses. For instance, social and mLearning activities can be incorporated into eLearning modules or become part of an instructor-led training. Moreover, these alternative solutions are an excellent blended learning approach to effective training.

In spite of its effectiveness, not all content is suitable for mobile learning. As a rule of thumb, whenever a course requires some type of a learning aid such as a glossary, an mLearning solution can be used. Pre-course presentations and reading materials, pre- and post-tests, and updated content can also be delivered via mLearning. For instance, if an eLearning module has already been created and after a few years all the information remains relevant but there are certain additions to the content, the mLearning solution will be a safe approach. Additionally, there are situations when something goes wrong and people need to learn how to solve a problem immediately. There is no time to go through the entire eLearning module, and there is certainly no time to attend a traditional learning session. In these cases, mobile and social learning are perfect ways to help people get what they need quickly and efficiently.

MLearning solutions work best for the following presentation methods:

- Job Aids
- Checklists
- Desk Reference Guides
- Podcasts
- Vodcasts
- Updates
- Social Networking
- Coaching
- Assessments
- Evaluations Surveys
- Games and Simulations
- EBooks

Mobile courses need to be created from scratch. You cannot simply convert your already existing eLearning course into a mobile one because, at the very least, it will not be displayed correctly on mobile devices. Instead, you will have to create two separate versions of the same course using the mobile first approach.

As you are creating mobile solutions for your eLearning courses, the questions below should guide you through the planning process.

- Why is a mobile solution needed for this course?
- Does your target audience use mobile devices?
- Does your target audience have access to mobile devices?
- What are the learning objectives?
- How will these objectives be evaluated?
- How often does the content change?
- Does the content already exist in any other format?

An instructional designer's job is to design learning experiences that help learners gain new knowledge and skills. Experienced instructional designers know what type of learning solution would best meet their learners' needs. The best way to get a feel of what works best for both social and mLearning is to try them yourself.

Test Your Knowledge

1. Web 2.0 is the second generation of the World Wide Web, focused on:
   A. Video conferencing and digital footprints
   B. Collaboration and information sharing
   C. Virtual world interactions
   D. Bulletin boards and email

2. Learning from and with other people using social media tools is called:
   A. Facebook learning
   B. Media learning
   C. Social learning
   D. Online learning

3. One of the best aspects of social learning is that the tools:
   A. Are limited to people in only certain geographic locations.
   B. Allow users to keep up with their social circles while they learn.
   C. Can use your private information to help learning organizations learn about their audience.
   D. Are free and open to people in multiple locations.

4. Instructional designers may post videos or blogs on social media prior to launching a course to:
   A. Build credibility among their peers.
   B. Establish a baseline of knowledge with their learners.
   C. Increase their revenue streams via advertising.
   D. Create a following of loyal learners.

5. The following are all excellent additions to a well-rounded blended learning approach EXCEPT:
   A. Using a Wiki to collect and share information among learners.
   B. Posting YouTube videos in conjunction with the course.
   C. Having learners turn in essays after the course over email.
   D. Writing blog posts as additional resources to a course.

6. Before delivering an eLearning course via a mobile device, an instructional designer should:
    A. Acquire both Android and iOS phones and tablets to test the solution.
    B. Review learning objectives to ensure that the mLearning solution is truly needed.
    C. Take some courses in mobile app development to make sure their courses are delivered effectively.
    D. Convert their eLearning courses to video-based training.

7. Should podcasts or vodcasts be a substitute to complete courses?
    A. No – they should be an addition to courses to enhance the learning.
    B. Yes – they should be able to stand on their own as a piece of learning.
    C. No – they should be used as a subsequent lesson to the course.
    D. Yes – they have been proven to be more effective than eLearning as a whole.

8. MLearning is NOT appropriate for:
    A. A learning aid
    B. Pre-course reading material
    C. An interactive learning module
    D. Just-in-time job aid

9. The mobile-first approach is:
    A. A method for developing learning when both mobile and eLearning versions are necessary.
    B. A method for developing learning which delays delivery of an eLearning module in favor of the mobile version first.
    C. A method for evaluating whether mobile versions need to be created alongside traditional eLearning.
    D. A method for evaluating whether mobile versions of a course are more effective than the traditional eLearning version.

Exercise 26

Think about your topic and your objectives. Then, decide whether you need to create a mobile learning solution to supplement your eLearning course. If you decide that you do need an mLearning solution, how are you going to approach its design?

Will there be a social learning component to your course? If so, what type of social learning tools would you use and why?

Chapter 28: Technical Training - Making Technical Content Stick

This chapter will cover:

- Technical Training
- Ways to increase retention of technical material,
- How to make technical training fun and engaging

Teaching technical concepts is not an easy task, and delivering technical information through eLearning is an additional hurdle to overcome. Online learners often tune out, click through text-heavy slides barely skimming information, and still get that satisfying "check the box" completion status on their assigned training—all without actually retaining a thing.

The core challenge of creating technical training is to translate very dry, mundane information into a memorable and engaging experience. The information must also clearly explain the inflection points where the learner should choose one option over another. How can you make sure your training hits both of these marks? Working with the right Subject Matter Experts (SMEs) will be central to your success. The learners will need context of where the technical information fits into their job, and this is where SMEs can help. Developing training that makes users relate to the technical information goes back to a cornerstone of sound instructional design—answering the learner's question, "What's in it for me?" Technical training ideally involves hands-on time with the new technology. Screencasts and screenshots can only teach users so much. By passively learning technical concepts through videos and demonstrations, then putting the acquired information to action, the learners will form stronger memories of the process they are absorbing. No matter how technical an employee's job may be, a robot cannot perform the job for them—the human skill of decision-making is what keeps them in a job. With that in mind, make sure your technical training has a human element, and allows the learner to apply information to real-world scenarios. Providing learners with an on-the-job scenarios and opportunities to practice, prepares them to successfully transfer their new knowledge and skills to their workplace.

In addition to providing the learner with hands-on exposure and relating the technical information to real-world scenarios, learners should be assessed for understanding the material. This can be done through simulations that test both theory and application. Multiple choice questions allow learners to guess responses. Games and simulations, on the other hand, provide the opportunity to apply information, make mistakes, correct them, and move forward. Support documents are critical for technical training retention, so building out robust reference materials should always be part of your training plan. Because technical training is very detailed, it is expected that the learner will not retain everything. Therefore, creating a downloadable quick reference guide is essential, as it will allow learners to review the information quickly, without needing to retake the entire course.

It is not a secret that most technical subject matter including training for new software, tools, or applications is boring. While all eLearning courses must be instructionally sound, fun, and engaging, technical training is much harder to design as the content is almost always dull and, at the same time, extremely critical for accurately performing the job. Furthermore, unlike soft skills training, which learners are often forced to take, technical training is typically needed to be able to perform tasks successfully at work.

So, what can instructional designers do to increase engagement and improve retention of the material? Here are a few tips and techniques that technical eLearning designers can use to captivate and challenge distance learners.

1. Design for Real-Life Applications – Learning to use the new Computer Aided Design (CAD) tool, or disassemble and assemble an aircraft engine can be extremely difficult, and often "dry" to comprehend, even when using animated videos and other multimedia content. This is because technical training focuses on walking the audience through various features, functionality, and bells-and-whistles of the product. However, if instead of focusing on the principles of the technical subject, designers made it about a real-life application—by adding simulations, examples, and scenarios—the course would become much less draining for the learner.

2. Keep it Short – While instructor-led technical learning sessions often stretch on for 60 minutes, distance learners are unlikely to stay engaged with the eLearning content for that length of time. Therefore, to retain the interest of an online learner, technical content should be designed in bite-sized segments—15-20-minute sessions.

3. Make it Interactive – While an in-class session may end with plenty of home assignments, online technical learners must be challenged in different ways. Simply assigning "required readings" at the end of each segment is not enough. To keep the learner engaged, designers must include interactive assignments, quizzes and hands-on exercises throughout the lesson—not just at the end of the course.

4. Make it Flexible – Most classroom courses start from Lesson 1 and proceed sequentially to the end of the course. Regardless of whether a learner finds specific content interesting or boring, they have to "suffer" through the entire course. To keep technical learners engaged, design content in segments that can be consumed based on learners' maturity and level of interest. That way, learners can drill-in or out of specific modules, skip the desired segment, or go back to review a previously completed content. This flexibility enhances the engagement levels and increases retention.

So, to make technical training interesting, instructional designers should focus on solving a real-life problem instead of highlighting technical concepts, theoretical constructs, sophisticated features or extensive functionality. For instance, instead of teaching how shapes, angles, and slopes are drawn using the CAD system, consider designing content that teaches these same concepts by using the system to build an office complex or construct a bridge.

By taking traditional instructor-led technical content, and relating it to the audiences' daily life through simulations and activities, instructional designers can make the course more relevant to the learner. As a result, the level of engagement and retention will significantly increase.

Unfortunately, many instructional designers design technical training the same way they design all other training courses. The problem, however, is that the goal of any technical training is not to "show and tell" (even in the interactive manner), but to "practice and do." Teaching learners how to use a new tool or application is not enough as doing so will not help you achieve the ultimate goal of a training program, which is to help learners obtain new knowledge and skills. In fact, if you teach your learners how to use the tool, they will most likely leave the class not knowing a thing. So, if you should not be teaching learners how to use a software, then what is your role as an instructional designer? Well, when designing a highly technical training, you need to focus on the reason why your learners need to know that piece of software and design your training around your learners' goals, not around the software and what it can and cannot do. Communication is key in attaining that goal. By working with Subject Matter Experts, asking the right questions, and conducting very thorough audience analysis, instructional designers can design highly effective technical training solutions.

When most people hear that they need to take another technical training course, they automatically expect to have another boring day. Nevertheless, technical training does not need to be boring. In fact, it should be interactive and offer as much hands on practice as possible. Technical training should be very engaging and personalized. If this is an eLearning course, consider offering different levels of interaction, so that learners can choose the most challenging level for themselves and practice their newly acquired skills. Also, be sure that all steps in the theoretical part of your course are clear, accurate and easy to follow. The worst thing that you can do is confuse your learners because you missed an important step in your presentation. Of course, as an instructional designer, it is not your job to know the tool well, but it is your responsibility to know how to communicate effectively with your Subject Matter Experts, so that you can obtain the most accurate information for your training materials.

Lastly, never assume that your learners will remember everything presented in the course and always include concise and complete job aids and desk reference guides that learners can use when they need a quick refresher.

Test Your Knowledge

1. What is the main challenge of technical training?
   A. Delivering training experience on time and within budget.
   B. Translating very dry, mundane information into a memorable and engaging experience.
   C. Finding the right tool that would support technical content creation.
   D. Using appropriate terminology to help learners understand the content.

2. What are some ways to increase engagement among technical learners?
   A. Keeping content short, interactive, and flexible.
   B. Demonstrating professionalism and effective communication.
   C. Designing linear navigation to force learners go through all sections of the course.
   D. Providing step-by-step written instructions.

Exercise 27

Think about your eLearning project. Does it have any technical aspects to it? If it does, what would you do to make your training more engaging? What would you do to ensure your training sticks?

Chapter 29: Copyright Protection In ELearning Design: What You Need to Know to Protect Your Work

This chapter will cover copyright protection in eLearning.

Case Study

Sam had been with the same eLearning company for about seven years. Though happy there, his wife obtained a job across the state and he found himself needing to quit. As he considered the process of applying to new jobs for the first time in a long while, he realized that he would need an updated portfolio. Unfortunately, he had signed NDA agreements for every course he had made for the company.

When he talked it over with his manager to see if anything could be done, he was disappointed to learn that the company could not make any exceptions. "We'd love to help you out," his manager said. "But those courses are company property, and we just can't afford them to be publicly available."

"I guess I'll have to come up with everything from scratch."

"Maybe, but there are other options, too," the manager said. She explained that there was a workaround: he could sanitize and redo his projects, making them unidentifiable, if he did not use any text, video, sound or images that he had no copyright for. He could keep the basic structure of the course, but rework the specifics to give potential employers the idea of what he had accomplished—as long as he obtained new copyrights for the assets he used, of course. Another option, she said, was to do pro-bono work for non-profits or other organizations, who would usually let him keep his copyright in exchange for the work.

Heartened, Sam thanked her. He was able to create a new portfolio without using any of the company's copyrighted courses.

When eLearning content designers create material for their courses, they invest considerable amount of time, skill, effort, and money into its production. If you are an independent designer, or running your own eLearning consulting business, you have much more at stake in your creations. As a result, there is often an implied understanding of "ownership" for the content. However, oftentimes content created through your toil and labor can be surreptitiously copied and used by someone else; depriving you not only of acknowledgement of ownership, but also of potential material and financial benefits that may have accrued to you. Copyright aims to put an end to such "misappropriation" of content that lawfully belongs to you. In most cases (though there are limitations and exemptions) such protection grants the original creator the right to own the content, and decide who can use, share or disseminate it.

Here is what you, as an instructional designer, should know about Copyright Protection in eLearning.

Your eLearning content, when properly copyrighted, enjoys protection under the Copyright Law of the United States. The Copyright Act of 1976 as subsequently amended since then, offers lawful owners the rights to safeguard their creations and, where legally permitted, enjoy the benefits of those creations.

Copyright protection in eLearning allows you to solely own protected content, and gives you the exclusive right to decide on distribution, sharing, or third-party use of the content. However, you should be aware that not everything you produce for an eLearning course might be copyrighted. If there is an express understanding that someone else (for instance, your employer or the institution you are developing the content for) will own the content, then you may not have any rights to what you have designed and created. If you are developing a course on your own (i.e. not on behalf of someone else who will legally own your creations), then you should consider using the copyright symbol—©—on all of your original works during the development phase of your eLearning content. When using the copyright symbol ©, it is not necessary for you to formally file for copyright protection. However, having a formal copyright assignment makes it easier to defend your title/ownership if material breaches of your copyrights do occur. Once copyrighted, your eLearning material receives special protections that make you its exclusive owner, allowing you ultimate control on its distribution, use and dissemination. Copyrighted content can also provide you special economic opportunities, as a result of which, you can monetize your works.

One very important thing to keep in mind is that the law does not protect the fundamental ideas that your content deals with—just the original (and unique) expression of your own thoughts.

A very pertinent aspect of copyright protection in eLearning content is enshrined in the Digital Millennium Copyright Act (DMCA) of 1998, which took the original copyrights laws and brought them into the digital age. DMCA is most relevant to you, as an electronic content designer and creator, because it offers you additional protection and remedies to safeguard your digital content from unintended or malicious use.

When designing your own eLearning courses, you may sometimes have the need to use content created by your peers, or content you download from the internet (public domain). The question is: Can you do that without running afoul of the Copyright Act? The answer is: Yes, but with certain limitations.

Most copyrighted content grants original creators *"exclusive right"* for only a limited duration (typically 50 to 100 years). Once exclusive right-unencumbered content enters the public domain, it may still be the originator's creation, but is limited by the **"Fair use"** guidelines.

Under *fair use*, original content can still be copied (in full or part) and used by others without the creator's permission. However, the use of such content must be done in a way that is not unduly "unfair" to the original creator.

If you are in need of content created by others, which you can use without infringing on other people's copyright, then you should start your search at the *Creative Commons (CC) archive*. While this resource may offer content that you can use under the "Fair Use" guidelines, you must always check with the creator about appropriate use.

When you do locate content that you believe can be used under "Fair Use," make sure you use this proprietary Fair Use Evaluator to ascertain whether your intended use is indeed "fair." The tool also produces a useful report that you can maintain as proof of your endeavors.

For additional information related to Creative Commons and a fair use evaluator tool, visit: http://librarycopyright.net/resources/fairuse/index.php

Note that if you come across unlawful use of your digital copyrighted content on the internet, you can file a *Legal Removal Request* at Google (other search engines and website owners are legally obligated to offer similar services) and seek for such content to be excluded from its search engine. You can officially apply for a Copyright here: https://www.loc.gov/

Copyright laws, like any other branch of legality, are rife with challenges with regards to interpretation, nuances and definitions. As a result, if possible, when facing copyrights issue, you should always consult with a copyrights lawyer before making any decisions related to your rights.

Test Your Knowledge

1. True or False Can all eLearning content be copyrighted?
   A. True
   B. False

2. What does "fair use" mean?
   A. Fair use means that eLearning content can be used and reused by anyone without any restrictions and for any purpose.
   B. Fair use means that only images from the course not the content can be freely reused for the purpose of teaching, scholarly research, or news reporting.
   C. Fair use means that any content that does not have the © symbol next to it can be reused in other eLearning courses for the teaching purpose.
   D. Fair use means that certain content can be used without obtaining permission for the purpose of teaching, scholarly research, news reporting, or review.

BONUS

Becoming an Instructional Designer: What does it take?

In today's consumer-driven economy, few fields of specialization are well defined and clearly remarked. That is because "specialists" today need to continually evolve to meet the changing demands of their professions. As they morph their skill sets to fulfill new and emerging customer requirements, the body of knowledge of their professions evolves too.

Instructional design is one such profession that has been evolving at a much faster pace than many other emerging digital-economy professions. Historically, an instructional designer supported the creation of, or participated in the selection of appropriate instructional materials. These creations or selections were subject to specific processes, and involved the use of time-honored educational psychology principles that resulted in the end deliverable. For instance, the instructional designer could:

- develop digital content for an online employee indoctrination program
- create user or operational manuals for a piece of heavy equipment
- produce decision-trees that 911 operators would use to triage an emergency call
- assist with producing supplementary course materials (e.g. quizzes, self-evaluation questions, etc.) for an IT Certification course.

As is apparent, the depth and breadth of ID-related activities is staggering, and the evolution of new-media and emerging tools and technologies makes the field even more challenging—more so than many related/similar professions. That is why breaking into the profession requires some creativity. So, let's take a look at some of the competencies needed to make it in the ID world.

Like all modern-day professions, instructional designers must possess a core set of competencies to break into the field.

1. **Communication** – Stems from being able to effectively "speak" through written, oral and graphical/visual media
2. **Staying current** – As evidenced by the ability to quickly learn and adopt newer ID tools, technologies and concepts as soon as they surface
3. **Probing mindset** – Refers to the innate ability to understand new and complex concepts, while being open to researching and learning about them

4. **Supporting Instructional Design Competencies** – Successful instructional designers need to be conversant in the methodologies of their chosen profession. For professionals who have a strong set of core competencies, acquiring or polishing the following additional traits will go a long way to make a successful career out of ID.

Let's take a look at some of these competencies:

1. **Planning and Analyzing** – Successful ID projects never start with development. Designers must have the ability to take a step back to plan and analyze what is needed of them. This means deciding:

   - What the content is
   - Who the content is for
   - How it must be delivered, and
   - What tools and technologies are best suited to get the job done.

2. **Designing and Developing** – Equipped with the plan and the analysis, the instructional designer should be competent enough to put together the necessary content using appropriate technologies, tools, techniques and strategies.

3. **Implementing and Managing** – A well-designed instructional package is only as good as how well its implementation/roll-out is managed. Key competencies for this role include collaboration, communication, scheduling and prioritizing, conflict and people management.

Success will ultimately hinge on creating the right environment for developing and receiving/consuming the content. The instructional designer should therefore master the skills of working across teams and using tools such as social media to engage trainers, Subject Matter Experts, and learners.

While the ability to promote a sense of "wanting to succeed" amongst all stakeholders is crucial, so too is the ability to recognize that training might not necessarily be the answer to the challenges faced by the stakeholder group.

Instructional Design Areas of Expertise

There is nothing wrong with being a Jack/Jill of all trades, but today's global economy calls for specialists. While some instructional designers prefer to specialize in a specific niche, others may build expertise in more than one area. Some popular areas of expertise to consider include:

- Curriculum Designer
- ELearning Developer
- Media Specialist
- Authoring Specialist
- Learning Management Specialist, and
- Project Manager

Within a specific niche, ID offers many choices for specialization too. For instance, expertise might be developed based on the type of media used (online training, games, videos, or classroom training). One may also specialize in the type of market segment, for instance Corporate, Government, or Not-For-Profit organizations. Still, other designers may prefer to become experts in servicing a specific audience, for instance Adolescents, Teens, Adult learners, Gamers, Stay-at-Home parents, or Do-It-Yourselfers.

Networking and Portfolios

Breaking into any field, especially if you are fresh out of a learning program, is difficult. However, if you take time to build your networks of contacts, you are bound to fare much better than someone who does not network. Networking is what will "spread the word" around for you, and open doors of opportunities that you would never otherwise be aware of.

Join as many networking communities as possible, including *Facebook, LinkedIn,* Twitter, and *Google Plus.* Attending Instructional Design seminars, *workshops* and *conferences* is great for in-person networking. Seek membership of professional associations, such as Association of Talent Development (ATD), Chief Learning Officer (CLO), Society for Applied Learning Technology (SALT), and International Society for Performance Improvement (ISPI), for additional networking and link-building opportunities.

A great resume is a good starting point for prospective employment seekers. However, if you want to start somewhere in the instructional design profession, chances are the first thing prospective employers will ask you is:

"So, what can you do for us?" That is where a picture paints a thousand words!

Do not just tell them what you can do—be prepared to show them your portfolio. Include a collection of works you may have previously produced. Time invested in developing and then continually updating your portfolio is well worth spending.

Now you know the importance of having a portfolio. However, you are probably asking yourself where to get samples to build your portfolio if you do not have any instructional design experience. Here is the answer: you do need to have experience to build your portfolio and apply to jobs, but you can get both experience and a portfolio relatively quickly without any formal job experience. Let's look at some ways to get content for your portfolio.

1. **Volunteer** – You can find an online organization that does not require you to travel to the location. ELearning for Kids is a global nonprofit foundation dedicated to free and fun online learning for kids of all ages. They now have courses for adult learners as well. ELearning for Kids is constantly looking for volunteers who can contribute their time and knowledge. The process for becoming a volunteer is simple, and they have all types of projects from basic storyboarding to developing courses to quality assurance. LINGOs (Learning in NGOs) is a not-for-profit consortium of more than 75 international humanitarian relief and development organizations. LINGOs engages companies and associations working in the field of technology assisted learning, and they always look for volunteers. Global Giveback is another organization that needs volunteers. To learn more and to get started, sign up for the Global Giveback Group on LinkedIn. There are many other organizations that are seeking volunteers. Simply spend time searching for them, explain who you are, and ask for projects. You can also consider contacting a university that has an instructional design or eLearning development program and see if they have or are aware of any volunteering or internship opportunities.

2. **Develop a course** – Another easy way to add a sample to your portfolio is to develop a course on any niche, and submit it to any eLearning provider. There are many eLearning companies that offer free courses and would be more than happy to have you donate your course to them. Some examples of these providers are ALISON and Carnegie Mellon University. By doing this, you will be able to showcase both your ability to design instructionally sound courses and develop lessons using eLearning and graphic design tools.

3. **Freelancing opportunities** – Businesses and Organizations often outsource work to freelancers. Since your goal is to build a portfolio, look for something that you can do, and offer to do the job almost at no cost to the outsourcer. This will be a win-win situation. The outsourcer will not

have to pay the fee he normally would for this service, and you will get a portfolio piece to showcase. Never offer to do anything you do not know how to do as this may result in a bad review or feedback.

4. **Create your own samples** – As you play with eLearning software, build prototypes that you can include in your portfolio. If you come across a project you really like, try figuring out how it was built, and consider rebuilding it yourself. Remember, if you do not know how to do something, help is always available from community members as well as on forums, blogs, and LinkedIn groups.

Now that we have talked about the sources you can use to build your portfolio, let's talk about different *artifacts* that should go into the portfolio. Below are some of the most common documents that most employers want to see in portfolios. If you have any other samples worth showcasing, feel free to include them too.

1. **Needs Analysis Document** – This document will show your employer that you know how to conduct research and that you are familiar with various data collection methods.

2. **Design Document** – Being able to create a design document is often a requirement in many organizations. This is a blueprint for both eLearning and face-to-face training. Most employers expect to see at least one design document to get an idea of how you design training exercises.

3. **Storyboards** – Always include at least one storyboard, and whenever possible, consider including different types of storyboards. For example, if one of your storyboards was created in Word and another one in PowerPoint, adding both of them to your portfolio will be beneficial.

4. **Facilitator and Participant Guides** – Typically, facilitator and participant guides are only necessary for developing face-to-face training and synchronous eLearning courses. However, even if the job you are applying for requires only the development of asynchronous eLearning, including these guides in your portfolio will show your prospective employer that you have a variety of skills and are able to develop training courses for any mode.

5. **Evaluation** – Consider including examples of all four levels of evaluation. If you have experience creating assessments, try to include some samples and document corrective feedback you provide to learners based on the response they select.

6. **Documentation or proof of programming, web design or graphic design skills** – Nowadays, both instructional designers and eLearning professionals are expected to know and be able to use eLearning development tools as well as graphic design,

image manipulation, and video editing tools. Lynda.com offers excellent training courses to help you acquire the needed skills. As you learn the tools and programs, consider creating short samples to display them in your portfolio.

7. **ELearning samples** – If possible, include a range of eLearning samples, and avoid including similar projects. You want to show your prospective employer that you are capable of handling different types of assignments. Including samples of both linear and nonlinear courses would be ideal. If you have created games or simulations, consider making them part of your portfolio too. The same goes for mobile learning, job aids, or any other materials you may have developed. Remember, more samples equal more experience, and more experience equals more opportunities.

8. **Writing /editing samples** – Good instructional designers must also be excellent writers and editors. If you have any published articles or papers, consider including them in your portfolio. If you do not have any formal publications, you can include any other writing samples. These can be scripts, unpublished papers, or even related blog posts. If you have edited someone else's work, it is a good idea to include a sample with your comments/feedback. If you do not have any writing or editing samples, consider volunteering as a writer/editor, or simply write something you are interested in or highly opinionated about, and make it part of your portfolio. It is best to include at least two types of professional writing – technical and conversational.

9. **Recommendations/ copies of certificates, endorsements, etc**. – As you are gaining experience through formal work assignments or volunteering, you are also expanding the network of professionals who can offer their recommendation about your knowledge and skills. Whenever possible, ask for a letter of recommendation or endorsement and include them in your portfolio. Do not trash those glowing emails you get from your colleagues or supervisors – they can help you get your next job. It is also recommended to include copies of certificates you earn, and add them as artifacts to your portfolio.

Obviously, there are many other artifacts that may enhance your portfolio. However, including too many of them may overwhelm your prospective employer. The best way to decide what to include and what to exclude is to make a list of all the items you have created as well as all the skills you want to showcase. Then, select your artifacts based on skills you have identified.

Avoid adding artifacts without explaining what skill they demonstrate and what thought process you followed to design them. Do not make your descriptions long or overly complicated. Simply adding few sentences or short paragraphs will help your prospective employer understand your ideas and instructional approaches. Before including artifacts in your portfolio, always ask for permission. Keep in mind that some projects may be proprietary, especially those done for government clients; therefore, you may not be allowed to display them in your portfolio. However, proprietary projects are not a decent excuse for not having a portfolio at all. You can always volunteer at organizations that will allow you to use projects in your portfolio. You can also blur out the text, displaying only the design elements, such as the organization of the lesson. Another alternative is to recreate your proprietary projects using any other content you may know or be interested in.

Now, let's talk about the format of your portfolio. There are two possibilities: you can either create an *electronic* or *paper-based* portfolio. First, let's look *at digital portfolios*. Below are some of the most popular tools you can use to create your electronic portfolio. While they are not listed in any particular order, VisualCV is probably the best one because it is easy to use and also because it can convert your digital resume/portfolio into a PDF file that you can easily print and bring to the interview.

- Silkapp
- Dropr
- Weebly
- Blogger
- DoYouBuzz
- Flavors.me
- VisualCV
- Webs
- Wordpress
- Wix

When it comes to the paper-based portfolio, your options range from inserting your artifacts into a three ring binder to investing in a professional portfolio binder. Regardless of the option you choose, consider purchasing sheet protectors to keep your portfolio pieces safe and clean as well as make your portfolio look more polished and professional. It is also a good idea to add dividers to separate the sections of your portfolio. This way, your portfolio will appear more organized.

It is suggested to have both electronic and printed versions of your portfolio. Your electronic portfolio can be easily accessible, you can update it almost effortlessly, and your prospective employer can always refer back to it when making his hiring decision. On the other hand, carrying a physical copy of your portfolio to the interview can immediately impress the interviewer and help you win that job!

Keeping your portfolio organized will help you find the items you want to show your prospective employer easily. Also, a well-organized portfolio will show you put some thought into it. There are many ways to organize your eLearning portfolio. Below are just some of them.

Put your documents in chronological order starting from the year you began working in the field and ending with the most up-to-date samples of your work. You can also categorize your artifacts based on the ADDIE model. This way, your portfolio will have five sections. The first section will be dedicated to analysis. Your analysis documents will go here. *The next section will be dedicated to design.* You will most likely include your design documents here. *Your third section will deal with all the pieces you developed* for your eLearning courses. You will also include your storyboards here. *The fourth section in your portfolio will present details* that deal with implementation of course material. If, for example, you did any work with LMS, you may want to include it here. If you were a presenter in any of the trainings you created, you can include sample videos or screenshots in this section. If the outcome of your course was a printed brochure, you can also include it here. *The fifth section should display your ability to conduct the four levels of evaluation* as well as include examples of assessment items you created. If you decide to organize your portfolio based on the ADDIE model, you may add another section at the end, showcasing those items that did not fit into the above categories such as recommendations and certificates of achievement.

Another good way to categorize your items is by creating sections for each type of work you have done. For example, you may have a separate section for your storyboards, writing samples, eLearning projects developed with various tools, and project management documents.

If during your career you were exposed to many different areas of expertise and wore many different hats, you may also consider organizing your portfolio according to the ten areas of expertise in the ATD Competency Model. These areas are:

- Performance Improvement
- Instructional Design
- Training Delivery
- Learning Technologies
- Evaluating Learning Impact
- Managing Learning Programs
- Integrated Talent Management
- Coaching

- Knowledge Management
- Change Management

Remember, there is no single best approach for organizing your portfolio. The method you select will mostly depend on the experience you have in the field, and on the items you want to showcase.

Summary

There are many decisions involved in creating an effective eLearning course. As you plan your training, you need to decide how many modules or lessons to include and split the content accordingly, paying close attention to objectives. For optimum retention, you should keep each lesson no longer than 20 minutes in length. Creating a storyboard is probably one of the most effective methods for organizing the material. Not only will storyboards lay out the content, but they will also serve as guidelines for programmers, multimedia specialists, and graphic artists who will be working on the course. Successful storyboard design will allow for visualizing the course and identifying gaps that need to be filled. In addition to separating and organizing the content, instructional designers should create a consistent navigation and layout of the lesson.

Another important step in the ISD process is going through the content and analyzing it for possible games and interactivities. By varying presentation of information as much as possible, instructional designers will be able to address the needs of most learners. For example, they can show a video clip for visual learners, create voiceover slides for auditory learners, and design a game or role-play for kinesthetic learners.

Whenever you are tasked with designing an eLearning course, the first step should always be conducting a needs analysis and reviewing the existing content. Then, based on the information gathered from the analysis, you can develop measurable learning objectives, keeping in mind that if the problem is not related to lack of knowledge or skills, even the best eLearning course will not solve it. When the content and objectives are in place, the decision about the presentation methods should be made. Some of these methods include:

- Video
- Audio
- Coaching
- Scenarios
- Role-plays
- Case studies
- Demonstrators
- Simulations
- Games
- Charts and diagrams
- Puzzles
- Assignments

- Activities and exercises
- Reading materials

Table 18 suggests methods for presenting different types of information.

Table 18 - Teaching Suggestions

Information Type	Methods
Facts, theories, procedures	• Competition games • Simulations • Activities and exercises • Case studies • Scenarios
Cognitive skills	• Demonstrations • Simulations • Coaching • Exercises • Role-play games • Adventure games
Making decisions or judgements	• Case studies • Role-plays • Adventure games • Detective games • Simulations • Scenarios
Reasoning and Analyzing	• Simulations • Games • Puzzles • Scenarios • Role-plays • Case studies

While ADDIE is the most commonly used ISD model, choosing the rapid eLearning approach may be wise as this method allows you to create training materials quickly and efficiently. As a result, clients will receive a quality product and spend significantly less money on it. Most of the time, if the course focuses on transmitting information, using a rapid eLearning tool is the best option. With rapid eLearning tools, you can save money by quickly adding audio, video, graphics, animations, and web objects without hiring expensive graphic artists, multimedia specialists, and computer programmers.

In addition to choosing the right development tools, you must consider technical issues such as the hosting of the course. You should also address SCORM and 508-compliance requirements.

When most people think of eLearning, they typically think of online courses; however, today's generation is so well versed in technology that eLearning is now available as podcasts and blogs. Educational software can be downloaded to mobile devices, iPods, and PDAs. This forces instructional designers to find ways to make their eLearning content available as mLearning. Nowadays, in addition to being able to learn from computers, the new generation wants to be able to download podcasts to smartphones and read blogs and forum postings pertinent to the topic. By incorporating social learning tools and making them part of the blended learning solution, you can add the collaboration element to lessons and address the needs of the younger generation at the same time.

The entire development process of the eLearning courses can be complex and overwhelming. By splitting the project into sections and putting check marks next to the already completed sections, you will ensure that all the important points are covered and the development of the course is moving in the right direction.

The proliferation of learning technologies has given rise to a number of approaches that instructional designers can use to deliver eLearning content.

Based on extensive research, the National Training Laboratories (NTL) developed an effective Learning Pyramid that demonstrates a clear relationship between the teaching method of choice, and content retention rates.

Your choice of how (the most effective approach) you wish to deliver learning, should be based on what (the content) you want to deliver (not the other way around!). Content Domain Analysis and Content Level Analysis should be conducted prior to selecting the instructional approach. Content Domain Analysis must be carried out in order to determine the fundamental objectives of the content. For instance, does the content address cognitive, emotional or physical characteristics of a learner? Based on the result of your analysis, you will be able to frame an overall instructional goal for the course-level content you are about to create. Content Level Analysis is used to determine how your content should be sequenced to achieve the domain level instructional goals.

Linear vs. non-linear analysis should also be conducted to analyze content for sequence. If you determine that the content must be delivered sequentially, then your delivery mechanism should include approaches that control the flow of your content, such as locked navigation. Rigidly controlled sequential "menu type" delivery would be ideal in such situations.

Related vs. non-related analysis helps to assess content for relevance. Where possible, grouping the delivery of related modules will have a positive impact on content retention. Use an approach that allows learners to view all related modules as a complete unit.

If after analyzing the content, you decided to package it as non-related modules, you should then consider providing learners with the opportunity to consume content at their discretion. For instance, allowing them to browse and review course lectures in any order they desire.

Analyzing pre-requisites is also a critical step in content review. If it is determined that there are certain prerequisites for the course, then these pre-requisites should be presented in a separate modules/units and delivered using a suitable approach, for example, through reading materials or pre-recorded lectures.

As a result of content analysis, instructional designers should have a clear understanding of the hierarchical structure and sequence of presentation methods. This understanding typically serves as a blueprint needed to determine the best delivery method—face-to-face, eLearning, mLearning, video-on-demand, gamification, podcasts, or a combination of instructional approaches.

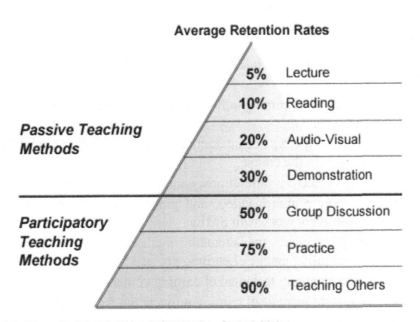

The Learning Pyramid*

Average Retention Rates

Passive Teaching Methods		
	5%	Lecture
	10%	Reading
	20%	Audio-Visual
	30%	Demonstration

Participatory Teaching Methods		
	50%	Group Discussion
	75%	Practice
	90%	Teaching Others

*Adapted from National Training Laboratories. Bethel, Maine

Conclusion

We have now come to the end of Instructional Design for eLearning: Essential guide to creating successful eLearning courses. However, as the fields of instructional design and eLearning continue to evolve, the learning journey will never end. You should always aim towards continuous professional development and constant acquisition of new knowledge and skills. In addition to introducing the major ISD theories and models, this book covered the basics of instructional design such as:

- learning theories,
- learning styles,
- motivation,
- memory, and
- the six principles of effective eLearning courses.

The book has also walked you through the course creation enabling you to:

- conduct needs analysis and gather data;
- design an effective eLearning lesson according to Gagné's Nine Events of Instruction;
- create design documents, storyboards, and scripts based on the instructional design best practices; as well as
- effectively implement and evaluate eLearning courses.

Moreover, after reading this book, you should be able to utilize your skills to:

- identify an eLearning authoring tool that meets specific project's requirements;
- decide on the type of interactivity and presentation method to be included in the course;
- design effective simulations, games, and learning scenarios;
- incorporate audio, video, and graphics in eLearning courses; productively work with SMEs;
- utilize project management methods and techniques to successfully manage eLearning projects;
- create engaging technical eLearning content;
- create and manage eLearning projects the Agile way; and
- identify the situations when eLearning courses can benefit from job aids, social, and mobile learning solutions.

As we have already discussed in this book, there is no single, unique approach to course design. All instructional designers have their personal preference for certain methods and techniques. As they gain experience, they also develop their own best practices. However, I hope that you will transfer the skills you gained from reading the Instructional Design for eLearning to the job and enhance the courses you develop with the suggestions and tools presented in this book.

To your instructional design and eLearning success!

Self-Evaluation

Use the checklist below to self-evaluate knowledge and skills acquired from this text.

Table 19 - Self-Evaluation Checklist

You should now be able to	Yes	No
Define the terms "instructional systems design," "eLearning," and "blended learning"		
Differentiate between CBT and WBT		
Explain advantages and disadvantages of eLearning		
Decide when eLearning is appropriate		
Name major contributors to the field of instruction design		
Describe most popular ISD models		
Describe the steps in the ADDIE model and apply them to the course design		
Apply the principles of major learning theories to your course design		
Define the concept of andragogy and describe Malcolm Knowles's six principles of adult learning		
Describe major learning style models and apply them to the training courses		
Describe the role of memory in eLearning design		
Describe cognitive load and apply it to your course design		
Conduct needs analysis using appropriate data collection methods		
Write SMART learning objectives using the A-B-C-D format and Bloom's Taxonomy		
Name the three learning domains		
Identify the stages of revised Bloom's Taxonomy		
Name the five stages of SOLO taxonomy and apply them to learning objectives		
Construct a lesson plan using Gagné's Nine Events of Instruction		
Create a design document		
Construct an eLearning storyboard and prototype		
Write voiceover scripts using plain language principles		
Create a style guide for the eLearning course		

Conduct alpha and pilot testing		
Name major LMSs and CMSs		
Design SCORM and Section 508-compliant eLearning courses		
Construct the five types of evaluations		
Create valid and reliable assessment items for you eLearning courses		
Construct intrinsic and extrinsic feedback statements		
Explain the levels of interactivity in eLearning		
Identify and apply interactive presentation methods to eLearning courses		
Apply the storytelling techniques to create games, simulations, and scenarios		
Describe the types of learning games		
Select the appropriate game type for the eLearning course		
Identify major eLearning authoring and development tools available on the market		
Select the appropriate software program for projects' needs		
Identify the types of videos in eLearning		
Explain reasons for including video and audio in eLearning courses		
Design screencasts for eLearning courses		
Explain the benefits of graphics in eLearning courses		
Identify and describe the types of graphics		
Apply Ruth Clark's visual design model to eLearning courses		
Explain the basics of color theory and typography		
Recognize most commonly used file sizes		
Explain the role and responsibilities of Subject Matter Experts in designing eLearning courses		
Communicate with Subject Matter Experts		
Collect information from Subject Matter Experts		
Use the IPECC model to manage eLearning projects		
Explain reasons for including job aids in eLearning courses		
Name the types of job aids and describe the appropriate use for each type		
Design learning experiences for Web 2.0 and mobile technology		
Describe eLearning copyright laws		
Create effective eLearning portfolio		

Test Your Knowledge – Answer Key

PART I Basic Elements of Instructional Design

Chapter 1 – Instructional Design and ELearning

1. The correct answer is A. Instructional Systems Design is a systematic approach to creating effective courses and training solutions.

2. The correct answers are B, C, and D. Most skilled instructional designers rely on various technologies and multimedia to enhance their courses. They focus on providing value to the organization by managing a project's time and cost, and know that the success of their learners is measured by their performance improvement. However, they do not need to be able to create a large number of courses in a short amount of time. In fact, highly interactive courses always require a lot of time to design and develop.

3. The correct answer is A. ELearning is a form of learning conducted via internet, Intranet, or CD-ROM. As instructional designers create their courses, they should carefully analyze the content and decide which modality best suits their needs.

4. The correct answers are B, C, and D. Successful eLearning courses must be interactive, energetic, and dynamic. Furthermore, they must appeal to the learner's auditory, visual, and tactile senses. In addition, eLearning can be either synchronous or asynchronous. However, successful eLearning courses do not necessarily have to be created using templates and pre-programmed multimedia interactions.

5. The correct answers are A, B, and D. Synchronous ELearning is done in real-time with a live instructor. Because of this, learners must attend the course at a specific time, and require a computer, internet connection, and access to audio and video conferencing. Furthermore, it is difficult to revisit content when all learning is done in real-time. However, synchronous eLearning does have the value of a real instructor and the ability to communicate with other participants in the course.

6. The correct answers are A, C, and E. Asynchronous ELearning is self-paced, allowing learners to go through courses as quickly or slowly as they desire. Some commonly used tools are forums, blogs, and webcasts.

7. The correct answer is B. Blended learning can help instructional designers address different learning styles, as it combines the needs of more traditional learners with the needs of the younger, so-called "net" generation.

8. The correct answers are B and D. With eLearning courses, the

learner can access courses anytime, anywhere, at their own pace. They can also go back and review course materials as needed.

9. The correct answers are A, B, and C. ELearning is not always a substitute for traditional classroom training. Unmotivated learners may not retain much information during a self-paced course. Also, if the course contains ambiguous information, the lack of immediate assistance may hinder learning. Furthermore, learners with low computer literacy may not fully benefit from the learning experience.

10. The correct answers are B and C. ELearning is overall cheaper than ILT. The development costs of eLearning are more expensive than ILT. However, implementation costs for eLearning are cheaper because they do not include the costs of paying the trainer, renting a training room, and printing hard copies of course materials.

11. The correct answers are A, C, and D. Many times, stakeholders want something that they do not really need. Finding vital information about the audience, the budget, and the goals of the training allow you to inform you and your stakeholders what type of solution is best for their needs. The skills determine whether an eLearning or traditional classroom training (or a combination) is best for the particular course. Geographic location helps you determine whether learners will need to travel to the course location or if all learners are in the same location. The overall costs of eLearning are lower than those of ILT; however, the budget will help you determine what costs you can and should include in your project.

Chapter 3 – Instructional Design Models

1. The correct answer is C. Top instructional designers do not follow any particular approach. Instead, they choose whatever technique best suits the specific needs of a course's audience and content.

2. The correct answer is C. ADDIE stands for Analysis, Design, Development, Implementation, and Evaluation.

3. The correct answer is B. In the design phase of ADDIE, you should write objectives and craft the structure and sequencing of the course. You also create a project management plan with deadlines, milestones, implementation details, and possibly budgeting.

4. The correct answer is D. The Seels and Glasgow ISD model places design within the context of project management, ensuring that a course stays within the time and budget constraints. In this model, the phases are Needs Analysis Management, Instructional Design Management, and Implementation of Evaluation Management.

5. The correct answer is B. This model incorporates the learner's needs, skills, and learning context into the course design. It is widely implemented by curriculum developers in higher education.

6. The correct answer is D. The Accelerated Learning Rapid Instructional Design (RID) model is ideal for those who work under tight deadlines, a limited budget, and constantly changing content.

7. The correct answer is B. Even though the RID model makes courses more interactive and engaging, it does not incorporate analysis and evaluation phases, which are crucial in the development of an eLearning course.

8. The correct answer is A. In the Preparation phase, learners are presented with learning objectives. During the Presentation phase, learners acquire new knowledge and skills. In the Practice phase, new knowledge and skills are integrated by incorporating games and other practice exercises. Learners also receive substantial corrective feedback. In the last phase, Performance, learners apply the new knowledge and skills and are rewarded for mastering the material.

9. The correct answer is C. Successive Approximation Model, or SAM, is an Agile instructional design model.

10. The correct answer is B. The SAM model focuses on prototyping more heavily than other instructional design models do. The model expects that mistakes will be made throughout the project and that stakeholders will change their minds or decide to make corrections along the way.

11. The correct answer is A. The Successive Approximation Model (SAM) was created by Michael Allen. It emphasizes collaboration, efficiency, and repetition.

Chapter 4 – Learning Theories

1. The correct answers are A, C, and D. There are three learning theories typically addressed within the scope of effective instructional design: behaviorism, cognitivism, and constructivism.

2. The correct answer is B. Each of the three learning theories has its strengths and weaknesses. To choose the theory that suits the needs of a specific course, you should take multiple aspects of learning into consideration, including their goals, learners, and situations.

3. The correct answer is B. Behaviorism is based on observable and measurable changes in behavior, and it assumes that the learner's behavior is shaped through either positive or negative reinforcement.

4. The correct answer is C. Cognitivism is considered an active learning process, believing that information is received, stored, and retrieved.

5. The correct answer is B. When cognitivists design courses, they focus primarily on the learner, and make learning meaningful through using learners' background knowledge.

6. The correct answer is C. Behaviorists concentrate on a change in behavior, not the visual elements of content.

7. The correct answer is A. Malcolm Knowles defined andragogy as "the art and science of helping adults learn", and he identified six principles of adult learning.

8. The correct answer is E. Knowles identified the six principles of adult learning as: Adults are internally motivated; they bring life experiences to new learning situations; they are goal and relevancy oriented, practical, and like to be respected.

Chapter 5 – Learning Styles

1. The correct answer is C. It is nearly impossible to create one perfect solution that would close the gap between all learning styles, but there are certainly ways to help you create courses to satisfy most learners' needs.

2. The correct answers are A, C, E, and F. In the Concrete Experience stage, instructors should serve as motivators. In the Reflective Observation stage, instructors should serve as experts. In the Abstract Conceptualization stage, instructors should serve as coaches. In the last stage, Active Experimentation, instructors should serve as facilitators.

3. The correct answer is D. Divergers prefer to learn through hands-on exploration, which the instructor should follow with constructive feedback. Convergers learn best through games and simulations. Assimilators prefer to learn through lectures, experiments, and conceptual models. Lastly, accommodators prefer to learn through hands-on activities, presentations, role-plays, and debates.

4. The correct answer is A. Generation Y, or Millennials, are individuals ages 18-28. They prefer eLearning to in-class lectures or workshops.

5. The correct answer is C. Generation X, learners ages 29-46, prefer eLearning. They enjoy experiential learning activities, and like self-study.

6. The correct answer is D. Besides preferring eLearning, Generation Y prefers to learn through social learning tools like blogs, podcasts, and mobile applications.

7. The correct answer is A. Traditionalists are individuals ages 66 and over. They prefer learning through lectures, and they do not like exercises such as role-plays and interactive gaming elements.

8. The correct answer is B. Understanding the VAK model is one way to cover the needs of most generations. To ensure better retention among learners, it is important to accommodate all three learning styles by adding at least one activity that fits each learning style.

Chapter 6 – Motivation

1. The correct answer is A. If a learner takes the course because they enjoy it or because they want to develop a particular skill, there is an internal drive, which describes intrinsic motivation. Extrinsic motivation describes learners who have external motivation, such as monetary rewards, certificates, or good grades.

2. The correct answer is A. Each of Maslow's five basic needs must be met before the person moves to the next basic need. These are physiological needs, safety needs, love/belonging needs, the need for esteem, and then the need for self-actualization.

3. The correct answer is D. It is highly recommended that learners get enough sleep and get a good breakfast before training so that their physiological needs are met. If those needs are not met, the learner will not gain from the training because the first basis need is not met.

4. The correct answer is C. When training is completed, learners expect to be able to utilize their newly acquired knowledge to grow on either a personal or professional level.

5. The correct answer is D. To make sure the learners' "What's in it for me?" question is answered, combine the internal and external needs and motivators. This helps ensure that learners are motivated to finish the course and thus, improve the results.

6. The correct answer is B. Keller focuses on a systematic approach to designing motivational learning, consisting of four steps: attention, relevance, confidence, and satisfaction.

7. The correct answer is B. Relevance is the second step in the ARCS model. In this step, you should demonstrate the importance and usefulness of the content through relevant examples and learning goals.

PART II Designing Instructionally Sound ELearning Courses

Chapter 7 – Needs Analysis and Data Collection Methods

1. The correct answer is C. The Analysis phase is an important part of instructional design. Through the needs analysis, you learn the reason for creating the course, the target audience, and the approach you need to take in designing the course. You also decide on media and delivery method, and whether the training is really a viable solution.

2. The correct answer is B. The three major types of analysis are audience analysis, performance analysis, and task analysis.

3. The correct answer is D. Sometimes, an instructional designer conducts a thorough needs analysis to determine that the performance issue

cannot be solved by a training course. If you do not conduct the audience analysis, you may develop a useless course. You may not address the real training need, wasting money, time, and resources.

4. The correct answer is C. The essence of the Five Why Technique is to continue asking the Why questions until you find the root cause of the problem.

5. The correct answer is B. If the performance gap analysis shows that the problem lies in knowledge and skills, you can proceed with the training. However, if the problem is with motivation, lack of tools, or lack of organizational support, realize that training will not solve a performance improvement issue.

6. The correct answer is A. Use the instructional analysis to break down the task of each instructional goal and help eliminate extraneous information.

7. The correct answer is C. The best method that suits the specific needs analysis depends on several factors, including the intensity of the analysis and the amount of time dedicated to the analysis. Whenever possible, try to choose several different methods to ensure accurate data collection.

8. The correct answer is B. When you do not have budget for needs analysis, you should at least consider reviewing relevant documents. However, you should understand that the information found in documents can be outdated, inaccurate, incomplete, and disorganized.

9. The correct answer is A. The primary advantage of Observation is that it allows instructional designers to see what people do and how they perform without relying on their readiness to provide information. However, the disadvantage is that people typically perform better when they know they are being observed.

10. The correct answer is C. Interviews work well for gathering information about current business needs, performance, and audience analysis. The biggest problem with interviews, however, is that they can be costly and time-consuming.

11. The correct answer is D. Surveys are commonly used for conducting needs analysis. They can help instructional designers obtain both qualitative and quantitative data.

12. The correct answer is C. Many people mark their answers without reading the questions, so data gathered from surveys are not always accurate. Also, participants do not have an opportunity to clarify questions. This means that with a survey, you must use clear and accurate wording in each question.

13. The correct answer is A. Dichotomous questions are yes/no questions. They do not provide enough information for analysis, but they do work well as screening tools to identify people eligible to participate in

the survey.

14. The correct answer is B. Open-ended questions allow participants to write out a detailed answer to the question.

15. The correct answer is B. Open-ended questions are effective because participants have to think about their answer before providing a response. They can provide a lot of valuable, qualitative information for analysis.

16. The correct answer is D. Start your needs analysis by defining your objectives. Then, look at the data. Determine your data-collection method for needs analysis. Then, start collecting your data. Last, use the data you collected and compare, organize, and analyze it.

Chapter 8 – Learning Objectives

1. The correct answer is B. Learning objectives are also called behavioral objectives, performance objectives, or course objectives. The main goal of objectives is to define the scope of the course and help learners focus on specific outcomes.

2. The correct answer is C. You should always write the objectives after conducting needs analysis.

3. The correct answer is A. All objectives should include four components, known as the A-B-C-D format. The components of the objectives are audience, behavior, condition, and degree.

4. The correct answer is B. When you write behavioral statements, try to avoid using verbs like *know* and *understand*, because these verbs are not measurable or observable. Instead, use verbs like *apply*, *classify*, and *explain*.

5. The correct answer is B. Degree is the level at which learners must perform the task. Some examples are without error, successfully five times, within one hour, and on two different issues.

6. The correct answer is B. Make sure you write measurable objectives. They should focus on the evaluation standards and include some type of measurement, such as standards. You, as the instructional designer, should be able to evaluate this assessment through evaluation.

7. The correct answer is A. Your objectives should be specific, measurable, attainable, relevant, and time-bound.

8. The correct answer is B. In 1956, educational psychologist Benjamin Bloom identified the three learning domains as cognitive domain, affective domain, and psychomotor domain.

9. The correct answer is D. Even though the goal of learning objectives is to help learners focus on their learning experience, most learners do not like to read a list of learning objectives and skip over it. In order for your

learners to truly benefit from the course, they need to know and understand the objectives. Objectives should not only be measurable and observable, but they should also be motivational and relevant, so making them interactive helps learners read and understand them.

10. The correct answer is A. When you use the word *learner* instead of *you*, the objective is less personal. Make your objectives personal. You should also incorporate scenarios because that adds meaning to your objectives.

Chapter 9 – Designing the Learning Experience

1. The correct answer is B. While Robert Gagne did identify a nine-step process known as the Events of Instruction, the book was called "The Conditions of Learning."

2. The correct answer is C. Start by gaining your learners' attention. This event is used to give learners a framework into which they can organize the lesson's content, and it also motivates learners.

3. The correct answer is A. In the last event of learning, instructional designers should provide the opportunity for learners to apply the outcome of their training in a real-world situation. This can include giving learners realistic assignments, practice activities, and exercises. The instructional designer can also provide a desk guide or job aid for future reference.

4. The correct answer is D. It is not always possible to incorporate all nine events into your lesson plan. The correct answer is C. Instructional design professionals use storyboards and prototypes to illustrate and communicate their ideas to team members and stakeholders, thus ensuring the outcome of efforts meets the highest standards.

Chapter 10 – Creating a Design Document

1. The correct answer is B. Create your design document during the design phase of the instructional design process. The goal of this document is to document the entire design process for a specific project, and it is based on the needs analysis. The document should include all the objectives and assessment items for the course.

Chapter 11 – Storyboarding

1. The correct answer is C. Instructional design professionals use storyboards and prototypes to illustrate and communicate their ideas to team members and stakeholders, thus ensuring the outcome of efforts meets the highest standards.

2. The correct answer is B. Storyboards are visual organizers that

illustrate and communicate ideas to others working on the course, such as graphic artists, multimedia specialists, and programmers. Most storyboards include text, visual, and audio elements that appear on every screen of an eLearning course.

3. The correct answer is A. Many instructional designers provide the storyboard templates to subject matter experts. The subject matter experts can then populate the content, thus allowing the instructional designer to arrange the content and add interactivities and assessments.

4. The correct answer is B. There are certain elements that are common to most storyboards. These are content, audio, graphics, and programming instructions or developer's notes.

5. The correct answer is C. Storyboarding is a time-consuming task, but it is a major timesaver in the end. It makes it easy for the subject matter expert to review projects and allow instructional designers to avoid rework. However, storyboards only work well for linear courses. Because many eLearning courses are nonlinear, storyboards can be confusing to subject matter experts and programmers.

6. The correct answer is A. Many instructional designers use rapid prototyping to develop an interactive model of the eLearning course. Rapid prototyping includes all the information found in storyboards, plus the overall course layout, including graphics buttons and navigation.

7. The correct answer is B. Semi-functional prototypes contain interactions and can be used as screenshots in storyboards. Nonfunctional prototypes do not have any functional elements but still have the look and feel of the actual course; they effectively communicate the functionality of the future course. Fully functional prototypes include most of the content, interactions, and assessments. They clearly demonstrate the entire course's functionality.

8. The correct answer is B. There are many tools you can use to build a prototype. You can use Articulate 360, Adobe Captivate, Adobe Flash, and others. If you do not have rapid eLearning tools available, you can use Microsoft PowerPoint to build a prototype.

Chapter 12 – Scripting Your ELearning Course

1. The correct answer is B. When you do not know the subject matter of the course you are developing, you ask questions and clarify statements to get all the information you need for creating a clear and effective script. Many subject matter experts know the content so well that they leave out important information, forget to mention crucial steps in the process, or provide unnecessary content.

2. The correct answer is C. Scripts are written to be heard, not read. Because of this, your writing style should be conversational.

3. The correct answer is A. To add a conversational tone to your script, consider using contractions in any written course materials that are meant to be read. You should also consider using pronouns to make the eLearning content more personal.

4. The correct answer is B. When you write scripts, use plain language principles. Use active voice instead of passive voice. Avoid run-on sentences. Avoid sentences that express more than one idea. Avoid misplaced modifiers. Avoid double negatives. Keep the subject and objects close to the verb. Be sure that when you write the script, it is easily read by your voice talent.

5. The correct answer is D. Always check your script for appropriate transitions. Incorporate pauses into the script to indicate any places where the voice talent should stop and give learners a chance to absorb the information. Also, use 12-point font and double-space the script to help the voice talent read the script more easily.

6. The correct answer is C. Proofread your script multiple times. This helps ensure that you do not still have errors in the script after recording it.

7. The correct answer is B. When you work with other professionals (editors, graphic artists, programmers), it can be difficult to maintain a consistent style. Because of this, it is important to create a standardized style guide for each project.

Chapter 13 – Quality Assurance

1. The correct answer is A. Before you submit your course to the client, you should alpha and beta test it. Doing both types of testing helps ensure the course's quality.

2. The correct answer is C. When you beta, or pilot, test the course, you release it to a small group of target audience, most likely subject matter experts, to ensure its quality and functionality.

3. The correct answer is D. The Quality Assurance Checklist helps you identify errors as you test your courses. You can also give this checklist to the subject matter experts to guide them through the problems they should look at when they conduct a course review.

Chapter 14 – Implementation

1. The correct answer is A. During implementation, you upload all the content into the Learning Management System (LMS), or the CMS.

2. The correct answer is C. The distribution method for the course might be a CMS, or Content Management System. It is often the main function of a Learning Management System.

3. The correct answer is B. After you upload a new eLearning course,

launch it and test to be sure it is fully functional. Ensure that all tools and equipment are readily available and work property, and that the learning application is fully operational. This means that you should check all slides, interactions, games, assessments, and external links.

4. The correct answer is D. SCORM is a set of technical standards that ensure the course works well with other eLearning software. It also ensures that the learning content and the Learning Management System communicate with each other.

5. The correct answer is A. A Reusable Learning Object is a course piece that can be used again in a different context, such as another course.

6. The correct answer is B. Section 508 is part of the Rehabilitation Act of 1973, which was amended in 1998. It requires that all electronic and information technology must be accessible by people with disabilities, meeting the needs of people with visual, auditory, and motor disabilities.

7. The correct answer is C. There are many ways to ensure content is Section 508 compliant, such as providing a text equivalent for every non-text element, offering synchronized captions for audio and video files, ensuring that all the information presented with color is also available without color, and avoiding elements that flash (text, graphics, or objects).

8. The correct answer is A. JAWS (Job Access with Speech) is a screen reader that allows visually impaired users to read the screen using a text-to-speech output or a refreshable Braille display.

Chapter 15 – Evaluation

1. The correct answer is B. Primarily, evaluation ensures that training courses improve learners' performance.

2. The correct answer is C. During the development phase, ask questions such as "What activities and interactions will result in the required performance?"

3. The correct answer is D. Formative evaluation occurs during all phases of the design process. Summative evaluation, on the other hand, is the process of reviewing a course after you implement it. It measures training outcomes.

4. The correct answer is B. In the 1950s, Donald Kirkpatrick established the four levels of evaluation. The first level is Reaction. In this level, you find out what learners think about the training.

5. The correct answer is D. In the second level of Kirkpatrick's model, Learning, you assess the extent to which learners gained knowledge and skills and whether they learned what was expected of them.

6. The correct answer is C. In the third level of the Kirkpatrick model, Behavior, you should measure the extent to which a change in behavior

actually occurred. When possible, measure the before and after behavior to determine whether the change took place.

7. The correct answer is A. Kirkpatrick's last level of evaluation is Results. Here, you measure whether the learner's performance was improved as a result of the training course. You also measure whether the organization benefited from that improvement.

8. The correct answer is C. Many theorists, including Kirkpatrick, have modified the original version of the Four Levels of Evaluation to better suit modern requirements. Jack Phillips added fifth step, known as Return-of-Investment, or ROI. According to Phillips, you should measure ROI between three and twelve months after the training.

Chapter 16 – Assessments

1. The correct answer is A. Assessments show both learners and management whether the learners mastered the knowledge and skills presented in the course. They help to draw attention to the most important elements in the content of the course, as well as determine the effectiveness of the course, among other things.

2. The correct answer is A. The goal is to accurately assess the knowledge and skills specified in the learning objectives. So that you can improve item validity, you should write assessment questions that focus on the application of the knowledge rather than just whether the learner comprehended the course.

3. The correct answer is D. Make sure your questions are clearly written and easy to understand and measure the outcomes as you intend to measure them.

4. The correct answer is B. Your assessments should be reliable, which means that they should produce consistent results over a period of time.

5. The correct answer is C. A multiple choice question typically consists of a stem, correct answer choice, and incorrect options. The incorrect options are known as distractors and should make sense, but be decidedly incorrect.

6. The correct answer is C. There are three major types of assessment items: diagnostic assessments, formative assessments, and summative assessments.

7. The correct answer is C. Diagnostic assessments are also known as pretests. They are done to find out how much learners already know about a topic, deliver various versions or levels of a course based on the diagnostic assessment, and allow learners to test out if they already possess adequate knowledge of the content. Diagnostic assessments shape learners' expectations about the content of the course.

8. The correct answer is B. Summative assessments are given at the end of the entire training course and check the learners' understanding of the overall content. These are also called posttests.

9. The correct answer is D. A multiple-choice question has a question stem, correct answer or answers, and distractors. Always indicate the number of possible correct responses in the instructions for the question. This helps avoid confusion among learners.

10. The correct answer is A. While it is tempting to include *All of the above*, *None of the above*, or *Both A and B are correct* as answer choices, learners know that these choices are almost always the correct response.

11. The correct answer is C. True/False questions are often used to measure an understanding of facts such as names, dates, and definitions. This type of questions is difficult to construct without making the correct response too obvious. They only assess learning at the knowledge level. Because of this, you should only use them to check the learner's knowledge of facts.

12. The correct answer is A. Matching assessments consist of a list of questions and statements and a list of responses. These assessments are effective because they can cover a lot of content at the same time. They also test learners' understanding of the material at the application level.

13. The correct answer is C. Free response questions are less commonly used than multiple choice, true/false, or fill-in-the-blank questions. However, there are many benefits to free response questions. They are easier to construct because the instructional designer does not have to worry about plausible distractors.

14. The correct answer is B. Some learners want to see assessments in courses, but they do not want to be graded. They are afraid of failure and tend to avoid taking scored assessments. There are also learners who feel that scoring assessments is not suitable for adult learners, because adult learners only need guidance, not scoring, to achieve better performance results.

15. The correct answer is B. It is imperative to provide corrective feedback because it allows learners to progress toward their goal and tells them whether they have mastered the content. Ensure that the overall tone of corrective feedback is friendly and supportive, even if the learner answered the question incorrectly.

16. The correct answer is A. To determine the type of feedback you provide, look at the type of course, presentation methods, and assessment instruments. Extrinsic feedback may be a good choice for multiple choice questions, but it may not work as well for a game as intrinsic feedback.

PART III Interactive ELearning

Chapter 17 – Interactivity in Your ELearning Course

1. The correct answer is B. Interactivity allows learners to become more involved with the content, thus providing better learning outcomes. It can include assessments, simulations, games, popup text boxes, expandable charts, graphs, tables, and animations.

2. The correct answers are A and C. Interactivity is an exercise or activity that helps the learner become more involved by discovering information and checking knowledge. An interaction can be a scenario where the learner is presented with a problem to be solved, role-play, content revelation after selecting a specific object, or a game that puts learners in a realistic setting so they can explore, try, succeed, and fail in a safe environment.

3. The correct answer is C. When learners actively perform tasks rather than passively sitting and reading or listening to something, they tend to retain more information. They are also less likely to make the same mistake again when they learn new material through trial and error.

4. The correct answer is D. The goal of any interaction is to process, encode, and store the material in memory. Most instructional designers incorporate one interaction for every ten or fifteen minutes of learning.

5. The correct answer is A. Passive interactions involve very limited interactivity. This can include an assessment at the end of a lesson or module. In this level, learners have no control over the course.

6. The correct answer is B. Level 3 interactions usually include animations, complex situations, and scenarios. This level of interaction finds a balance between reasonable development time and active learning.

7. The correct answer is C. Most courses involving complex and real-time interactions are not Section 508 compliant. Therefore, if you need to meet accessibility requirements, your course will be limited to Level 1 and 2 interactions.

8. The correct answer is A. ELearning courses can be either linear or non-linear. Linear courses require learners to complete the entire training, and are usually used for mandatory training courses, including compliance training.

9. The correct answer is D. Non-linear navigation is also known as branched navigation. In this type of navigation, learners can jump from one section to the next in any order they desire.

Chapter 18 – Simulations and Games

1. The correct answer is C. A learning game is an activity in an eLearning course that improves the learning process and motivates the

learner to complete the course. It can be an excellent learning aid.

2. The correct answer is C. Learning games clarify difficult concepts and help learners practice the newly acquired knowledge and skills. They give the learner an opportunity to practice and apply what they learned in the course. Learning games also spark interest, which leads to increased motivation, understanding, and retention.

3. The correct answer is D. Casual games engage learners and reinforce the learning objectives in a fun way. These can include drag and drop, sequencing, and matching.

4. The correct answer is A. Serious games are usually simulations with other elements of game design. They help achieve measurable and sustainable changes in the learner's performance or behavior.

5. The correct answer is B. A simulation is also called a branching scenario. This is usually a scenario that allows the learner to go through situations that they will likely encounter in real life.

6. The correct answer is D. When approaching a learning game design, mimic the elements found in typical video games. Elements of a good game include rules, score, rewards, strategy, message, challenge, risk, levels and titles, and feedback.

7. The correct answer is A. Rewards add excitement to the learning experience. You can give away medals, badges, and assign points as learners complete levels of the game or provide correct responses to questions.

8. The correct answer is B. The message is responsible for communicating objectives and goals of a lesson. You can hide your messages in the game, allowing players to discover them as they go.

9. The correct answer is C. Risk is an important part of game design. Learners want to have a sense of risk. Design games to make failure possible, but avoidable. This ensures that, regardless of how players move, failure is not their final result.

10. The correct answer is B. Corrective feedback can be either direct or indirect. A congratulatory message is direct feedback to the learner.

11. The correct answer is A. When you assign scores throughout the game, you provide indirect feedback to the learner. Whether you use direct or indirect feedback, make sure that it does not interrupt the flow of the game.

12. The correct answer is D. A virtual world is an immersive 3D only environment where users can interact with other users and characters. Learners can experiment, plan, collaborate, learn from mistakes, and take risks, all while learning new skills. Some popular examples are Second Life, Active Worlds, and There.

13. The correct answer is D. Virtual Worlds allow learners to collaborate. They design lectures, demonstrations, and other experiences in

the Virtual World environment. Trainers can post slides, audio, video presentations, and even self-paced tutorials. All of this allows for both synchronous and asynchronous learning experiences.

14. The correct answer is B. Avatars are an effective way to engage learners, often used to provide feedback and remediation. They can ask questions and lead discussions, helping learners progress. They can also act as an instructor or a learning mate, depending on the purpose of the game.

15. The correct answer is C. Storytelling can be a learning tool that teaches, motivates, and entertains, all at the same time. Stories provide learners with the facts, using realistic situations, and evoke an emotional response.

Chapter 19 – ELearning Authoring Tools

1. The correct answer is A. Adobe eLearning Suite is a toolbox for creating eLearning courses. It includes several Adobe products: Captivate, Flash, Dreamweaver, Photoshop, Acrobat, Presenter, and Audition.

2. The correct answers are A, B, and D. The three types of eLearning authoring tools are PowerPoint plugin authoring tools, desktop authoring tools, and cloud-based authoring tools.

3. The correct answer is D. Cloud-based authoring tools. Cloud-based tools are tools that eLearning developers can access over the internet via a secure hosted system. One popular example is Articulate 360.

4. The correct answer is C. Desktop authoring tools are installed on the desktop. They offer more flexibility to eLearning designers, but there is a learning curve. Some of the most popular are Captivate, and Lectora.

5. The correct answer is A. Lectora is a very powerful eLearning tool. It is capable of producing high quality interactions. Some people do not consider it a rapid authoring tool because there is a higher learning curve than with other rapid eLearning tools.

6. The correct answer is D. Cloud-based tools are very user friendly. Everyone on the team can easily access them and update the course when necessary. They allow instructional designers with limited technical skills to create great-looking eLearning courses and assessments. You can easily upload images, video, and audio.

7. The correct answer is A. Camtasia Studio is a video-based screen capturing software program. The screen captures are directly recorded in a digital format with high quality audio.

8. The correct answer is B. Before deciding on the appropriate development tool, consider the budget, learning curve, and content requirements. One tool may be perfect for creating simulations, but it may not work for software demonstrations. It is best practice to add as many

eLearning tools as possible to your arsenal and use each one based on the needs and requirements of the course.

Chapter 20 – Video in ELearning

1. The correct answer is C. Short video clips are clips from YouTube or another source that are relevant to the content. Keep in mind that most courses benefit from short videos of no more than five minutes. If the video is longer, try to break it into a number of shorter chunks.

2. The correct answer is B. Videos with talking heads can be boring. Avoid them whenever possible. However, they can be beneficial for introducing a course or serving as a guide throughout the course.

3. The correct answer is D. You can use a video to add a scenario by having the learners watch a role-play or situation that illustrates points from the course. Then, you can ask the learner what they would do in this situation, or identify what went wrong.

4. The correct answer is C. When shooting videos, the camera is the most important piece of equipment. Choosing the best camera for your needs helps ensure a good quality video.

5. The correct answer is A. Optical zoom costs more than digital zoom, but it also produces a better quality video when you need zooming capabilities.

6. The correct answer is A. A teleprompter displays the script, which allows the presenter to concentrate on delivery rather than memorization of a script. Reading from a teleprompter requires practice to sound as natural as possible. Learners should not realize that the presenter is reading.

7. The correct answer is C. If you cannot hire professional actors, keep in mind that the presenters may not feel comfortable on-camera. Leave plenty of time for rehearsal, and pay attention to the presenters' tone of voice, facial expressions, speech rate, and gestures. Also pay attention to their attire and overall appearance.

8 The correct answer is D. A screencast is a recording of a computer screen that is converted into a movie. Screencasting is becoming increasingly popular for the development of software and information technology-related training courses. Use screencasts for demonstrations of online tools, websites, and catalogues.

9. The correct answer is D. Treat screencasts as videos. After you receive a screencast script from your SME, ask for access to the tool and walk through the steps. Note any inconsistencies or missing steps, and then discuss them with the SME. Walk through the steps as many times as possible before you record the final version. Make sure the desktop that you record is clean -close all documents, websites, and other windows on your computer.

Chapter 21 – Audio in ELearning

1. The correct answer is B. A good quality microphone is essential for recording optimum quality audio. For narration, use a unidirectional microphone because it does not pick up any distracting audio from other directions.

2. The correct answer is A. Start your recording with a sound check, and avoid any movement that could be picked up by the microphone (such as page turning).

3. The correct answer is D. Recording outside of a recording studio is often associated with ambient noise, which distracts from the learning experience. Make sure your recording environment is as quiet as possible. Unplug all unnecessary machines and hang a "Do Not Disturb" sign. You can also use a small room or sound booth.

4. The correct answer is C. Most learners cannot read the text on the screen and listen to the audio at the same time. If the client wants to have both on-screen text and audio, give learners the option to turn the audio off. This allows learners to take the course in public places without disturbing other people.

Chapter 22 – Graphics in ELearning

1. The correct answer is A. If your course is visually appealing, it will help draw the learner's attention. Visual learners, in particular, find graphics beneficial for understanding, analyzing, and processing information.

2. The correct answer is C. When most of the photos in the course are realistic, avoid using cartoonish drawings for some graphics. This helps ensure a consistent overall course design.

3. The correct answer is B. Decorative graphics look appealing, but they do not add any instructional value – avoid them in your course. This type of graphic is usually used on book and course covers.

4. The correct answer is C. Organizational graphics help learners organize the information that you provide in the course. The best examples of organizational graphics are charts and graphs.

5. The correct answer is A. Use relational graphics when you want learners to see the relationship between the numbers presented in the content. In other words, use them to show the quantitative relationship of variables. A good example of a relational graphic is a pie chart.

6. The correct answer is A. A transformational graphic shows changes over time. Include these graphics to show how objects are affected by a

process. Examples are timelines and before/after images.

7. The correct answer is A. High-resolution graphics look nice and crisp, but take up a lot of space and take a long time to load. Start with the highest possible resolution. Then, you can resize the image as much as possible to take up the least amount of space.

8. The correct answer is C. The file type you use for images depends on the client's needs and priorities. The most commonly used image files on the web and in eLearning are PNG, JPG, and GIF.

9. The correct answer is A. If you need transparent images, use a PNG.

10. The correct answer is B. JPGs are smaller in size and therefore load more quickly than PNGs. Use them if the stakeholder wants the course to load quickly.

11. The correct answer is B. Graphics in your eLearning course should be Section 508 compliant. Whenever possible, describe them with alternative text that conveys the same information as the image.

12. The correct answer is A. The aim of the Visual Design Model is to help instructional designers without graphic experience envision the appropriate art for their courses. The five phases of the model are to define goals, define context, design a visual approach, identify the communication function needed to match the content type, and apply the principles of psychological instructional events.

13. The correct answer is B. When you define the context, you should identify the target audience, delivery methods, learning environment, and constraints.

14. The correct answer is D. Understanding color theory can help you create better graphics. The color wheel organizes the primary, secondary, and tertiary colors.

PART IV Advancing Your Instructional Design Skills

Chapter 23 – Working with SMEs

1. The correct answer is B. All people are subject matter experts in one area or another, but a SME is an individual who has knowledge about a specific area or topic.

2. Both A and B are correct. Most of the time, SMEs provide either too much or too little information. It is your job to include the right amount of information in the course. Some SMEs want to share everything they know, and believe that every piece of information is important. To ensure that they provide only relevant information, check the content to see if it meets the intended objectives. If it does not, go back to the SME and ask relevant questions to get more information so you can satisfy all the course

objectives.

3. The correct answer is C. Break the information into three categories: must know, need-to-know, and nice-to-know. The information the learner absolutely needs to obtain the knowledge or learn the skill is the must-know information.

4. The correct answer is B. Sometimes, a SME can have a difficult time organizing all the information he or she wants to share. You can use a mind map or graphic organizer to help them organize their thoughts.

5. The correct answer is D. Materials used in a classroom version of the course can be adapted to the eLearning environment. However, they will have to be modified or even reformatted to meet the eLearning requirements. These materials are most likely missing information needed to understand the content. In this case, the SME can help you fill in the gaps where necessary.

6. The correct answer is A. When dealing with a SME, it is crucial to use effective communication. Inform the SME of the goals and objectives of a meeting ahead of time. Prepare interview questions in advance. Also, consider eMailing a list of the questions to the SME. All of these tactics will help your meeting with the SME be more productive.

7. The correct answer is D. Most SMEs are not familiar with instructional design theories and terminology. Consider explaining terminology in layman's terms whenever possible. In the long run, using terms with which the SME is not familiar can cost more time and money.

Chapter 24 – ELearning Project Management

1. The correct answer is A. ELearning projects involve both training and technology. Because of this, they may be more difficult to manage than other projects.

2. The correct answer is C. IPECC is the most commonly used model in project management for all types of projects. It stands for Initiating, Planning, Executing, Controlling, and Closing.

3. The correct answer is A. During Initiation, project managers present their vision, define goals, state expectations, and define the scope of the project. Conduct a Business Requirements Analysis so that you can fully understand the requirements and desired project outcome.

4. The correct answer is D. A project charter is a document serving as a contract between an eLearning project manager and the client. It is the foundation of any project, and it should be as comprehensive as possible.

5. The correct answer is B. Planning is probably one of the most important phases in project management. It ensures that the project is delivered on time, within budget, and within scope. In this phase, refine the

scope, assemble the team, and identify the specific tasks and activities to be completed. Then, write a project plan.

6. The correct answer is A. During the controlling phase, make necessary corrections and adjustments to the schedule, based on any problems that occurred during the previous three phases. Also during this phase, monitor the scope, schedule, budget, and risks for the project.

7. The correct answer is D. Several tools can help you and the rest of the team deliver projects on time. A Gantt chart is a horizontal bar chart that enables project managers to organize the events identified during the planning phase.

Chapter 25 – ELearning Development Agile Project Management

1. The correct answer is B. Agile approaches the development process in short iterative cycles called sprints, usually lasting two weeks.

2. The correct answer is C. The nature of Agile enables stakeholders to be engaged earlier in the development process; they see results in as little as two weeks. Because of the short iterations, developers can address changes and defects quickly.

3. The correct answer is B. Agile project managers are responsible for managing the team's environment. They should also encourage the team members to make decisions. Rather than managing cost, time, and scope of the project, the main role of an Agile project manager is to facilitate the team and empower them to achieve results.

4. The correct answer is A. Fundamental eLearning design principles such as identifying learning objectives, structuring the course, storyboarding, designing individual modules building the user interface, and creating the content, are not compromised when Agile is successfully implemented. Instead, Agile helps to bring these fundamental building blocks together. It also manages the entire development process so the final product is delivered more quickly and to the highest standards.

Chapter 26 – Job Aids

1. The correct answer is C. Job aids allow individuals quick access to information required to complete a task efficiently. They help individuals apply new skills to real-world problems without having to refer back to long training courses.

2. The correct answer is B. Include only the must-know content so that individuals have the material they need the most. Use short, descriptive words that are easy to understand. Incorporate simple, clear, illustrative graphics. Consider including highlights, boxes, and arrows that emphasize

the text. Use only relevant information, and make the job aid easily available through either a download in the lesson or a mobile application.

3. The correct answer is D. Most training courses contain so much information that it is impossible to retain all of it. Job aids serve as reference, reminder, and refresher tools, allowing employees to work faster so they do not have to stop and think of the next step.

4. The correct answer is A. The Electronic Performance Support System (EPSS) is any software program within a larger application that guides people through completing a task. It is, basically, an electronic job aid.

Chapter 27 – Web 2.0 and Mobile Learning

1. The correct answer is B. Web 2.0 is used to describe the second generation of the World Wide Web. This generation focuses on collaboration and information sharing.

2. The correct answer is C. Social learning is a way for learners to learn from other people and with other people using social media. Some potential tools are Facebook, Twitter, YouTube, LinkedIn, blogs, and wikis.

3. The correct answer is D. Social learning is often used for informal collaborative learning. Social learning tools are free and they allow people to connect with others and share or obtain knowledge.

4. The correct answer is B. Some instructional designers post videos or blogs with the information they want their learners to know before starting the course. Instructional designers also use social learning tools to share links with additional resources before, during, or even after the learning event.

5. The correct answer is C. When you design a blended learning course, you can create a wiki or blog, and then have learners contribute opinions or reflect on their learning. Another way to use blended learning is to upload relevant videos to YouTube, and have the learners watch and comment on them before the learning event.

6. The correct answer is B. Mobile Learning, or mLearning, focuses on learning with mobile devices, like smartphones, tablets, and eBook readers. mLearning can reach a large number of people at the same time, as well as provide just-in-time training. However, you should review learning objectives before delivering an eLearning course via mobile device, ensuring that the mLearning solution is truly needed.

7. The correct answer is A. Do not use podcasts or vodcasts as a substitute for a complete course. Instead, use them as an addition to the course, enhancing the learning experience.

8. The correct answer is C. mLearning can be effective, but not all content is suitable for mLearning. If a course requires a learning aid such as a glossary, you can use an mLearning solution. Pre-course presentations and reading materials, pre- and post-tests, and updated content can also be delivered via mLearning.

9. The correct answer is A. You must create mobile courses from scratch. You will have to create both eLearning and mobile versions of the same course using the mobile-first approach.

Chapter 28 – Technical Training – Making Technical ELearning Stick

1. The correct response is B. Translating very dry, mundane information into memorable and engaging experience is the main challenge of technical training.

2. The correct answer is A. Keeping content short, interactive, and flexible are some of the best ways to increase engagement among technical learners.

Chapter 29 – Copyright Protection In ELearning Design: What You Need to Know to Protect Your Work

1. The correct answer is B. False. Not everything you produce for an eLearning course might be copyrighted. For example, if someone else will eventually own the content, then you may not have any rights to what you have created.

2. The correct answer is D. Fair use means that certain content can be used without obtaining permission for the purpose of teaching, scholarly research, news reporting, or review.

Instructional Design and ELearning Glossary

Abraham Maslow's Hierarchy of Needs – a theory that states there are five basic human needs that must be satisfied for internal motivation to occur. These needs are physiological, safety, belongingness, self-esteem, and self-actualization.

Accelerated Learning Rapid Instructional Design (RID) – a model for creating courses under tight deadlines with limited budget and constantly changing content.

Action Mapping – one of the newest instructional models developed by Cathy Moore. Its goal is to increase efficiency and performance.

ADDIE – the classic model that most instructional designers use. ADDIE stands for Analysis, Design, Development, Implementation and Evaluation.

Adobe ELearning Suite – a toolbox for creating eLearning courses, which includes Adobe Captivate, Adobe Flash, Adobe Dreamweaver, Adobe Photoshop, Adobe Acrobat, Adobe Presenter, and Adobe Audition.

The Agile approach – an approach based on short iterative full-cycles that deliver usable components of the courseware and introduce a goal oriented, action-driven efforts.

Alpha testing – the initial quality assurance test that involves usability testing to confirm the course works the way it should.

Alternative text – also known as Alt-text. When users mouse over a visual, alternative text pops up and provides a description of that visual.

Andragogy – the term coined by Malcolm Knowles. It is an adult learning theory that believes that adults learn differently from children and describes assumptions about adult learners.

Animation – a simulation of movement created by showing a series of visuals.

ARCS Model – a model of motivational design pioneered by John Keller. It is a systematic approach to designing motivational learning. It consists of the following four steps for promoting motivation in the learning process: attention, relevance, confidence, and satisfaction.

Assessment – the evaluation of comprehension and ability of the learner to do something as a result of a training course.

ASSURE – a model that assumes the course design uses different types of media. The model is used for designing eLearning courses. ASSURE stands for Analyze Learners, State Objectives, Select Media and Materials, Utilize Media and Materials, Require Learner Participation, and Evaluate and Revise.

Asynchronous ELearning – a self-paced learning experience that allows learners to go through courses as quickly or as slowly as they desire.

Audience analysis – a process of collecting information about learners' background, experiences, and motivators.

Authoring tools – software programs used for developing, editing, testing, and arranging eLearning courses.

Avatars – a graphical representation of a character.

Backlog – is an Agile term referring to a list of tasks that need to be completed before a release of the project.

Behaviorism – a learning theory based on observable and measurable changes in behavior, which assumes that learner's behavior is shaped through positive or negative reinforcement.

Beta testing – the second phase of the quality assurance process, also known as Pilot testing. Beta testing requires a group of users who review the eLearning course for errors and ensure the course works the way it should.

Big Data – a very large data sets that can be analyzed to reveal associations, trends, and patterns.

Blended learning – a combination of several media such as eLearning and mobile learning in one course.

Blog – short for web log. It is a website where an individual writes entries on a regular basis.

Bloom's Taxonomy – was pioneered by an educational psychologist, Benjamin Bloom. In his taxonomy, Bloom identified three learning domains: cognitive, affective, and psychomotor. Instructional designers use these domains for writing measurable and observable learning objectives.

Camtasia Studio – a video-based screen capturing software program.

CBT – an acronym that stands for computer-based training. It is a form of education where learners take training courses while on the computer.

Chunking – refers to breaking learning content into small manageable pieces.

Cloud-based Authoring Tools – are tools that eLearning developers can access over the internet via a secure hosted system. The main benefits of these tools is that they do not require IT configurations, special set-ups or licenses. Many eLearning developers turn to these tools because they allow collaboration with colleagues, and can be accessed anywhere.

Cognitive load – There are three types of cognitive load: intrinsic load, germane load, and extraneous load.

Cognitivism – a learning theory that assumes an existing knowledge structure is used to process new information and believes the information is received, stored, and retrieved.

Complex Interactions – Level 3 interactions that include animations, complex simulations, and scenarios.

Constructivism – a learning theory that focuses on how learners construct knowledge based on their prior experience. Constructivists believe in experiential, self-directed learning.

Content Management System (CMS) – often the main function of a Learning Management System, which acts more like a database.

Corrective feedback – information provided to learners regarding their performance to help them progress toward their goal.

Creative Commons – an organization dedicated to making creative works available for others to recreate or share.

Data collection methods – methods used to gather information for different types of analysis. Some examples of data-collection methods include surveys, interviews, and focus groups.

David Kolb – an American educational theorist who developed the learning style inventory.

Delivery methods – a method of transferring a lesson to learners. Some of the delivery methods include CD-ROM, ILT, CBT, and WBT.

Design document – documents the entire design process for a specific project. It provides all the necessary information about the course to instructional designers, graphic artists, multimedia specialists, programmers, project managers, and all other team members and stakeholders.

Desktop authoring tools – authoring tools installed on the desktop. Some of the most popular ones are Articulate Storyline, Captivate, and Lectora.

Diagnostic assessments – pretests used to determine learners' initial knowledge of the material prior to the training course.

Dick and Carey systems approach – a model based on theoretical principles of learning and Robert Gagné's conditions of learning and focus on selecting and organizing appropriate content for each module.

Donald Kirkpatrick – a father of evaluation, who created the four levels of evaluation: reaction, learning, behavior, and results.

Dr. Sivasailam "Thiagi" Thiagarajan – internationally recognized expert in learning games for personal and company development.

EBook reader – a device used to read digital eBooks.

Eight types of motivational appeals – Fear, Humor, Warmth, Shame, Reward, Pride, Ingratiation, and Guilt. These appeals can either push or pull an individual's performance.

ELearning – a form of learning conducted via internet, intranet, network, or CD-ROM. eLearning gives people an opportunity to learn just about anything at any time and place.

ELearning Copyright – a legal right that allows the creator of an original work to distribute their intellectual efforts.

Electronic Performance Support System (EPSS) – any computer software program within a larger application that guides people through completing a task. It is an electronic job aid.

Enabling Objectives – objectives that support the terminal objectives. They define the skills, knowledge, or attitudes learners must obtain to successfully complete terminal objectives. Enabling objectives are more specific than terminal ones.

Evaluation – a process that ensures that training meets the standards and expectations. Evaluation helps instructional designers identify strengths and weaknesses of the course, and confirms that all course objectives have been met and the business goal has been achieved.

Experiential learning – a process that allows learners to develop knowledge and skills from their own experience rather than from formal training courses.

Extrinsic feedback – a direct type of feedback that comments on the learner's performance in a straightforward way.

Extrinsic motivation – refers to performing activities with a goal to get something at the end such as monetary rewards, certificates, or good grades.

Face-to-face training – a method of delivering training in the classroom setting with live instructor.

Fair use – A legal doctrine, which states that copyrighted materials may be used without permission of the owner assuming that this use is fair and does not inhibit any profits.

Five Why technique – a way to gather information about performance gap and root causes. The essence of this technique is to repeatedly ask the Why questions until arriving at the root cause of the problem.

Flash player – a plug-in software that adds functionality to the web browser.

Formative evaluation – a process that occurs in all phases of the course design, and ensures that training stays on track while it is being developed.

Forum – an online message board where ideas on a particular topic can be shared.

Four-Door (4D) ELearning model – a simple model developed by Dr. Sivasailam "Thiagi" Thiagarajan that allows eLearning professionals to develop eLearning courses cheaply and rapidly for different types of learners.

Gagné's Nine Events – a nine-step process known as the events of instruction. These nine-steps are:

- Gain attention
- Inform learners of objectives
- Stimulate recall of prior learning
- Present the content
- Provide guidance
- Elicit performance
- Provide feedback
- Assess performance
- Enhance retention and learning transfer

Gantt chart – a horizontal bar chart that enables project managers to organize the events identified during the planning phase.

Generational learning styles – learning preferences based on generation. The four generational learning styles are traditionalists, baby boomers, generations X, and Y or millennials.

HTML – a Hypertext Markup Language used for creating websites.

Implementation – delivery of a course.

Instructional Systems Design – also known as ISD. It is a systematic approach to creating effective training courses.

Interactivity – an exercise or activity that allows the learner to become more involved with the content by discovering information and checking knowledge through assessments, simulations, and games, as opposed to simply reading text on the screen.

Interface – refers to the "look and feel" of the course.

Intrinsic feedback – indirect feedback that immediately lets learners know they made a mistake, and allows them to make adjustments based on that feedback.

Intrinsic motivation – refers to internal drives and desires such as gaining new knowledge and skills.

IPECC – the most commonly used model in project management. It is used for all types of projects, not just for eLearning projects. IPECC model stands for Initiating, Planning, Executing, Controlling, and Closing.

Jack Phillips – pioneered the fifth level of evaluation known as Return-of-Investment or ROI, which compares the monetary program benefits with the program costs.

Job aid – a tool that allows individuals to access the information required to complete a task quickly and efficiently.

Kemp's Instructional Design Model – is an instructional design model created by Jerrold Kemp. The model is based on the principle that the instructional designer should not only look at the learning objectives when creating a learning system, but should also consider other factors, such as the personality and characteristics of the learner, the needs of the learner, the learner assessment, and instructional resources.

Kolb's learning cycle – composed of four stages: concrete experience, reflective observation, abstract conceptualization, and active experimentation. Kolb developed learning styles based on his four-stage learning cycle. These styles are convergers, divergers, assimilators, and accommodators.

Learning – a process of gaining knowledge and skills.

Learning game – an activity inserted into any learning module with the goal to improve the learning process and motivate the learner to complete the course.

Learning goals – goals that provide information about the purpose of the course.

Learning Management System (LMS) – a software application used to plan, implement, and assess learning process. LMS allows instructors and administrators to create and deliver content to the maximum number of people, monitor participation, and assess performance.

Learning objectives – measurable and observable statements that define the scope of the course and help learners focus on specific outcomes. Learning objectives describe the knowledge, skills, or attitudes that learners should demonstrate after completing the course. Objectives should be written using the A-B-C-D format. The A-B-C-D format stands for Audience, Behavior, Condition, and Degree.

Limited interactions – Level 2 interactions that give learners more control over the sequence of a course.

Linear navigation – set up in a way where learners must go through the entire section until they can move to the next one. Linear navigation requires learners to complete the entire training.

Long-term memory – a location in the brain where the information is stored permanently.

Malcolm Knowles – a theorist of adult education who pioneered the concept of Andragogy and identified six principles of adult learning.

Media – refers to audio, video, animations, and graphics in an eLearning course.

Merrill's principle of instruction – also known as the First Principles of Instruction. It is an instructional theory developed by M. David Merrill and derived from earlier learning theories and models. This theory is based on hands on experiences.

Mobile learning – also known as mLearning is a subset of eLearning that focuses on learning with mobile devices such as smartphones, tablets, and eBook readers.

Multiple Intelligences theory – a theory pioneered by the psychologist, Howard Gardner. According to his theory, people are born with certain aptitudes used to learn new information and solve problems. Gardner's Nine Intelligences are:

- Linguistic Intelligence
- Logical/Mathematical Intelligence
- Musical Rhythmic Intelligence
- Bodily/Kinesthetic Intelligence
- Spatial/Visual Intelligence
- Naturalistic Intelligence
- Intrapersonal Intelligence
- Interpersonal Intelligence
- Existential Intelligence

Needs analysis – a process of collecting information to determine the needs that must be addressed in a training course.

Non-linear navigation – also known as branched navigation, allows learners to jump from one section to the next in any desired order.

Passive interactions – Level 1 interactions that involve very limited interactivity such as assessment at the end of the lesson or module.

Performance analysis – a process of collecting information to identify and close the gap between the current and the desired performance.

Personalized ELearning – technique that provides the ability to customize the learning environment and many other aspects of the entire learning experience.

PERT chart – a project management tool used to schedule, organize and coordinate tasks within the project.

Podcast – an audio recording of a training program.

PowerPoint plugin authoring tools – tools that use PowerPoint as the authoring environment such as Articulate Studio

Presentation methods – techniques used to present learning material such as video, audio, scenarios, and games.

Prototype – an interactive model of an eLearning course that contains the overall course layout including graphics and structural elements.

Quality assurance – refers to ensuring the quality of an eLearning course.

Raptivity – a rapid interactivity building tool.

Real-Time interactions – Level 4 interactions that involve all the elements of Levels 1, 2, and 3 plus very complex content, serious games and 3D simulations.

Reliability – refers to the ability of the same measurement to produce consistent results over a period of time.

Remediation – refers to providing specific performance feedback whenever necessary.

Repurposing – refers to restructure of the already existing content into a different format to accommodate a different delivery method.

Return on Expectations (ROE) – an approach to creating and demonstrating the degree to which organization's expectations have been satisfied.

Reusable Learning Objects (RLOs) – course pieces that can be reused in a different context such as another course.

Robert Gagné – an American educational psychologist best known for his conditions of learning for training applications. He developed a theory that states there are five major levels of learning including verbal information, intellectual skills, cognitive strategies, motor skills and attitudes.

Robert Mayer – one of the key contributors to the field of instructional design, who developed behavior learning objectives.

ROI model – Jack Phillips added a fifth step to the already existing four levels of evaluation. His fifth level is known as Return-of-Investment or ROI. It compares the monetary program benefits with the program costs and should be measured about three to twelve months after the training.

Ruth Colvin Clark – an instructional design and workforce learning specialist who developed the six principles of effective eLearning courses and, together with Chopeta Lyons', created a Visual Design model.

SCORM – an acronym that stands for Shareable Content Object Reference Model. SCORM is a set of technical standards that ensure the course works well with other eLearning software.

Screen reader – software that reads the text on the computer screen.

Screencasts – the recording of a computer screen and converting this recording into a movie.

Script – a written text for audio narration.

Scrum – an iterative and incremental development framework for managing Agile projects

Section 508 – part of the Rehabilitation Act of 1973, and amended in 1998, which mandates that all electronic and information technology must be accessible by people with disabilities.

Simulations – scenarios that allow learners to go through real-life situations.

SMART objectives – focus on the result rather than activities and allow learners to measure their own success. SMART stands for Specific, Measurable, Attainable, Relevant, and Timely.

SnagIt – a screen-capturing tool that creates highly engaging images, presentation videos, tutorials, and training documents.

Social learning – a subset of eLearning, which refers to learning from and with other people using social media tools such as Facebook, Twitter, YouTube, LinkedIn, Blogs, and Wikis.

Sprint – an Agile term referring to a specific period of time during which certain amount of work has to be completed.

Storyboards – visual organizers instructional design and eLearning professionals use to illustrate ideas and communicate these ideas to team members.

Storytelling – a learning tool that teaches, motivates, and entertains learners by telling a story.

Style guide – a standardized guide for writing eLearning documents or designing learning experiences.

Subject Matter Experts (SMEs) – individuals that have knowledge about a specific area or topic.

Successive Approximation Model (SAM) – an Agile instructional design model created by Michael Allen, a recognized pioneer and leader in the design of interactive multimedia learning tools and applications. The model emphasizes collaboration, efficiency, and repetition. SAM assumes that mistakes will be made throughout the process and focuses on iterative design with frequent early evaluation.

Summative evaluation – a process of reviewing a course after implementation. Summative evaluation measures training outcomes in terms of learners' opinion about the course, assessments results, job performance, and return of investment (ROI) to the organization.

Synchronous ELearning – a type of eLearning that is done in real-time with a live instructor.

Task analysis – a process of collecting information to identify knowledge and skills needed to accomplish instructional goals.

Teaching – a process of transferring knowledge and skills to learners.

Technical training – a process of teaching employees how to complete the technical components of their job.

Template – a form that provides the structure of the document and used to populate information in appropriate fields.

Terminal objectives – describe what the learners are expected to be able to do by the end of the course. Terminal objectives focus on the results not processes.

Usability – refers to the ease of use of a learning course.

User Stories – is an Agile term referring to a detailed description of user's requirements for a specific project.

VAK Model – a model that describes the three learning preferences-and how people learn. Some people learn best from lecture (audio), others learn best from visuals (visual), yet others prefer hands-on activities (kinesthetic).

Validity – refers to measuring what the assessment instruments intended to measure.

Virtual Worlds – immersive 3D online environments in which users can interact with any other users and characters.

Vodcast – a video-based podcast.

WBT – an acronym that stands for web-based training. WBT courses run off the internet and are intended for synchronous and asynchronous delivery.

Web 2.0 – a term used to describe a second generation of the World Wide Web focused on collaboration and information sharing. Web 2.0 technologies are comprised of wikis, blogs, social networking tools, content hosting services, and podcasting.

WIIFM – an acronym that stands for "What's in it for me?" It is a technique used to design motivational courses that learners can relate to.

Wikis – collaboration websites to which anyone within the community of users can contribute to.

References

CPLP learning system. Alexandria, VA: ATD Press, 2015.

Allen, Michael W., and Richard Sites. Leaving ADDIE for SAM an agile model for developing the best learning experiences. Alexandria, Va.: ASTD Press, 2012.

Clark, Donald. "Instructional System Design (ISD) Handbook (ADDIE)." Colocation | Broadband Wireless | Dedicated Servers | Web Design & Development | DSL | Web Hosting | Infinity Internet. http://www.nwlink.com/~donclark/hrd/sat.html (accessed January 17, 2017).

Clark, Donald. "Bloom's Taxonomy of Learning Domains." Colocation | Broadband Wireless | Dedicated Servers | Web Design & Development | DSL | Web Hosting | Infinity Internet. http://www.nwlink.com/~donclark/hrd/bloom.html (accessed February 7, 2017).

Clark, Ruth Colvin, and Richard E. Mayer. E-learning and the science of instruction: proven guidelines for consumers and designers of multimedia learning. 4th ed. Hoboken, NJ: Wiley, 2016.

Clark, Ruth Colvin. Evidence-based training methods: a guide for training professionals. Alexandria, Va.: ATD Press, 2014.

Clark, Ruth Colvin, and Chopeta C. Lyons. Graphics for learning proven guidelines for planning, designing, and evaluating visuals in training materials. 2nd ed. San Francisco: Pfeiffer, 2011.

Hodell, Chuck. ISD from the ground up: a no-nonsense approach to instructional design. 4th ed. Alexandria, VA: ATD Press, 2016.

Hodell, Chuck. "The Subject Matter Expert's Role in Training and ISD." In SMEs from the ground up a no-nonsense approach to trainer-expert collaboration. Alexandria, VA: ASTD Press, 2013. 1-14.

Kirkpatrick Partners. "The One and Only Kirkpatrick." The Official Site of the Kirkpatrick Model. http://www.kirkpatrickpartners.com/ (accessed March 15, 2017)

Malamed, Connie. "The eLearning Coach - Instructional Design and eLearning: The eLearning Coach." The eLearning Coach - Instructional Design and eLearning: The eLearning Coach. http://theelearningcoach.com/ (accessed May 16, 2017).

"Mobile Learning Guide Part 1: Designing it right | Elearning Reports." Custom E-learning Training & LMS Solutions Kineo. http://www.kineo.com/elearning-reports/mobile-learning-guide-part-1-designing-it-right.html (accessed May 10, 2017).

Moore, Cathy. "Instructional design: How to write motivational learning objectives." Training design ideas from Cathy Moore. http://blog.cathy-moore.com/2007/12/makeover-turn-objectives-into-motivators/ (accessed April 11, 2017).

Quinn, Clark N., and Marcia L. Connor. Engaging learning: designing e-learning simulation games. San Francisco, CA: Jossey-Bass, 2005. Ward, Desirée, and Diane Elkins. E-learning uncovered: from concept to execution. Jacksonville, FL: Alcorn Ward & Partners, 2019.

Index